The Business
of the State

The Business of the State

WORLD BANK GROUP

ISBN (paper): 978-1-4648-1998-8
ISBN (electronic): 978-1-4648-1999-5
DOI: 10.1596/978-1-4648-1998-8

Cover design: Bill Pragluski, Critical Stages, LLC

Library of Congress Control Number: 2023948000

Contents

Boxes

Figures

Maps

Tables

Foreword

State participation in economic activity is not new. Ownership or control of commercial firms by the government is more widespread in countries with a history of central planning, but it can be found around the world. In recent years, we have observed a renewed upswing in the use of state-owned companies to achieve various objectives.

The reasons for this renewed enthusiasm for state firms among country policy makers are diverse, and some have clear merit—at least conceptually. State-owned enterprises have been traditionally mobilized to tackle natural monopolies and strategic sectors with national security implications, and to ensure universal access to services. These roles could become more valuable at a time when new technologies are strengthening network effects and widening digital divides.

Other, new roles are receiving attention as well. By minimizing layoffs, increasing investment, or waiving the payment of utility bills, state-owned enterprises might have cushioned the impact of the global financial crisis and the COVID-19 pandemic. Also, with so many businesses of the state operating in the energy, transportation, and construction sectors, their social orientation could in principle be tapped to drive decarbonization efforts. And with geopolitical tensions on the rise, state ownership in strategic sectors may seem integral to national de-risking strategies.

But can the business of the state really deliver on these ambitious agendas? Answering this question is challenging because data-driven research on state-owned enterprises has been sparse for the past quarter century.

This new report aims to help fill this knowledge gap. It does so by taking a fresh look at the commercial footprint of the state around the world, unpacking its changing institutional modalities, analyzing its implications for economic dynamism at the firm and sector levels, and assessing its track record on the macroeconomic and environmental fronts.

State-owned firms have characteristics that make them intrinsically different from private firms. They usually face a softer budget constraint and a more lenient regulatory environment; they also have social mandates going beyond a narrow profit motive. Whether these characteristics lead to better or worse aggregate outcomes depends on how they interact with the market imperfections and institutional failures of the broader economy.

The report builds on strong empirics. Its preparation involved the assembly of a new database of 76,000 firms with state ownership covering 91 countries, the analysis of detailed firm-level data from 14 of them, and leveraging of regulatory reviews in 66 countries. The report is also innovative in considering all firms with at least 10 percent ownership by any government organization, not just those with majority ownership by the central government.

The results show that over time the footprint of the state has become much vaster than previously thought, but also much more diffuse. The often-sprawling business of the state includes a large number of commercial firms in which the state has a minority stake but is still influential. Moreover, state ownership rights are often held by subnational governments, other state-owned enterprises and holdings, and sovereign wealth funds, including from other countries.

In most countries, the private sector is prevalent in industries such as food, construction, and hospitality, among many others. Thus, it was surprising to see through the findings of this report that almost 70 percent of the businesses of the state operate in these types of competitive markets. Careful regulatory analysis also reveals that, even in these competitive markets, firms with state ownership are often granted exclusive rights, protected by quotas, and exempted from economywide laws.

The firm-level analysis, in turn, shows that firms with state ownership are generally less dynamic than comparable private firms. And they often affect the overall performance of the sectors they operate in by reducing entry by new firms, thus weakening competition and long-term growth.

As for their social objectives, firms with state ownership pay significantly higher salaries than comparable private firms—even after controlling for the characteristics of their workers. And those in the energy, transportation, and construction sectors tend to be less "green" than their private sector counterparts.

The patterns just described are not universal. In every area, the report highlights examples of businesses of the state successfully addressing important development issues. But it also shows that the good, the bad, and the ugly coexist, at times within the same country.

At a more practical level, the report proposes a 10-point scorecard to help determine whether a specific business of the state could be part of the solution . . . or is rather part of the problem. Some of these points refer to the characteristics of the firm itself, others to that of the sector it operates in, and yet others to the broader institutional environment. Based on the responses, an aggregate score can be computed for each state-owned firm.

Axel van Trotsenburg
Senior Managing Director for Development and Policy
World Bank

Acknowledgments

This report was led by Mariem Malouche, Birgit Hansl, and Mary Hallward-Driemeier, under the overall guidance of Pablo Saavedra (vice president), Mona Haddad (global director), and Martha Martinez Licetti (practice manager) of the World Bank Equitable Growth, Finance, and Institutions (EFI) Practice Group. The team benefited from guidance and support from Indermit Gill (former vice president, EFI, and current World Bank chief economist), Ahmadou Moustapha Ndiaye (EFI director, strategy and operations), and Gaurav Nayyar (acting EFI chief economist).

The core team of authors comprised Stephan Apfalter, Alex Ciborowska, Seidu Dauda, Maciej Drozd, Mary Hallward-Driemeier, Annette De Kleine Feige, Soulange Gramegna, Birgit Hansl, Martha Martinez Licetti, Mariem Malouche, Graciela Miralles, Dennis Sanchez Navarro, Sara Nyman, Georgiana Pop, and Francis Ratsimbazafy.

Background papers for this report were prepared by Ufuk Akcigit, Reyes Aterido, Rodrigo Barajas Aparicio, Sara Brolhato, Seyit Cilasun, Xavier Cirera, Ana Paula Cusolito, Seidu Dauda, Alberto di Maio, Roberto N. Fattal-Jaef, Esteban Ferro, Mary Hallward-Driemeier, Mariana Iootty De Paiva Dias, Fausto Patiño Peña, Georgiana Pop, Akshat V. Singh, Antonio Soares, François Souty, Trang Tran, and Maria Vagliasindi.

The following colleagues contributed to the case studies presented in this report: Tobias Akhtar Haque, Adnan Ashraf Ghumman, Davit Babasyan, Yeraly Beksultan, Ruxandra Luciana Brutaru, Andrei Busuioc, Maxwell Bruku Dapaah, Bernard Drum, Senidu Fanuel, Henri Fortin, Elena Georgieva-Andonovska, Kjetil Hansen, Mariana Iootty De Paiva Dias, Rafay Khan, Salamat Kussainova, Jinkook Lee, Vinayak Nagaraj, Paul Phumpiu Chang, Marlon Rolston Rawlins, Charles Schlumberger, Qurat ul Ain Hadi, Dusko Vasiljevic, Marius Vismantas, and Bakhrom Ziyaev.

The team gratefully acknowledges the contributions from Martin Rama to the standalone overview of the report. The team benefited from input and technical guidance provided by the following experts and professors: Ufuk Akcigit, Richard Carney, Sunita Kikeri, William Mako, and William Megginson.

The team would like to thank the peer reviewers Rabah Arezki, Kevin Carey, Paulo Correa, Marianne Fay, Tanja Goodwin, Eva Gutierrez, Matias Herrera Dappe, Mariana Iootty De Paiva Dias, Ivailo Izvorski, Somik Lall, Daniel Lederman, Gaurav Nayyar, Denisse Pierola, Habib Rab, Marc Schiffbauer, Immanuel Frank Steinhilper,

Andrew Stone, and Maria Vagliasindi, as well as the members of the EFI State-Owned Enterprises Working Group for their valuable feedback. The team is also grateful to Asli Senkal, Dana Vorisek, and Shu Yu for their review of the report.

The team is thankful for contributions and advice from Fernando Blanco, Christian Eigen-Zucchi, Eric Anthony Lacey, Mellany Pintado Vasquez, Andre Proite, Frederico Gil Sander, Emilia Skrok, and Robert Johann Utz. The team also benefited from multiple conversations and valuable comments provided in the context of the development of the report from Alexandre Arrobbio, Tania Begazo, Alexander Berg, Loic Chiquier, Eva Gutierrez, Jesko Hentschel, Arturo Herrera Gutierrez, Douglas Pearce, Jean Pesme, and Rob Taliercio.

The team is thankful for the administrative support provided by Rachel Fano, Osongo Lenga, Loretta Ann Grace Matthews, and Barbara Nalugo. It also thanks Cindy Fisher, Patricia Katayama, and Mark McClure of the World Bank's publishing team. The report was edited by Bruce Ross-Larsson and Elizabeth Forsyth and proofread by Sherrie Brown and Honora Mara. The support provided by the communications team, Chisako Fukuda, Elizabeth Price, and Nandita Roy, is gratefully acknowledged.

This report is part of a programmatic engagement on the Business of the State (BOS) led by Martha Martinez Licetti since 2020. The BOS program has been made possible thanks to encouragement and guidance from EFI senior management during 2020–23, including Ceyla Pazarbasioglu, Caroline Freund, Indermit Gill, Mona Haddad, and Pablo Saavedra. In addition to the BOS report, the BOS program includes the collection of BOS data, methodology, and operational tools to analyze the role of the state in markets. The BOS data team has been led by Ana Paula Cusolito (2020), Andrea Dall'Olio (2020–22), Tanja Goodwin (2020–22), Mariem Malouche (2021–22), and Dennis Sanchez Navarro (2022 to present). The core team members of the BOS database are Dennis Sanchez Navarro, Jan Orlowski, and Fausto Patiño Peña. The extended team is comprised of Ana Cristina Alonso Soria, Davida Connon, Seidu Dauda, Maciej Drozd, Nejra Hadziahmetovic, Ryan Kuo, Regina Onglao-Drilon, Francis Ratsimbazafy, Juan Felipe Rodrigo, Carla Scarlato, and Goran Vranic. The team is thankful to EFI regional directors, program leaders, practice managers, and country teams for their support in building the database.

OVERVIEW

Introduction

Debates over the role of the state in business are not new, but there is a growing interest among policy makers in leveraging state-owned enterprises (SOEs) to attain development goals, and the stakes are high. The state, as an owner of businesses, is both competing and collaborating with the private sector at the firm level, market level, and economywide. Whether in the end it crowds private economic activity in or out has profound implications for investment and growth.

The drivers of this renewed interest in SOEs can only be speculated upon, and they are most probably diverse. Around the world, effective responses to major economic disruptions—from the global financial crisis to the COVID-19 (coronavirus) pandemic to natural disasters—have often involved SOEs spending more, undercharging or temporarily not charging for their services, or restoring damaged infrastructure. Action to reduce greenhouse gas emissions and address climate change will almost certainly have to involve SOEs, given their heavy presence in sectors such as energy, transportation, agriculture, and raw materials—and it could be facilitated by their public service mandate. Moreover, recent geopolitical tensions have brought national security concerns to the forefront, encouraging some policy makers to assert control of key networks and strategic inputs.

When thinking about relying on SOEs to attain development goals, policy makers in different countries are sensitive to various considerations. But beyond the specifics, it seems that they increasingly perceive SOEs as part of the solution, rather than as part of the problem.

The key issue this report discusses is when is this perception correct, and when could it lead to costly dead ends? Or, put differently, what are the complementary policies and institutions that are needed for SOEs to deliver the good economic outcomes that are hoped for? And if the right circumstances are not in place, and cannot be established quickly, what else should governments do?

Answering these questions is challenging for two reasons.

First, although state presence in the economy is not new—and is not likely to end—the way the state is engaging in commercial activities is evolving. According to the definition in OECD (2015, 16), "any corporate entity recognised by national law as an enterprise, and in which the state exercises ownership, should be considered as an SOE." But what this means in practice is not straightforward.

When the definition above was translated into data, SOEs were traditionally understood to be commercial enterprises with majority (if not total) state ownership by the central government (IMF 2020). However, state ownership increasingly involves diverse stakeholders, from line ministries to subnational governments and from sovereign entities to other SOEs. On top of this heterogeneity, partial privatization has led to a greater reliance on minority state ownership. And, in parallel, various forms of indirect state control have emerged.

The state may be less visible in these structures than in the traditional majority ownership by the central government, but the structures are not necessarily less effective in terms of state control. For example, the state can still exert decisive influence on the decisions of an enterprise through "one share, one vote" rules, or by using veto power, or by appointing board members (Bognetti 2020; Megginson, López, and Malik 2021a, 2021b).

Moreover, there is a growing internationalization under way, with companies fully or partially owned by the state expanding operations in overseas markets, and governments increasingly using vehicles such as sovereign wealth funds to invest in foreign firms. Collectively, state-owned investors, including public pension funds and state-owned banks, have become the third-largest holders of financial assets globally, after only banks and insurance companies (Megginson, López, and Malik 2021a, 2021b). As a result of this internationalization process, commercial enterprises in one country may be controlled—partially or totally—by the state of a different country.

These new developments make the overall state ownership more multilayered and the true level of state control and influence more complex to assess than in the past. Because these new forms of ownership are seldom captured in a systematic way, the true state footprint has become more invisible and the frontier between state-owned and genuinely private firms more blurred.

In this report, the broader set of commercial enterprises that have the state as an important stakeholder are called businesses of the state (BOSs). Compared to the standard definition of SOEs, this set also includes firms with minority, indirect, or subnational ownership.

A second reason why answering the questions addressed by this report is challenging is that there has been relatively little analytical work on SOEs for several decades now, with the effects of emerging forms of state ownership being among the least studied. The dearth of recent studies is even more striking in a context in which new mandates—such as addressing climate change—are being vested on these enterprises.

In the 1980s and 1990s, at the time of structural adjustment programs, most analytical work focused on privatization—including alternative divestiture mechanisms (World Bank 2020). This was followed by research on how to unbundle infrastructure services in the presence of significant returns to scale or network externalities (Megginson and Netter 2001). And then considerable attention went into mechanism design for public-private partnerships, including timebound concessions and management contracts (Kikeri and Kolo 2005).

Robust economic theory often underpinned these analyses. However, their implementation proved challenging because of politicization of the process, weak institutional and competition frameworks, and lack of conducive policy and regulatory environments.

Thus, in some European countries, privatization conducted at discount prices created a class of powerful oligarchs, turning public opinion against it (Nellis 2001). In parts of Latin America, the successful unbundling of infrastructure services was subsequently undone by newcomer governments (Andres et al. 2008). And, from Buenos Aires to Manila, private concessions for urban water became a source of acrimonious political tensions and were eventually canceled (Kikeri and Kolo 2005).

The mixed record of this long history of efforts at reform obviously calls for humility, which is why over the past couple of decades the focus has shifted from divesting state ownership to strengthening its corporate governance. The key idea is that improving public service delivery and resource allocation requires SOEs to be managed more like private firms. By following similar professional standards and practices as their private counterparts, the argument goes, SOEs should become more efficient and the fiscal burden to support them would be reduced. This is why most of the recent analytical work on SOEs has been on the underlying rules, processes, and institutions that should govern the relationship between enterprise managers and government owners (World Bank 2014).

This report makes three contributions to the ongoing debates on SOEs.

First, it leverages a new and very detailed firm-level data set of enterprises—not only SOEs—in which the state is a stakeholder. The cross-country data fill an important data gap, help assess the true extent of BOSs in a very large number of middle- and low-income countries, and provide a clearer picture of the state's footprint along a series of dimensions—including the number of enterprises, their revenue, and their employment. The firm-level data allow analysis of how business performance and sector dynamics are affected by various forms of state ownership.

Several stylized facts emerge from the analysis of these new data. The broad BOS definition used more than quadruples the number of firms identified as having state ownership compared to earlier estimates. The share of sectors with state involvement is also much higher than previously thought, and BOSs are surprisingly common in areas such as manufacturing and hospitality services. And indirect forms of ownership by the state have become widespread, accounting for half of BOSs' total revenues and one-third of their employment.

Other stylized facts refer to the performance of enterprises themselves. BOSs have lower levels of productivity than private firms with similar characteristics, and the growth rate of their employment is generally lower as well. But they pay higher wages. A greater state presence in commercial activities is also associated with lower aggregate productivity and reduced firm entry, as reflected in fewer young firms, or a lower share of economic activity accounted for by young firms.

A second contribution of this report is to propose a clear analytical framework to think about the consequences of relying on BOSs to attain specific development goals. Such a framework does not have the theoretical complexity of the analyses underpinning mechanism design for privatization, or public-private partnerships. However, by identifying the key differences between BOSs and private enterprises, and the way these differences interact with the rest of the economy, this framework helps understand when relying on BOSs may lead to the desired outcomes and when it is likely to fail. The report also puts in perspective the choice of state intervention as a market player as opposed to adopting other policy instruments to address market failures in competitive markets.

An important difference between BOSs and wholly private enterprises is that the former often face a softer budget constraint. The support they receive from governments may take multiple forms, from permanent subsidies to temporary transfers to capital injections to debt bailouts. This easier access to resources may help attain social goals in the short term, such as making access to services affordable. But it often leads to an uneven playing field with private firms and undermines the incentives for BOSs to become more efficient—both harming longer-term economic prospects. Moreover, BOSs receiving state support tend to become dependent on it, undermining their service delivery and economic viability over time, as well as creating explicit and implicit fiscal costs and more public debt.

BOSs also tend to be granted more advantageous regulatory treatment relative to private firms. They may enjoy preferential access to inputs, be protected from new entrants, or be allowed to exercise monopoly power. This more lenient treatment may have an economic rationale in a few strategically important activities, but it is difficult to justify in competitive sectors.

Importantly, BOSs differ from privately owned firms in that they are mandated to deliver on social goals. The argument in this case is that relying exclusively on the private sector would lead to underdelivery. But, in reality, many BOSs also appear to cater to other nonprofit objectives that are clearly less socially desirable, such as artificially supporting greater employment or using better salaries and benefits for political patronage.

The third contribution is to identify the circumstances under which the distinctive features of BOSs lead to better or worse aggregate outcomes. The approach in this case is akin to a second-best analysis, in which the imperfections of private markets and the peculiarities of BOSs may offset or reinforce each other, so that more state ownership may lead to better or worse aggregate outcomes.

This ambiguity makes it clear that the report does not take an ideological stance on BOSs being good or bad on their own. However, the report also discusses that the first-best policy response rarely requires mobilizing state ownership. Fiscal and regulatory policies can tilt the incentives faced by private firms so that they provide universal access to services or help protect the environment. And, when confronted with macroeconomic fluctuations, fiscal policy and monetary policy are better suited to stabilizing an economy than a softer—and costlier—budget constraint for BOSs.

That said, BOSs are unlikely to go away, so the report concludes by discussing the circumstances under which relying on them can be viable. It first notes that a prerequisite to relying on BOSs is to have transparent and reliable information on their finances and performance, which is not always the case. But there are also characteristics of the BOSs themselves, of the markets they operate in, and of the broader economic environment that can make a significant difference in the expected outcomes.

Based on the degree of information transparency and on these three layers of characteristics, the report proposes a simple scorecard to help decision-makers assess whether they should expect good, bad, or ugly outcomes.[1] The scorecard is simple in that it gives equal weight to each of the 10 indicators it includes and allows for some subjectivity in their measurement. But the replicability of the scores should lead to healthy debates on whether and how to rely on BOSs, and hopefully create the impetus for reforms that would eventually support better aggregate outcomes.

A Spreading Business of the State

The mere decision of what to call an SOE can be the source of heated conversations. And these are not just hair-splitting arguments among statisticians: the criteria used for measurement do matter for both economic analysis and policy guidance.

Given the steady emergence of more indirect and less visible forms of state ownership, a broad definition is used in this report. In what follows, BOSs include all firms with at least 10 percent ownership by a public sector entity. This is regardless of whether the public entity is the central government, a local government, or another company—operated domestically or across borders (Dall'Olio et al. 2022b). Only a subset of these firms matches traditional definitions of SOEs, which have focused on direct, majority ownership of domestic firms by the central government.

Building on this broad definition, a novel database—the World Bank Global Businesses of the State (BOS) database—was especially assembled for this report.

It allows assessment of the prevalence and nature of BOSs across a large number of countries. Connecting this BOS database with a firm census, which follows firms with different forms of state ownership over time in selected countries, allows a comparison of economic performance with fully private firms as well as an assessment of BOSs on sectoral performance (box O.1).

The analysis of this database and other country firm-level census data show four important stylized facts:

1. State Participation in Markets Is Widespread, Especially in Competitive Markets

The cross-country BOS database, through its expanded definition and its greater geographic coverage, more than quadruples the number of firms identified as having state ownership compared to earlier estimates. As a result, the share of sectors in which firms with state ownership can be found expands considerably, relative to the standard SOE definition (figure O.1).

The state's footprint in the economy can be measured through the revenue of the enterprises it owns, normalized by gross domestic product (GDP) to get a sense of scale. (Value added would be a preferable indicator, but information on inputs is not widely available.) Based on this measure, BOSs' revenues are equivalent to 17 percent of GDP on average.[2]

Although SOE definitions vary by country, the gap between BOSs and SOEs is nonetheless informative. This gap is relatively important across all regions and income levels, but it is wider in some of the larger economies. The gap is most significant in countries in Europe and Central Asia, which is not surprising given their long history of central planning. Beyond this region, India, Indonesia, and Viet Nam also stand out. Elsewhere, the gap is significant in a few economies from Latin America and the Caribbean (especially Argentina, Brazil, and Colombia), the Middle East and North Africa (the Arab Republic of Egypt), and Sub-Saharan Africa (South Africa and Uganda).

The BOS database also reveals that the state's presence is widespread in competitive markets, such as manufacturing, hospitality, and retail—all activities that can be served efficiently by the private sector. This finding contradicts the standard perception, based on traditional SOE definitions, that state participation is concentrated in natural monopolies and network industries (such as energy, telecommunications, and transportation), or the financial sector.

In reality, competitive markets account for almost 70 percent of BOSs. When adding partially contestable markets, such as utilities among others, these shares reach 82 percent. In some countries, such as Brazil, Costa Rica, Côte d'Ivoire, Jordan, and Senegal, more than 30 percent of total BOS firm revenues come from manufacturing activities alone.

A Novel World Bank Global BOS Database

The new World Bank Global Businesses of the State (BOS) database assembled for this report is the most comprehensive data set on businesses of the state across 91 countries and covers most four-digit sectors in the standard Statistical Classification of Economic Activities in the European Community (NACE). These sectors range from agriculture to mining and quarrying to manufacturing to wholesale trade and services. The financial sector is included as well. However, education, human health and social work, public administration, pension funds, libraries and cultural patrimony activities, activities of households as employers, and activities of extraterritorial organizations are excluded from the cross-country database.

In all, about 76,000 enterprises with state ownership of 10 percent and more were identified in the 91 countries covered by the database. These firms were identified at the central and subnational levels and include subsidiaries (Dall'Olio et al. 2022a). The BOS database includes information on revenues and employment. These data are more comprehensive for about half of the countries. The cut-off date for the BOS data used for this report was February 2023.

It should be noted that the Russian Federation alone accounts for 36 percent of these enterprises, so many of the analyses in the report are replicated excluding it, to avoid distorting the results. Nevertheless, the BOS database still underestimates the full presence of the state because it does not (yet) include all the ownership links through sovereign wealth funds, and businesses of the Chinese state, including through the Belt and Road Initiative.

The Global BOS database assembled for this report can be further disaggregated along several meaningful dimensions. One of them refers to the extent of market competition firms face or could face given the inherent features of the respective economic activity (Dall'Olio et al. 2022b). In this respect, it is important to distinguish between natural monopoly markets (where it is not economically viable for more than one firm to operate, as in some infrastructure sectors), partially contestable markets (economic sectors characterized by some form of market power, externalities, or other market failures such as underprovision of services, like aviation and banking), and competitive markets (such as the manufacturing of food products and apparel).

Another informative breakdown of the Global BOS database is by the sectoral intensity of greenhouse gas emissions. High-emitting sectors include mining, oil, gas, and the chemical industry (including production of petrochemicals, fertilizers, and plastics); some manufacturing activities (pulp and paper, cement, steel, and aluminum); transportation (rail cargo and passenger, air, freight and logistics, sea, and water transportation); selected agricultural activities (cattle farming, rice growing, and logging); and power generation.

The report focuses on the economic efficiency of BOS firms in the real sector, whether they tend to be more, or less, productive than private firms, as well as the impact of state presence on market dynamics. The role and specific performance of state-owned financial institutions, including state development banks, are not covered in this report. Therefore, the recommendations included in this report are not attributable to such institutions.

The Footprint of the State in Commercial Sectors Is Bigger than Traditionally Thought

Percentage of sectors with BOSs and SOEs in selected countries, by region

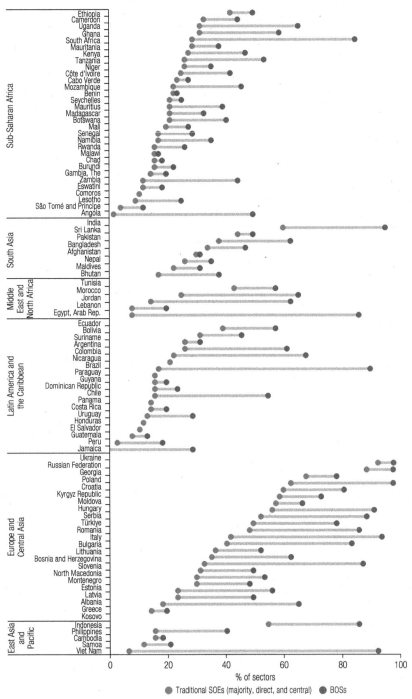

Source: World Bank Global Businesses of the State (BOS) database.

Note: The horizontal axis reports the share of sectors in which firms with state ownership are found out of 77 NACE two-digit code sectors. The blue and red markers use the SOE and BOS definitions of state ownership, respectively. When information on ownership is not available, it is assumed that the BOS firm is centrally owned. BOSs = businesses of the state; SOEs = state-owned enterprises.

Globally, about one-fifth of BOSs operate in high-emitting sectors. But, again, slightly more than half of these BOSs can be found in competitive markets with a weaker economic rationale for state participation, like the growing of rice, the raising of dairy cattle, the manufacturing of cement, or the casting of steel and iron.

The gap between BOSs and SOEs is larger in extractive industries and smaller in power generation. The former account for 27 percent of BOS firm revenues in high-emitting sectors and the latter for 37 percent. However, from an employment perspective, transportation is the most significant of the high-emitting sectors, accounting for half of all BOS firm employment. By contrast, extractive industries account for only 4 percent of employment in high-emitting sectors.

2. Indirect and Complex Forms of State Ownership Are Remarkably Common

The Global BOS database documents how extensive indirect, subnational, and minority ownership by the state is (figure O.2). Although wholly and majority-owned firms remain more prevalent in numbers, enterprises with minority state ownership generate half of BOSs' total revenues and one-third of their employment. In countries such as Eswatini, Madagascar, Mozambique, São Tomé and Príncipe, Slovenia, Türkiye, and Viet Nam, the state has blocking minority stakes under country corporate law in more than one-fifth of BOSs. And, in Botswana, Egypt, Jordan, Mauritius, Mozambique, Uruguay, and Viet Nam, more than 60 percent of BOSs have an indirect state presence.

On average, 46 percent of BOSs operate at the subnational level, with the share being higher in Europe and Central Asia and in Latin America and the Caribbean. In Colombia, over 87 percent of about 700 companies with state participation are linked to subnational governments. Many subnational BOSs operate as providers of local utilities; however, many are also present in competitive markets, such as real estate, hospitality, and manufacturing. By contrast, BOSs operate mostly at the central level in countries affected by fragility, conflict, and violence.

Reporting lines have also become more blurred. About 8,000 enterprises in the BOS database have more than one owner. Indirect ownership of BOSs through subsidiaries is significant too. On average, among 30 countries with good data coverage, mixed ownership accounts for 60 percent of all BOS firms' revenues and 40 percent of their employment. Indirect state presence is especially important in Botswana, Egypt, Jordan, and Viet Nam.

Some 70 percent of the BOSs identified in the BOS database are corporatized, and thus potentially managed as commercial enterprises. However, the share falls below 50 percent in the Middle East and North Africa, as well as in Bolivia, Ecuador, Ethiopia, Lebanon, Moldova, and Serbia. And, even in countries with centralized management and oversight, some BOSs fall beyond the state's purview. For instance, Petroperu, the

Indirectly and Minority-Owned BOSs Account for Much of State Ownership, 2019

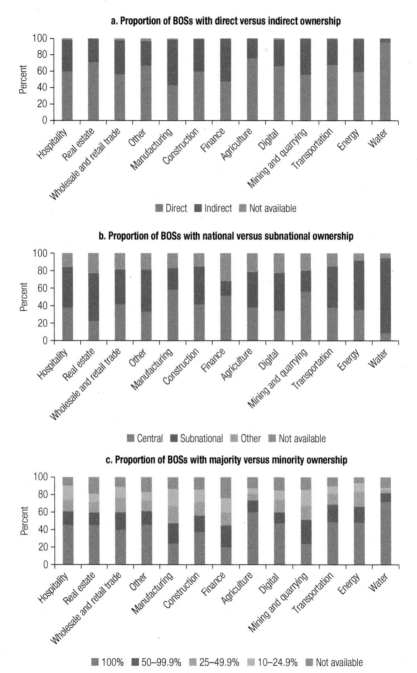

a. Proportion of BOSs with direct versus indirect ownership

Legend: ■ Direct ■ Indirect ■ Not available

b. Proportion of BOSs with national versus subnational ownership

Legend: ■ Central ■ Subnational ■ Other ■ Not available

c. Proportion of BOSs with majority versus minority ownership

Legend: ■ 100% ■ 50–99.9% ■ 25–49.9% ■ 10–24.9% ■ Not available

Source: World Bank Global Businesses of the State (BOS) database.

Note: Indirectly owned BOSs are owned by the state through another company; directly owned BOSs are owned by a government or state agency. Minority-owned BOSs have state ownership of 10–49.9 percent; majority-owned BOSs have state ownership of 50–100 percent. Subnational BOSs are owned by a subnational government entity; national BOSs are owned by the central government. BOSs = businesses of the state.

largest SOE in Peru is not under Fonafe, the government institution in charge of monitoring SOEs.

More than two-thirds of countries have BOSs with a presence abroad. In all, over 7,200 BOSs run operations across borders through subsidiaries or indirectly owned companies. About 40 percent of these companies originate in Italy, but Angola also has over 400 subsidiaries in a diverse set of sectors across 52 countries. Other economies with a strong foreign presence are Botswana, Costa Rica, Greece, India, Jordan, Mauritius, and Slovenia. The top destinations of foreign investments by BOSs are the United States, the United Kingdom, Brazil, and Spain.

Several BOSs are owned by sovereign wealth funds, especially in resource-rich countries that aim at better managing revenue windfalls across generations. The median number of subsidiaries owned by such funds at least doubled over 10 years, from 20 to 45 subsidiaries when using the 50 percent state ownership threshold, and from 89 to 277 subsidiaries at the 10 percent threshold level used by the cross-country BOS database. Most of the increase was driven by Singapore and China, whereas Malaysia and the United Arab Emirates have consolidated their ownership above the 50 percent threshold. Moreover, sovereign wealth funds have increased their investment in BOSs over time. They owned 446 unique BOSs in 2010 and about 2,600 by 2020.

3. BOSs Tend to Be Larger and Pay Higher Wages Compared to Their Private Counterparts, and Their Performance Depends on the State Footprint

New empirical analyses conducted for this report using a cross-country panel data set for 14 eastern and central European countries, and five country studies using census data, show that BOSs are generally larger and more capital intensive than their private sector counterparts (figure O.3). Importantly, the relative performance of BOSs varies with the extent and nature of state ownership. BOSs with substantial private ownership are generally more efficient than those with majority or sole state ownership. And BOSs that are indirectly owned by the state are often more efficient than those that are directly owned.

Overall, BOSs generate higher revenues, employ more workers, and pay higher wages than private firms in the same sectors. This is true in all 5 countries for which census data at the firm level are available, as well as in the 14 countries in eastern and central Europe with panel Orbis data. Where data on assets are available, BOSs also tend to have higher rates of capital per worker.

A wage premium is found in almost all countries, ranging on average from 3 percent to 22 percent. Across countries the premium is higher for firms that are fully

FIGURE 0.3 **BOSs Are Much Bigger than Privately Owned Firms in Terms of Employment and Sales**

Relative size in terms of employment and sales for BOSs compared to private firms, selected countries, 2019

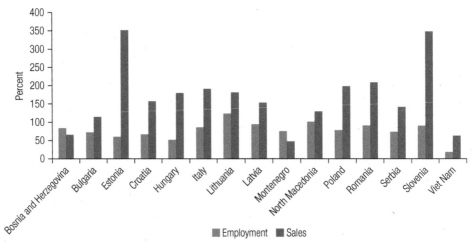

Source: Original figure for this report.

Note: This figure shows that for Romania, for example, sales in BOSs are on average more than double those in private firms (within the same two-digit NACE code and controlling for firm age and country). BOSs = businesses of the state; NACE = Statistical Classification of Economic Activities in the European Community.

or majority-owned by the state. Among firms with minority state ownership, there is not a significant premium.

Paying higher wages could be consistent with BOSs having social goals, or with incumbent workers capturing rents, or simply with BOSs attracting higher-quality workers. In Brazil, the only country with census data providing information on both employers and formal employees, controlling for differences in workers' quality reduces the wage premium from 18.5 percent to 4.5 percent, but it does not make it disappear.

4. Sectors with a Larger State Footprint Are Less Dynamic

The analyses conducted for this report also show that a greater state presence in commercial activities is associated with lower aggregate productivity for most countries. The effects are not just statistically significant: in many cases they are large, especially in competitive markets. This result could be expected, given that BOSs underperform their private counterparts. However, effects at the sector level are more consistent across countries than are the effects at the level of individual firms, suggesting that there are additional forces influencing sector dynamics.

FIGURE O.4 A Stronger State Presence Is Associated with Lower Firm Entry and Higher Market Concentration

Percentage change in entry rate of new firms and in market concentration when the BOS firm is present in sectors, selected countries, various years 2007–19

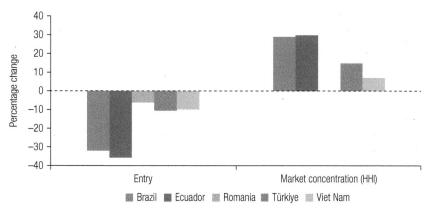

Sources: Akcigit and Cilasun 2023 (Türkiye); Cirera, Brolhato, and Martins-Neto 2023 (Brazil); Dauda, Pop, and Iootty 2023 (Romania); Ferro and Patiño Peña 2023 (Ecuador); and Hallward-Driemeier, Aterido, and Tran 2023 (Viet Nam).

Note: This figure shows that in Brazil, for example, doubling the state's share in a sector is associated with 30 percent less entry. Entry is based on the rate of entry of new firms in Romania and Türkiye and on the share of revenues accounted for by young firms (under age five) in Brazil, Ecuador, and Viet Nam. Market concentration is measured using the Herfindahl-Hirschman index (HHI). The years covered vary by country: 2016–19 for Brazil, 2011–19 for Ecuador and Romania, 2015–19 for Türkiye, and 2007–19 for Viet Nam. All effects are statistically significant except for market concentration in Romania.

One such force is reduced firm entry (figure O.4). In four of five countries with census data, a greater presence of the state is associated with either fewer young firms (Romania and Türkiye) or a lower share of economic activity accounted for by young firms (Brazil and Viet Nam). Across all five countries, doubling the state's share in a sector is associated with 5–30 percent less entry, with the impact being larger in competitive sectors. Conversely, in the case of Viet Nam, the rolling back of state presence was associated with more substantial firm entry.

A related consideration is the effect on market structure. Again, in four of the five countries, a greater state presence is associated with higher market concentration, independent of the sector. And, across all five countries, doubling the state presence in a sector is associated with up to a 30 percent higher concentration.

There is also evidence of less labor reallocation when the presence of the state in a sector is significant. This is so across the 14 pooled countries in eastern and central Europe, as well as in Romania and Viet Nam, whereas in Brazil, Ecuador, and Türkiye the relationship is not statistically significant.

The impact of state ownership on other dimensions of market dynamism is more muted. In particular, the empirical analyses do not reveal any systematic association between state presence in a sector and rates of investment by BOSs, or by average private firms in that sector due mainly to country heterogeneity and different policy and regulatory frameworks.

Why State Ownership Matters

The broadening of state participation in commercial activities, and the emergence of complex ownership arrangements, calls for revisiting the role of the state in business. Whether this role is positive or negative remains a topic of hot conceptual debates. But rather than relying on first principles and trying to prove that state ownership is good or bad in general, this report embraces an empirical approach to shed light on the circumstances under which positive or negative outcomes prevail.

Empiricism alone is not sufficient, however. In interpreting the four findings described above, it is important to keep in mind that how much the state chooses to own and which sectors and firms it invests in are not random events. Governments seek to be proactive because they want to address apparent or evident market imperfections or for political economy considerations. Economic rationales for and final effects of SOEs are market-specific.

Given the potential selection biases, the four stylized facts uncovered are descriptive in nature, not necessarily entailing true causation. To make sense of them, a tractable analytical framework is needed. The framework used in this report is inspired by second-best theory (Lipsey and Lancaster 1956).[3]

Real-world economies are characterized by multiple market imperfections and institutional failures that government interventions seek to correct. State ownership of commercial enterprises is one important instrument in the government's toolkit. However, BOSs are also characterized by features that distinguish them from private firms. How these features affect aggregate outcomes critically depends on how they interact with market imperfections and institutional failures in the rest of the economy. Because distortions may neutralize or amplify each other, a basic result of second-best theory is that government interventions may not have the same consequences as in a first-best world.

To various degrees, depending on countries and sectors, BOSs are characterized by at least three distinguishing features: (1) they are often supported by fiscal resources, explicitly or implicitly; (2) they tend to benefit from a more favorable regulatory environment, and may even influence it; and (3) maximizing profits is not their only, or even their main, objective. These features, in turn, have important implications.

A Soft Budget Constraint

BOSs' accounts and government fiscal structures are often intertwined, although not necessarily in a direct or transparent way. Indeed, many governments provide direct monetary transfers to BOSs, particularly BOSs fulfilling public service obligations, or to their customers through explicit subsidies or tax exemptions. The transfers can also be indirect, taking the form of privileged access to land, subsidized credit, or essential infrastructure services. And they may be implicit, as when governments offer debt guarantees in good times or bailouts and recapitalizations in bad times (La Porta and Lopez-de-Silanes 1999; Vickers and Yarrow 1998).

In the literature on SOEs, this combination of direct, indirect, and implicit transfers of resources is known as a soft budget constraint (Kornai 1986). Softness may be a permanent feature; for example, the government may consistently subsidize the price of services provided by BOSs to offset their high cost to the population. But it can also be seasonal, as when BOSs are called on to contribute to countercyclical investment and employment policies during periods of crisis.

No doubt, there can be benefits associated with this more flexible access to resources by BOSs. For example, in the case of utilities, permanent subsidies to electricity and drinking water—if well targeted—could favor households of more modest means and support better social outcomes. Similarly, following natural disasters—such as floods and earthquakes—the soft budget constraint may allow BOSs to maintain or recover basic services in times of hardship.

However, there are also costs associated with these potential benefits, and they can be significant. For example, the total operating expenditures of 135 infrastructure SOEs in 19 countries averaged 3.1 percent of GDP between 2009 and 2018. These expenditures were partially supported through fiscal injections amounting to 0.24 percent of GDP for power and roads, 0.12 percent for airlines and airports, and 0.04 percent for railways (Herrera Dappe et al. 2023). And this is without counting the value of privileged access to land, services, or credit.

The actual amount of the transfers could be one order of magnitude bigger than these figures suggest, because resources are often channeled through the demand BOSs face. For example, there may be tax breaks on electricity consumption, or on natural gas for residential heating, or on exploration for oil. In 2022, subsidies to the consumption of energy—a sector with a heavy state presence—were estimated at about 1 percent of GDP (IEA 2023). The figure would be much higher if the environmental and health costs of fossil fuel energy consumption were added to the subsidies themselves (IMF 2021).

Emerging forms of state ownership make the total bill associated with the soft budget constraint even more blurred. In countries with significant natural resource exports, governments are increasingly taking stakes in firms through sovereign wealth funds. Globally, assets under management by these funds have grown from less than US$1 trillion in 2000 to over US$11 trillion in 2022 (Megginson and Malik 2022). Sovereign wealth funds have a variety of objectives, but their bountiful resources clearly represent an advantage for the beneficiary BOSs (Divakaran et al. 2022; Gelb et al. 2014).

Relying on BOSs to counter economic fluctuations has reduced fiscal space. Data collected for the World Bank Subsidies and State Aid Tracker show that, during the recent COVID-19 pandemic, many governments deployed fiscal programs that far exceeded state support to firms during the global financial crisis of 2007–08. In many developing countries, public debt levels were already high to begin with, but in some they have reached unsustainable levels because of these large-scale countercyclical policies (Freund and Pesme 2021). With emergency support to BOSs having a high likelihood to become sticky, a further build-up of fiscal risks and sovereign debt crises cannot be ruled out.

The soft budget constraint can thus have important economic downsides. The transfers received by BOSs need to be financed, which requires higher tax rates either in the present or in the future, because the additional public debt needs to be serviced. Higher tax rates penalize economic activity and can be expected to crowd out private sector employment and investment. This cost is more widespread and diffuse than the benefits from the soft budget constraint, but it is not less real.

The soft budget constraint has other important implications for economic efficiency. Resource transfers to BOSs result in unfair competition with private sector firms. For example, in Romania, BOSs are, on average, four times more likely to receive government subsidies than private firms, irrespective of their productivity levels (figure O.5). The odds for BOSs with majority, direct, or local state ownership receiving subsidies are even higher.

Even in the absence of direct transfers, state participation can have a signaling effect to businesses and partners indicating that the firm is backed up by the government, providing it with a clear comparative advantage (Dewenter and Malatesta 2001; Nguyen, Do, and Le 2021; Shleifer 1998; World Bank 1995).

And, even when government support is allegedly provided to all firms, as was often the case during the COVID-19 crisis, transfers can be tilted in ways that affect the level playing field. The nature of government support can be different as well. For example, during the COVID-19 crisis, government purchase of equity was the most frequent measure for schemes targeted to BOSs, followed by grants and loan guarantees. Private firms, however, rarely benefited from purchase of shares and debt alleviation, suggesting that government support was on more generous terms in sectors with higher levels of state ownership.

FIGURE O.5 **Government Subsidies Favor Firms with State Ownership: The Case of Romania**

Probability of a BOS firm receiving a subsidy relative to a private firm, 2011–19

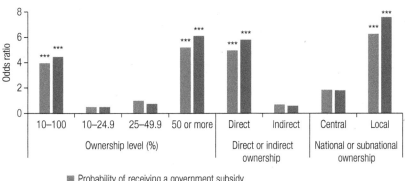

Source: Dauda, Pop, and Iootty 2023.

Note: This figure shows that in Romania BOSs are, on average, four times more likely to receive government subsidies than private firms. Asterisks represent significance levels. Indirectly owned BOSs are owned by the state through another company; directly owned BOSs are owned by a government or state agency. Minority-owned BOSs have state ownership of 10–49.9 percent; majority-owned BOSs have state ownership of 50–100 percent. Subnational BOSs are owned by a subnational government entity; national BOSs are owned by the central government. BOS = business of the state.

One of the most detrimental consequences of the soft budget constraint is to undermine the incentives faced by BOSs. Because of direct, indirect, and implicit government transfers, BOSs can afford to be less efficient, to provide higher wages and benefits to their workers, and to delay potentially painful adjustments in the event of adverse shocks (Pop and Connon 2020). Continued support may also be linked to increased risk taking and moral hazard by BOSs (Dam and Koetter 2012; Hryckiewicz 2014; Marques, Correa, and Sapriza 2018; OECD 2010; Poczter 2016).

A Favorable Regulatory Environment

In order to fulfill their mandates, BOSs are often granted advantageous treatment relative to private firms, such as preferential access to inputs and market protection from new entrants, thereby preserving dominant positions and increasing the costs to compete or discriminating against other firms. Governments may also provide implicit advantages, such as market rules and policies that in principle apply to all market players but in practice protect the position of BOSs or dampen competition in markets in which BOSs are present. SOEs frequently receive such advantages, particularly in middle-income countries as confirmed by the product market regulation data (figure O.6).

The economic rationale for this more favorable regulatory treatment varies across sectors. State involvement seems to be more easily justified in some infrastructure sectors, where a combination of high entry barriers and positive externalities may

FIGURE O.6 SOEs Often Receive Advantageous Treatment

Advantages available to SOEs over private firms, by country income level

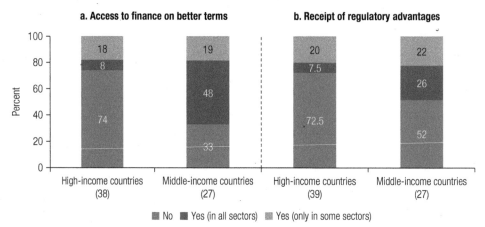

Source: Organisation for Economic Co-operation and Development (OECD) product market regulation (PMR) questionnaires, 2018; OECD and World Bank PMR questionnaires, 2013–22.

Note: PMR indicators measure the regulatory barriers to firm entry and competition in a broad range of key policy areas. SOE = state-owned enterprise.

deter private participation. In the energy sector, this logic would apply, for example, to transmission, which is a natural monopoly, whereas generation can be deemed partially contestable.

At the other end, sectors such as hospitality, real estate, and trade have less justification for regulations enshrining state participation. Nevertheless, it is not unusual to find legal or de facto monopolies in sectors that could otherwise be operated under competitive conditions by the private sector. Examples include meat production in Botswana, cardboard production in Bolivia, and fertilizer provision in The Gambia. In such cases, the regulatory advantage of BOSs is associated with unfair competition with private firms.

These less defensible regulatory advantages typically reflect a conflict of interest. As a policy maker the government has a broader responsibility toward the public. Its regulation of the market and its enforcement of competition law should thus aim at increasing economic efficiency and ensuring a fair distribution of its benefits. However, as an owner of BOSs, the government has an interest in maximizing their revenues and distributing them in politically advantageous ways.

These conflicting roles raise the possibility that the state may make decisions that advantage BOSs over their competitors. Blurred lines between public interest and financial gain call for a careful review of the regulatory environment in which BOSs operate. This is especially needed in competitive markets, where there is not a strong economic rationale for state participation. And the review needs to go beyond the letter

FIGURE O.7   Restrictive Market Regulations Are Correlated with State Ownership

State involvement and restrictive regulations, by country income level, 2018

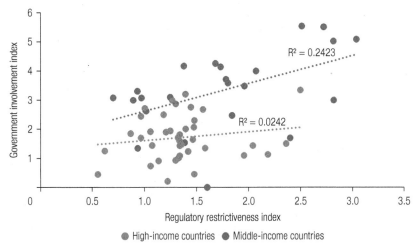

Source: Analysis of the Organisation for Economic Co-operation and Development (OECD) product market regulation (PMR) indicators and the OECD and World Bank PMR indicators; OECD PMR questionnaires, 2018; OECD and World Bank PMR questionnaires, 2013–22.

Note: PMR indicators measure the regulatory barriers to firm entry and competition in a broad range of key policy areas. The data cover energy, communications, and transportation in 39 high-income countries and 23 middle-income countries. The government involvement index measures the degree of state ownership and government control. The regulatory restrictiveness index measures barriers to competition resulting from the presence of anticompetitive regulation or the absence of pro-competition regulation.

of the law, because the state may not adequately protect against anticompetitive behavior or prevent undue exercise of market power by the businesses it owns.

In high-income countries, the state has been replacing direct participation in network sectors (such as energy, communications, and transportation) with indirect interventions, putting in place regulations that would enable private entry and expansion (figure O.7). In middle-income countries, governments have also moved to private ownership but still lag advanced economies on the necessary regulations to support sound market competition and hold dominant firms in check.[4]

A hint at the regulatory advantage BOSs may benefit from is protective tariffs, a restrictive trade policy instrument applied to sectors that are competitive by nature. In more than half of the countries for which product market regulation data are available, tariffs are higher in sectors where BOSs are present, compared to sectors where all domestic suppliers are private firms.

Regulatory advantages in competitive and partially contestable markets can be expected to have a negative impact on economic performance. Even in the absence of financial support by the state, the perception that BOSs could have an easier time getting procurement contracts, or avoid having to meet full regulatory standards, could discourage more efficient private sector firms from entering the market and lower capital mobilization (Shleifer 1998; World Bank 1995).

Regulatory advantages also challenge standard performance measures. For example, a positive relation between state ownership and profitability has been found in sectors where state dominance is high and competition is low (Liljeblom, Maury, and Hörhammer 2020). Firms in which the state holds a golden share have also been found to be more profitable (Kočenda and Svejnar 2003). However, it is not clear whether this higher profitability is driven by efficiency or by government support (Le and Buck 2009; Yu 2013).

Country-level studies provide hints that regulatory advantage is at play. In China, the larger the market share and market power of SOEs is, the lower is the probability of entry of more productive private firms (Brandt, Van Biesebroeck, and Zhang 2012). And, in Poland, SOEs are found to have less financial liquidity and lower inventory management than their private sector counterparts, yet their return on assets is higher (Kabaciński, Kubiak, and Szarzec 2020).

Nonprofit Objectives

State involvement in business is often associated with delivering development objectives, such as providing universal services, contributing to the social contract through employment, expanding access to finance, or driving the energy transition. These motivations are generally perceived by the public as valid justifications for the presence of SOEs in the economy (Vagliasindi, Cordella, and Clifton 2023).

Defensible economic arguments for BOSs not to focus only on their profitability include addressing market failures that could lead to an undersupply of specific goods or services, tapping positive externalities and offsetting negative ones, exercising government control over strategic sectors for national security purposes, and catalyzing investments in new markets when there are first-mover constraints (Bernier, Florio, and Bance 2020; Chang 2002; Mazzucato 2011; Millward 2011).

There is some evidence that BOSs effectively deliver on social goals. For example, in China, SOEs perform better than private firms for pollutants covered by government targets and they perform similarly for the unregulated pollutants (Wang, Liu, and Zhan 2022). The difference suggests that BOSs can be responsive to policy requirements.

However, this example may not necessarily be the norm. A deep dive into the cement industry conducted for this report using annual company and industry data shows that BOSs in the high-emitting cement sector exhibit significantly higher carbon dioxide emissions than their private peers, particularly among the top 10 companies. And in renewable energy, a sector in which commercially viable solutions are available, investments have been driven by the private sector. These findings complement existing research that shows that SOEs in the energy sector are also often financially challenged and have weaker environmental performance than their privatized peers (Asane-Otoo 2016; Harrison et al. 2019; Meyer and Pac 2013). More generally, BOSs' ability to raise resources for new less-carbon-intensive investments or climate adaptation can be constrained by government-imposed prices and their poor financial performance.

The mechanisms at play are informative about the true motives of BOSs. Across 46 countries, a significantly negative relationship exists between market concentration and investments in renewable energy, suggesting that large utilities use their market power to keep out competitors that engage in renewable energy generation (Prag, Röttgers, and Scherrer 2018). This may reflect a determination to maintain the value of sunk-cost investments in fossil fuels by avoiding—and potentially opposing—investments in renewable generation capacity.

A more realistic view of BOSs must therefore recognize that their nonmonetary goals are not necessarily aligned with the public interest. Their jobs represent an important source of political patronage, and their workers may have sufficient leverage to capture higher wages and benefits. Rather than minimizing emissions or ensuring universal service, BOSs could well maximize their own payroll.

The Good, the Bad, and the Ugly

The differences between BOSs and private firms are not in themselves good or bad. Depending on how these differences are leveraged by policy makers, and how they interact with market imperfections and institutional failures in the rest of the economy, BOSs can support good, bad, or ugly aggregate outcomes, which explains why making a case in favor of BOSs, or against them, would be misguided. The relevant question is under which circumstances can good, bad, or ugly outcomes be expected.

From Effective to Wasteful Resource Mobilization

The COVID-19 pandemic illustrated how budget resources can be quickly mobilized through BOSs to address crises or natural disasters. Thus, in Brazil and Indonesia, state-owned aircraft manufacturers were requested to produce ventilator prototypes (World Bank 2021). In El Salvador, the government allowed a three-month deferral of utility payments without having utilities cut off and approved a one-time US$300 subsidy to approximately 75 percent of all households in the country. In Colombia, free water access was provided for over 1 million people without payment. In Serbia, all citizens were granted deferral of the payment of energy bills without surcharges. And, in Angola and Nigeria, governments negotiated with utility companies not to shut off energy supply for nonpayment and to introduce more flexible payment plans.

Temporary financial support to large BOSs may also stabilize employment during crises, thus cushioning social impacts (Kopelman and Rosen 2014). For example, during the COVID-19 crisis, few BOSs furloughed or fired their staff (IMF 2021). As a result, their employees were significantly less likely to have lost their jobs or to have seen their incomes reduced, compared to their private sector counterparts (EBRD 2020). By financially supporting large and at times critically important BOSs, governments may thus have prevented deeper declines in aggregate demand.

However, temporary support was also provided to private firms during the COVID-19 crisis, and some governments went out of their way to avoid discriminating against them. For example, a majority of countries provided resources to airlines to help them navigate the downturn. Yet, to ensure a level playing field, in Norway state support was granted to all airlines holding a Norwegian air operator certificate, and in Sweden to all airlines having a Swedish commercial air transportation license, irrespective of their ownership (Pop and Coelho 2020).

Such evenness was not the norm, however. Out of 112 state support schemes for the air transportation sector in 66 countries, almost 40 percent exclusively targeted BOSs. Among monetarily quantified relief measures for airlines provided by governments or government-backed entities, BOSs received 68 percent of the support, compared to 32 percent for private airlines (Martinez Licetti, Sanchez-Navarro, and Perrottet 2020). And several studies have challenged the view that BOSs performed better than private firms during the COVID-19 crisis (Bortolloti, Fotak, and Wolfe 2022; Herrera Dappe et al. 2023; Jie et al. 2021).

From Market Discipline to Uneven Playing Field

Governments can instill competitive behavior in BOSs through adequate competition legislation and regulation. To avoid the abuse of dominance by vertically integrated public incumbents, governments may limit entry of BOSs into market segments where competition is possible.

Merger control has been another important tool to limit the anticompetitive effects of market consolidation. In Hungary, the competition authority blocked the acquisition by the national telecommunications company of a small regional telecom operator that later grew to become a European player. Similarly, in Namibia, the acquisition of the second-largest mobile operator by the largest public telecom incumbent was allowed on the condition of separating the management and shareholding of both companies.

Good practices also call for BOSs not to act as regulators and market players at the same time. For example, a conglomerate owned by the government of Singapore is the direct owner of many commercial companies at home and abroad. Among other firms, it owns a golden share in Singapore Airlines, a prestigious and successful air carrier. However, this conglomerate is not involved in market regulation, nor in the management of Singapore's international airport, which serves as the airline's main hub.

Unfortunately, examples of BOSs benefiting from regulations that distort competitive markets and affect private sector development are numerous throughout the world. For example, in Nepal, a fully owned BOS that accounts for 63 percent of dairy product output benefits from bans on foreign direct investment and on imports of competing products. And, in Ethiopia, shipments require the letter of credit issued by a fully owned BOS, giving this BOS the monopoly on shipments, especially imports.

Other examples include those where the regulatory role is carried out by the BOSs themselves. In South Africa, a BOS firm that is the owner and operator of all major commercial ports also acts as the port sector regulator. In Ethiopia, a BOS firm that is the sole importer of fertilizer in the country is directly involved in its price regulation and market allocation. In Kenya, a BOS firm involved in seed research and production sits on the regulatory committee that makes decisions about permits and certifications required for private peers. And, in Viet Nam, a BOS firm that is one of several market participants in the oil and gas sector can by law influence investment decisions for all firms in the industry. Similar examples can be reported for Angola in relation to cement and for Serbia for intercity bus transportation. In some cases, beyond a regulatory role, the challenge is conflict of interest. In Egypt, the telecommunications regulator falls under the authority of the ministry in charge of communications and information technologies, which also owns 80 percent of the biggest telecom operator.

From Virtuous to Disturbing Nonprofit Objectives

Because of their public service mandates, BOSs can be levers for governments to effectively advance societal goals despite the lower profitability associated with them. This unique ability to internalize development objectives has been manifest in the energy transition, as countries strive to meet their commitments on climate change mitigation and adaptation. However, government effectiveness can be undermined when BOSs are used to achieve other goals such as revenue generation or employment, creating tensions between mandates.

For example, in less than 15 years, a vertically integrated BOS utility in Uruguay led a dramatic reduction in the country's carbon footprint. By the end of 2019, Uruguay not only supplied 98 percent of its total electricity consumption out of clean energy sources but had also become a net exporter of energy to neighboring Argentina and Brazil. Still, despite potentially having one of the lowest generation costs in the world thanks to its clean generation matrix, the utility's electricity was among the most expensive for both households and firms. This is the result of a different—nonprofit—objective of this BOS, namely to raise revenue for the government (World Bank 2022).

Tensions between mandates for BOSs can be found elsewhere. Mexico's first three clean energy auctions, held in 2016 and 2017, were seen as an unqualified success, bringing major new solar and wind developers into the market and delivering stunningly low prices. However, in 2021, the energy reform that had helped spur the country's early clean energy growth was rolled back. The changes were intended to benefit Mexico's fossil fuel–dependent BOS utility, which was no longer required to purchase energy for basic supply via auctions, and could instead buy from its own power plants, even if the energy generated is dirtier and more expensive (Vagliasindi 2023).

BOSs around the world are often less virtuous than their governments' climate change commitments may suggest. In South Africa, for example, generation by the 100 percent state-owned monopolist electricity company relies on coal, the production of which often dominates local economies and provides highly desirable jobs (Ruppert Bulmer et al. 2021). Generation projects based on solar and wind energy have been awarded after fierce competition, and their generation cost is 40–50 percent cheaper than those of the new state-owned coal-fired plants (Montrone, Ohlendorf, and Chandra 2022). However, these projects were delayed by the state-owned utility.

Similarly, in Indonesia, about three-quarters of coal production is purchased by a 100 percent state-owned electricity company that owns 73 percent of installed generation capacity. The nonprofit objective in this case seems to be social, because coal mining jobs pay more than most other sectors and employment is highly concentrated in two remote regions (Ruppert Bulmer et al. 2021). Employment objectives can openly clash not only with environmental goals but also with health and safety considerations.

Finally, the reliance on BOSs in the energy transition should not deter private investment. Across the world, the private sector has been the major driver of investment in renewable energy generation. To decarbonize the energy sector, many countries will have to liberalize markets, pursue ambitious BOS reforms, and create level playing fields between private and state-owned actors.

When Are Good Outcomes More Likely?

While state business ownership is likely to continue, what it accomplishes very much depends on how BOSs interact with the rest of the economy. The features that distinguish them from private firms—a softer budget constraint, a more favorable regulatory environment, and nonprofit objectives—may make them useful tools for economic policy.

But these features may also get compounded with the economy's market imperfections and institutional failures and come at a cost in terms of growth and jobs. The impact of state participation in markets on an economy is therefore shaped by the type of public-private ownership characterizing BOSs, by the structure of the markets they participate in, and by the broader policies and institutions that regulate state ownership.

At the Enterprise Level

State ownership can take multiple forms. How large the share of a firm's equity belonging to the state is, which agencies or bodies exercise the rights associated with such share, and how those agencies or bodies influence day-to-day decisions at the enterprise level all matter for BOS performance.

As revealed by the empirical analysis conducted for this report, minority state-owned firms often perform better than those with majority or sole state ownership. There is also some evidence that firms that are directly owned have lower growth rates than those owned indirectly. These regularities suggest that a greater detachment of state authorities from BOS firm management—leaving more wiggle room for their private partners to make business decisions—is associated with greater efficiency.

Which state agency or body is in charge is relevant too. The exposure of BOSs to state influence is greatest when ownership rights are exercised by a line ministry and lowest when they are exercised by a specialized agency that operates at arm's length from the government.

However, across a sample of 69 countries for which information is available, only a small percentage use arm's length specialized agencies. Instead, more than half of the countries have line ministries in charge, with the proportion being higher in relatively less developed countries. Higher-income countries are also more likely to have safeguards to ensure that BOS firm chief executive officers are appointed by board members rather than by public authorities, which reduces the likelihood that day-to-day decision-making will be influenced by government (figure O.8).

Politicians are not the only possible source of influence on BOSs. Pressures to depart from their intended mandates may also arise from the inside. BOSs provide some of the most coveted jobs in developing countries. In many cases, their employees are covered by protections against termination or pressures to perform akin to those enjoyed by civil servants. Their salaries and benefits—from annual leave to health care to old-age pensions—tend to be more generous than in the private sector.

These privileges may be attributed to the willingness of the government to set higher standards as a reference for aspirational private sector employers. But they are as likely to stem from insider pressure, aimed at capturing the rents made possible by the soft

FIGURE 0.8 How State Ownership Rights Translate into Managerial Decisions

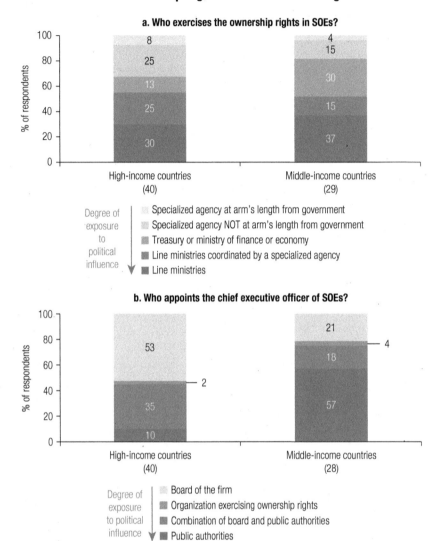

a. Who exercises the ownership rights in SOEs?

Degree of exposure to political influence ↓
- Specialized agency at arm's length from government
- Specialized agency NOT at arm's length from government
- Treasury or ministry of finance or economy
- Line ministries coordinated by a specialized agency
- Line ministries

b. Who appoints the chief executive officer of SOEs?

Degree of exposure to political influence ↓
- Board of the firm
- Organization exercising ownership rights
- Combination of board and public authorities
- Public authorities

Source: Organisation for Economic Co-operation and Development (OECD) product market regulation (PMR) questionnaires, 2018; OECD and World Bank PMR questionnaires, 2013–22.

Note: PMR indicators measure the regulatory barriers to firm entry and competition in a broad range of key policy areas. SOE = state-owned enterprise.

budget constraint and by the market power provided to BOSs by natural monopolies and a favorable regulatory environment.

Measuring the wage premium associated with employment in BOSs raises methodological challenges, because their workers may differ in unobservable ways from private sector workers (Arnold 2022; Bales and Rama 2002; Gindling et al. 2020). However, the regulatory framework applying to a BOS firm provides some hints to the potential for rent capture by insiders. This potential is higher the more protected

BOS firm jobs are, and the less likely it is that the BOS will be allowed to go bankrupt and close operations.

Measures that subject BOSs to market discipline and competitive neutrality can improve BOSs' performance, while achieving their public service obligations. In Morocco, the government makes agreements with BOSs on key performance indicators and scope of activities called *contract programs* (Article 7 of Law 69-00). In the case of the national airline, these contract programs provide incentives to respond to market forces and drive the company toward profitability, while offering adequate compensation for its public service obligations.[5]

At the Sector Level

Around the world, BOSs operate in a range of sectors that differ both in their market structure and in the way competition among market players is regulated. In some sectors, fixed costs and returns to scale are such that only one firm—the natural monopolist—can be expected to operate. In others, there is potentially more than one supplier, or at least the incumbent can be challenged by new entrants. In principle, BOSs are more prevalent in natural monopolies and in sectors with public service obligations. But the cross-country BOS data assembled for this report show that this is not the case.

Across the 91 countries covered by the BOS database, the vast majority of BOSs operate in competitive or partially contestable markets (figure O.9). Because BOSs in natural monopoly markets tend to be larger and more capital intensive, the share accounted for by competitive or partially contestable markets is highest when the metric chosen is number of firms and lowest when it is the employment level.

Unless market regulation ensures a level playing field, a strong BOS firm presence in competitive or partially contestable markets runs the risk of undermining private sector entry, favoring market consolidation, and slowing down innovation. An analysis of the World Bank's latest data collected on anticompetitive laws and policies across 10 countries and seven key economic sectors shows that regulatory restrictions are more frequent in sectors with BOSs. Restrictions are found in three out of four sectors with a BOS presence. For example, BOSs often benefit by being granted exclusive rights, being protected by quotas and price controls, being involved in regulating the sector, and being exempt from economywide laws. Where these explicit and implicit advantages are combined, BOSs may enjoy full control over the market in which they operate.

The challenge for regulators is to foster efficiency and prevent the exercise of excessive market power. Whether they can do so depends on how the regulatory environment handles the potential conflict between the state as a regulator in the public interest and the state as a self-interested market player. Anticompetitive regulations are less likely when regulations are designed and enforced by a specialized agency that operates

FIGURE 0.9 **Most Business Activity by the State Is in Competitive or Partially Contestable Markets**

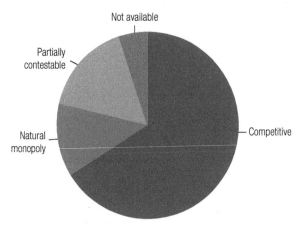

Source: World Bank Global Businesses of the State (BOS) database; 91 countries.

at arm's length from BOSs. This kind of separation is unfortunately less frequent in middle-income countries than in high-income countries.

The conflict between the state as a regulator and as a business owner disappears when BOSs operate in foreign markets, whose competition rules are set abroad. Internationalization can thus become an explicit policy to expose BOSs to market discipline and to improve their global competitiveness. About 70 percent of countries in the BOS database have state-owned companies with a presence abroad, with operations across borders run through subsidiaries or indirectly owned businesses—including sovereign wealth funds. These companies are in principle subject to greater market discipline than BOSs operating exclusively within borders. However, these firms should not benefit from government subsidies and credit guarantees, which would tilt the playing field in their favor abroad.

At the Economywide Level

Good outcomes are more likely when other parts of the government machinery help BOSs keep focused on their mandates while preventing them from creating unwarranted risks for the rest of the economy. For example, a soft budget constraint may help BOSs attain their objectives quickly, but an excessively loose constraint may undermine their drive for efficiency and end up imposing a disproportionate burden on taxpayers. Similarly, oversight exercised at arm's length may give BOSs the flexibility they need to be nimble, but weak oversight may result in the accumulation of hidden debts and contingent liabilities. And not trying to influence day-to-day decisions may avoid political interference, but not intervening at all may reduce incentives for good performance by managers and workers.

In the end, the overall quality of governance in a country is bound to determine whether BOSs deliver good, bad, or ugly outcomes. Preventing an excessively loose budget constraint requires good fiscal institutions that are able to transfer resources to BOSs when justified, but to condition support on performance and to assess that targets are indeed being met. Avoiding situations in which BOSs need to be bailed out requires solid debt management capabilities so that their liabilities and risks can be evaluated in real time. And providing incentives for the management of BOSs to perform as expected requires strong accountability mechanisms, including the ability to reward or dismiss those in charge of delivering, from chief executive officers to technical cadres and workers.

There is some evidence pointing to the important role played by the broader institutional setting in which BOSs operate. Thus, widespread gaps in BOS firm performance across Europe and Central Asia have been attributed to a large extent to differences in governance (IMF 2019). Across 30 countries in this region, the effect of BOSs on economic growth in the period 2010–16 has been found to be neither positive nor negative in general, but the sign depends on the countries' institutions. The impact is more beneficial when institutions are strong and more detrimental when they are weak. These effects become statistically significant in the low- and high-end tails of institutional quality (Szarzec, Totleben, and Piątek 2022). And whether BOSs are leaders or laggers in climate action depends on enabling factors, including sound institutions and regulations (Isungset 2022; Talukdar and Meisner 2001).

Finally, the institutional capacity and the implementation of competitive neutrality across markets matter when transitioning BOSs to private sector players. Governments have several measures at hand to implement this transition effectively for the benefit of consumers and businesses (box O.2). Effective pro-competition regulation of incumbents that were former BOS monopolies is essential to facilitating an adequate transition.

BOX O.2

The Subsidiarity Principle of Business of the State and Market Reforms: The Case of Peruvian Telecommunications Markets

According to the subsidiarity principle, the state plays a subsidiary role in the provision of economic activities. This principle is grounded in both economic and social considerations. The state's resources are limited and must be assigned to the most valuable objectives. The principle of subsidiarity represents a limit to state action in the market, as it establishes that the state can only intervene in the market with a business of the state firm if the private supply is insufficient or nonexistent. If private agents are interested and capable of supplying goods and services to attend demand, then the best means for the state to intervene in those markets is by supervising

(Box continues on the following page.)

The Subsidiarity Principle of Business of the State and Market Reforms: The Case of Peruvian Telecommunications Markets *(continued)*

and controlling the behavior of those private agents. Meanwhile, the direct intervention of the state focuses on (1) supplying essential goods and services that will not be provided by private agents, that is, the social role of the state driven by distributive and welfare objectives; or (2) those activities that, according to the country's highest rank laws, cannot be performed by the private sector. In parallel, complementary regulatory reforms are implemented for goods and services to be provided in a competitive manner. Deregulation is also implemented in such a way that the business environment gives incentive for entry and operation of a competitive private sector.

In line with this principle, in Peru, during 2001–02, Indecopi's Free Competition Commission analyzed state-owned enterprises (SOEs) in a variety of sectors, including the postal service, commercial aviation, ship building, and the commercialization of coca leaves, which helped reform these sectors and bring private investment. Similarly, for the case of the opening up of the telecommunications sector, a strong regulatory and institutional framework was established to guarantee a proper transition from the SOE dominant player. The concession contract for the provision of telecom services was granted to a private player, initially for a five-year period, including a national monopoly in fixed telephony and domestic and international long distance.

During this period, the concessionaire was to expand and improve fixed telephony service, public service telephony, and universal service obligations in rural areas. Competition was permitted in other services, including mobile telephony, pay phones, beepers, and cable television. Additionally, the contract set specific investment goals to build the infrastructure (new lines) and thus decrease the price and increase the quality of service for consumers. The concession contract included an explicit competition clause. The clause stipulated that the concessionaire was obliged not to abuse its dominance position, not to engage in tying practices, not to discriminate in allowing other service providers access to the network, and to eliminate cross-subsidies between long distance and local telephony services. The telecom regulator played a fundamental role in the transaction. It participated in all the final stages of the privatization and renewal of contracts to make sure that the contract adhered to competition principles.

This resulted in successful bidding for the concession, over US$2 billion (almost four times more than the minimum asked price), an additional 1.19 million phone lines in the first five years, reduction of cross-price distortions between services (that is, rebalancing of rates) with a recomposition of the structure of operating earnings, completion of calls from 35 percent to over 95 percent, digitization of the network from 30 percent to over 90 percent, significant reduction in the cost and time of installing a phone line (from more than US$1,500 and several years to get a fixed line), more efficiency in the number of employees, and reduction in the allocation of its costs to wages and salaries, which was estimated at about 40 percent. The impact on consumer welfare was also significant. An important regulatory improvement after privatization was the guidelines established by the ministry and regulator for the full opening of the market, setting up rules for new market concessions to competing firms, tariff policies such as application of the total factor productivity factor to reduce rates, cost-based models to set interconnection rates, interconnection policy, access to infrastructure and essential facilities, new obligations for expanding network connectivity and its penetration, spectrum access, network digitization and quality of service, and revision of compliance with competitive regulations.

Sources: Congreso de la Republica del Perú 2002; Government of Peru Decreto Supremo 020-1998-MTC; OECD 2004; Torero 2002; Torero et al. 2003; UNCTAD 2004.

A Practical Guide for Policy Makers

The new evidence generated for this report, together with the findings from previous studies, provides guidance on whether and how to rely on BOSs as a tool for development policy. This is a time when policy makers around the world seem increasingly upbeat about the contribution state ownership can make to development objectives. Offering a few clear principles and some practical checks to implement them could help make the most out of BOSs, while at the same time highlighting the potential risks and proposing the most pertinent reform options to improve expected outcomes.

By relying on the broad BOS definition used in this report, this guidance should also help policy makers bring to the surface the least visible parts of the state's involvement in business, and hopefully trigger healthy country-level discussions on the most appropriate way forward.

First-Best Policies Rarely Require State Ownership

When deciding whether to rely on BOSs to attain specific development objectives, a first question concerns the economic rationale for the state's involvement in business. According to the subsidiarity principle, the state's duty is to perform only those socially valuable tasks for which private supply is not feasible or is clearly insufficient. From this perspective, BOSs should not displace private businesses that are fully capable of meeting social needs.

The first step in any protocol related to BOSs should therefore be to identify the least distortive policy alternative to attain specific social goals. This requires understanding the trade-off between the benefits from state ownership and its potential unintended consequences, recognizing that state participation in the production of goods and services is not always necessary to solve market imperfections or address institutional failures.

For example, BOSs can be used as a countercyclical policy tool, helping to stabilize delivery and employment during downturns or mitigating negative shocks. However, the first-best instruments to cushion economic fluctuations are fiscal and monetary policy. In a downturn, governments can spend more on physical infrastructure and social programs, and they can transfer resources to households to support their consumption. Monetary authorities can also use interest rates and banking regulation tools to facilitate access to credit for firms.

Encouraging BOSs to expand their activity may seem compelling as well, especially because they most often pay higher wages and offer more stable job opportunities and are therefore seen as providing better jobs. However, because BOSs face less budgetary discipline and less competitive pressure than their private sector counterparts, resources are likely to be used less efficiently than if they were directly channeled to households or firms. Besides, the greater scale of BOSs' activity may be politically difficult to unwind after the downturn is over, eventually absorbing significant public resources.

BOSs can also be used as an industrial policy tool, solving some market failures in emerging sectors and jump-starting economic activity in laggard areas. However, other policy instruments are likely to achieve the same goals with lower risks of resource waste or political capture. Subsidies can make private firms internalize the positive network spillovers they generate in emerging sectors, or their positive externalities in laggard areas. Direct support to universities may compensate for the difficulties in appropriating the benefits from basic research. And advance purchase commitments may make private innovation efforts toward social goals become profitable.

In principle, BOSs could step in and tap their own resources to offset the losses from sectoral and local spillovers, incomplete property rights on new ideas, or sunk costs on risky innovation projects. But there is no guarantee that they will be as efficient as private firms in undertaking these tasks. With a softer budget constraint, a more favorable regulatory environment, and weak incentives to perform, BOSs may not be sufficiently nimble to identify the projects with the strongest economic potential, and to adjust and change course along the way as needed. Accountability, incentives, and expectations about return are typically different between private and public ownership of capital.

Finally, BOSs are often used to deliver on socially valuable tasks that are not privately profitable, such as providing service coverage for lower-income households and those in remote areas, or advancing the decarbonization of the economy. However, the financial resources needed to accomplish goals could be channeled through the demand side rather than the supply side. Universal service coverage may be mandatory for utilities, with the budget filling the gap where it is unprofitable. And taxes, subsidies, and standards can provide incentives for the adoption of green technologies by the private sector.

The question in this respect is whether the public resources devoted to these social goals will be more effectively used if they are channeled through BOSs than through private firms. When it comes to service delivery, there is a risk that public utilities will be overstaffed relative to their private counterparts, and that their responsiveness to customers will be lower. As for climate-related goals, BOSs may be large and operate in network sectors (such as energy, telecommunications, and transportation), but they are still just a few economic units, whereas taxes on carbon emissions or standards for carbon-saving technologies apply to all firms.

Toward Greater Transparency on Companies with State Ownership

The cross-country BOS database assembled for this report underscores the significant information gaps that remain on the extent of state ownership of firms, on the support these firms receive—explicitly or implicitly—and on their performance. Even at the central level, some countries do not have information on the number of jobs or revenue

FIGURE 0.10   State Footprint Is Often Unknown Due to Lack of Information

Share of BOSs not reporting employment data, select countries

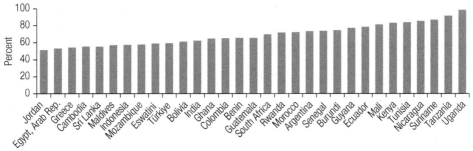

Source: World Bank Global Businesses of the State (BOS) database.
Note: BOSs = businesses of the state.

generated by companies with state investments. For example, 31 countries in the database lack employment information for half or more of their BOSs (figure O.10). Data are even more scattered in relation to other indicators, such as fiscal transfers or outstanding debt, which are necessary to get a full reading of the state's footprint in the economy. And data are frequently unavailable for BOSs that do not directly report to the central government.

More transparency on BOSs is essential to ensure accountability, to support a level playing field at the sector level, to allow for a sustainable fiscal situation at the aggregate level, and to provide confidence to private investors.

More transparency is especially important in countries with a large state presence, with conglomerate groups whose operations are not easy to grasp, and with sovereign wealth funds. To understand the true extent of the state footprint in commercial sectors, it is indeed crucial to consider indirect ownership stakes in other firms, across markets, and in value chains. Uncovering these ownership links should unveil upstream and downstream relationships and vertical integration issues that can inhibit competition and create fiscal risks.

Making BOSs' operations transparent requires the full and timely disclosure of their financial reports. But it is also important to gain a clear picture of the advantages granted by the state to each BOS firm in the form of direct transfers, consumption or production subsidies, tax exemptions, and other preferential treatment. Transparency also involves the explicit costing of the public service obligations for each company with state ownership, as well as an assessment of its contingent liabilities.

A Scorecard to Predict Outcomes and Identify Risks

Although state ownership of commercial businesses is rarely the first-best policy response to any development challenge, governments still choose to rely on their BOSs to attain social goals. For example, first-best policies may be difficult to implement for technical reasons, and putting them in motion may take time for political reasons. Given that BOSs are ubiquitous in developing countries, using them as a second-best policy tool could be defensible.

Whether good outcomes can be expected from this choice, and the ensuing risks contained, depends on the characteristics of the BOSs and on the way they interact with the rest of the economy. Therefore, it is worth assessing the strengths and weaknesses of individual BOSs before deciding to rely on any of them for economic policy.

The findings in this report suggest that governments should systematically set targets and measure the performance against them of individual BOSs along four major dimensions: (1) transparency, (2) firm characteristics, (3) the structure of the market in which they operate, and (4) the broader institutional environment. Table O.1 presents an illustration of a simple scorecard that can be adapted to each country context and BOS firm, complemented with specific key performance indicators (KPIs). KPIs go beyond financial performance indicators and should include efficiency measures. Efficiency KPIs measure the degree of efficiency in using resources (labor, management, and capital) to generate output and revenue (for example, labor productivity and utilization of production capacity).

This scorecard should be implemented in the context of the following five guiding principles for governments to engage with BOSs: (1) develop a nationwide mapping of BOSs under various line ministries and agencies and in different sectors to monitor performance and fiscal costs; (2) apply the subsidiarity principle (focus direct participation only on markets where private supply is insufficient or nonexistent—see box O.2); (3) put in place strong institutions to regulate markets, ensure separation between commercial and noncommercial roles of BOS firms, and address the risk of capture by insiders; (4) ensure competitive neutrality of regulations and policies and their enforcement, including labor regulations, as well as direct and indirect support, between BOS firms and privately owned firms; and (5) prepare phase-out strategies for BOSs not needed anymore.

A practical way to conduct this assessment is to give a rating ranging from 0 to 10 to each of the indicators under the four headings in the table. By construction, the sum of these ratings is a score ranging from 0 to 100. The larger the aggregate score, the higher the probability that good outcomes will be attained and the lower the risk of bad—or even ugly—consequences for the rest of the economy.

This aggregate score is not a statistically rigorous predictor, but rather a heuristic tool. The assessment methodology assumes that all 10 indicators carry the same weight and that credible ratings can be produced for each of them, which is of course questionable. But the methodology has the advantage of being replicable, so that different experts, think tanks, or researchers in a country can produce their own BOS firm

TABLE 0.1 A Scorecard of the Strengths and Weaknesses of Individual BOSs

Dimension	Indicator	Rating
Data transparency and performance monitoring	1. Financial reports are timely, reliable, and publicly available. Direct and indirect government support is quantified and systematically monitored. Debt and its service are adequately documented. BOSs' efficiency and performance with specific key performance indicators (KPIs), execution of performance contracts, and achievement of other goals (for example, sustainability and resilience) are monitored. KPIs include the return on equity and equity/assets ratio, dividend policy, share of employment, portfolio value, labor productivity, and utilization of production capacity.[a]	0–10
Company characteristics	2. State ownership rights are exercised by a specialized agency rather than by a line ministry. The BOS firm has a competitively selected private partner with a stake in its performance. Board members representing the state are appointed based on professional rather than political criteria.	0–10
	3. The management of the BOS firm is appointed based on professional rather than political criteria. Sound corporate governance principles are followed. The personnel of the BOS firm are subject to the same labor regulations that apply to private firms. Dismissal for underperformance is feasible.	0–10
	4. The commercial and noncommercial activities of BOSs are clearly separated, and the costs of each activity can be properly identified and allocated. The commercial activity of BOSs yields rates of return like comparable private businesses over a reasonable period to prevent private sector competitors from being undercut.	0–10
Sector characteristics	5. The sector is a natural monopoly or is characterized by positive or negative externalities. Some potential for contestability by private entrants exists.	0–10
	6. The agency in charge of regulating the sector operates at arm's length from the company. Efficiency, equity, and security are its most important goals.	0–10
	7. Effective competition policies apply to the sector. Mergers leading to anticompetitive effects are prevented, and abuse of significant market power is penalized. Regulatory neutrality applies (for example, equal treatment for corporate and commercial law).	0–10
Institutional context	8. Transfers of resources from the government are linked to well-specified mandates. The BOS firm is not automatically supported if it underperforms. The compensation paid by the public authorities to the BOS firm for the delivery of public service obligations is transparent and limited to the minimum necessary to avoid cross-subsidization. Mechanisms of adjustments and compensation should balance out the BOSs' preferential access to finance through state-owned banks or government guarantees. The transfers to BOSs are assessed, monitored, and captured in published subsidies data.	0–10
	9. The buildup of contingent liabilities by the BOS firm and its potential to create systemic risk are adequately assessed, regularly monitored, and captured in overall contingent liabilities disclosures.	0–10
	10. There is reasonable control of corruption in the country, including disclosure of beneficial ownership for procurement contracts. The chances that the BOS firm will be used for private gain are limited. The access of the BOS firm to public contracts and their overall treatment during public procurement is open, transparent, and nondiscriminatory.	0–10
Overall	Aggregate score	0–100

Source: Original table for this report.

Note: BOSs = businesses of the state.

a. A good practice is to evaluate the fulfillment of individual BOSs against financial and nonfinancial targets set by the state-owner and disclosure of noncommercial assistance (OECD 2022).

rankings, compare the results, and identify where disagreements lie. And this replicability, in turn, should allow for some research on which indicators are associated with better outcomes in practice.

By itself, this discussion could make the business of the state in a country more visible and help build consensus on the strengths and weaknesses of its various BOSs. The rating exercise would also provide guidance on whether specific BOSs could or should be used for policy purposes. And it would help identify the areas where further policy reforms are needed to maximize the chances that good outcomes will be attained.

A Sunset Path When Bad Outcomes Are Likely

Rating the strengths and weaknesses of individual BOSs allows for a triage of reform options. Those with a high score can be used as policy instruments when first-best options are out of reach or take time to implement. BOSs with intermediate scores may call for action to improve their overall rating through measures ranging from improving their corporate governance to strengthening the independence of the regulators for the markets they operate in.

The weakest scores across the 10 indicators should guide the identification of the most appropriate reform measures for each of them. The implementation of such measures should be guided by a set of reform principles that apply across markets. But measures would also need to be tailored to the types of markets where BOSs operate—in competitive, partially contestable, and monopoly markets.

In many cases, however, the prospect for individual BOSs to reach a decent rating in the short to medium term may be slim. Given the reported overreach of state ownership into economic activities, especially in the aftermath of the COVID-19 crisis, charting a sunset path for these weak BOSs should be a central tenet of development policy. Options in this case range from divestiture and greater private sector involvement to outright closure.

Private actors can be mobilized through various mechanisms. Management contracts retain state ownership but delegate operational decisions to private investors for a specific period. They are particularly useful when service delivery involves a public good for which the delivery is relatively straightforward to monitor, as in the case of waste management. Public-private partnership arrangements and concessions transfer assets or stakes to the private sector. They are especially well suited for BOSs in sectors such as transportation, power generation, or telecommunications.

A common feature of these mechanisms is to bring private skills and expertise into companies with state ownership. Concessions and especially public-private partnership arrangements also attract private investment. In all cases, however, an element of subsidization may be needed to cover universal service obligations and positive externalities from the activity of the BOS firm, if any. Regulation may also be needed to ensure that the public interest is safeguarded as management or ownership is transferred to private actors.

In all cases the design of a sunset path should be geared toward strengthening market discipline. The rich experience accumulated with the privatization of state assets is valuable for identifying good practices but also common pitfalls (box O.3). Embedding competition considerations within the process itself and monitoring the market ex post can ensure that the intended outcomes are achieved.

BOX 0.3

Lessons from Privatization Episodes around the World

Until around 2005, privatization efforts were dominated by governments in Europe selling utilities, telecoms, airlines, and energy companies; but more recently it is governments in emerging markets that have been divesting stakes in national oil companies, manufacturers, infrastructure assets, and, especially, banks. Europe's share of global privatization proceeds decreased from roughly half around 1999 to less than 25 percent by 2009. More recently, Brazil, China, India, the Russian Federation, and Türkiye have become major privatizers—although the United States led globally for a few years by selling bank stakes acquired during the global financial crisis (Megginson, López, and Malik 2021a).

A review of businesses of the state (BOSs) reform episodes in seven countries, conducted for this report, sheds some light on the motivation for these efforts. The countries covered were Costa Rica, Ethiopia, Kazakhstan, the Republic of Korea, Pakistan, Serbia, and Uzbekistan; and the episodes considered focused mainly on privatization and accountability between the 1970s and the 2000s. The reforms' main goals were to address fiscal burdens and risks, to contain political influence and vested interests, to fight corruption, and to respond to citizens' demand for better service delivery. In several cases, there was also a will to increase the space for the private sector.

As for the mechanisms used, China has been unique in privatizing BOSs by allowing them to raise capital by selling newly issued primary shares to investors. State ownership is thus diluted indirectly by increasing the total shares outstanding rather than by having the state sell its shareholdings to investors. This approach significantly increased the size and liquidity of China's stock market. Sales have been relatively small in other emerging markets. This might reflect partial divestment strategies but could also result from multiple tranches of public share offerings spread over several years with the goal to not overwhelm the stock market's absorptive capacity and to maximize long-term sale proceeds (Megginson and Malik 2022).

On the one hand, data confirm that privatization did reduce losses and improve financial performance. However, success varied across sectors and gains were unevenly distributed. The main beneficiaries were generally the new owners, and losses were often suffered by workers, consumers, and other stakeholders. There were also legitimate concerns about opacity and corruption in privatization processes (ADB 2020).

(Box continues on the following page.)

On the other hand, improvements to BOS oversight and governance did not consistently lead to better performance. For example, six state-owned airlines whose corporate governance was strengthened with World Bank support continued to face challenges. Over time, experiences such as these led to the growing recognition that traditional corporate governance reforms are not a replacement for facilitating market discipline and creating sustainable business models.

A major concern in charting a sunset path for weak BOSs concerns their personnel. The performance of these companies may be underwhelming, but their jobs remain coveted because of the higher pay, better benefits, and stronger job security. And they tend to be overstaffed. In places where BOSs are significant employers, entire communities may be affected.

In Brazil, for example, employer-employee matched data that allow controlling for individual characteristics show that relative wages declined by about 10 percent in the first two years after privatization (Arnold 2022). In Sweden, they fell by about 4 percent in the first two years and by 9 percent during the third and fourth years (Olsson and Tåg 2021). In Viet Nam, matching privatized firms with similar ones that were not privatized shows a significant initial decline in employment, followed by a somewhat lower but still sustained decline in the following years (Hallward-Driemeier, Aterido, and Tran 2023). And, in Poland, the reduction in coal mining jobs generated persistent economic challenges in the surrounding communities (Ruppert Bulmer et al. 2021).

Not adequately addressing the associated losses may be perceived as unfair and may also undermine the political viability of reforms. This requires paying explicit attention to the scale and composition of public sector downsizing, the amount of compensation to be provided to redundant workers, and the support affected communities may require (Rama 1999).

Notes

1. The good, bad, and ugly categorization is borrowed from Laeven and Valencia (2010).

2. Revenues based on 43 countries with high firm-level data coverage.

3. The general theorem for the second-best optimum states that, if there is introduced into a general equilibrium system a constraint that prevents the attainment of one of the Paretian conditions, the other Paretian conditions, although still attainable, are, in general, no longer desirable. In other words, given that one of the Paretian optimum conditions cannot be fulfilled, then an optimum situation can be achieved only by departing from all the other Paretian conditions. The optimum situation finally attained may be termed a second-best optimum because it is achieved subject to a constraint that, by definition, prevents the attainment of a Paretian optimum.

4. The product market regulation indicators were designed and collected by the Organisation for Economic Co-operation and Development for some countries and jointly collected with the World Bank for other countries.

5. Royal Air Maroc is in charge of connecting certain parts of the country by maintaining unprofitable routes for which it receives compensation from the regions; however, regions can enter into these types of agreements with other carriers.

References

ADB (Asian Development Bank). 2020. "Reforms, Opportunities and Challenges for State-Owned Enterprises." Asian Development Bank, Manila.

Akcigit, U., and S. M. Cilasun. 2023. "State-Owned Enterprises in Türkiye." Background paper for this report, World Bank, Washington, DC.

Andres, L. A., J. L. Guasch, T. Haven, and V. Foster. 2008. *The Impact of Private Sector Participation in Infrastructure: Light, Shadows and the Road Ahead*. Washington, DC: World Bank.

Arnold, D. 2022. "The Impact of Privatization of State-Owned Enterprises on Workers." *American Economic Journal: Applied Economics* 14 (4): 343–80.

Asane-Otoo, E. 2016. "Competition Policy and Environmental Quality: Empirical Analysis of the Electricity Sector in OECD Countries." *Energy Policy* 95: 212–23.

Bales, S., and M. Rama. 2002. "Are Public Sector Workers Underpaid? Appropriate Comparators in a Developing Country." *Semantic Scholar*. https://www.semanticscholar.org/paper/Are-Public -Sector-Workers-Underpaid-Appropriate-in-Bales-Rama/693e6ab3c0a30e1c9ee373111f81fa 5cc4590637.

Bernier, L., M. Florio, and P. Bance, eds. 2020. *The Routledge Handbook of State-Owned Enterprises*. London: Routledge.

Bognetti, G. 2020. "History of Western State-Owned Enterprises: From the Industrial Revolution to the Age of Globalization." In *The Routledge Handbook of State-Owned Enterprises*, edited by L. Bernier, M. Florio, and P. Bance, 25–44. London: Routledge.

Bortolotti, B., V. Fotak, and B. Wolfe. 2022. "Government Share Ownership and Innovation: Evidence from European Listed Firms." BAFFI CAREFIN Centre Research Paper 2018-72, University of Turin, Turin, Italy.

Brandt, L., J. Van Biesebroeck, and Y. Zhang. 2012. "Creative Accounting or Creative Destruction? Firm-Level Productivity Growth in Chinese Manufacturing." *Journal of Development Economics* 97 (2): 339–51.

Chang, H.-J. 2002. *Kicking Away the Ladder: Development Strategy in Historical Perspective*. London: Anthem Press.

Cirera, X., S. Brolhato, and A. Martins-Neto. 2023. "Businesses of the State in Brazil: Employment and Impact on Business Dynamism." Background paper for this report, World Bank, Washington, DC.

Congreso de la Republica del Perú. 2002. "Informe Especial de Investigación – El Proceso de Privatización de las Empresas." Lima.

Dall'Olio, A., T. Goodwin, M. M. Licetti, A. C. Alonso Soria, M. Drozd, J. Orlowski, F. Patiño Peña, and D. Sanchez-Navarro. 2022a. "Are All State-Owned Enterprises (SOEs) Equal? A Taxonomy of Economic Activities to Assess SOE Presence in the Economy." Policy Research Working Paper 10262, World Bank, Washington, DC.

Dall'Olio, A., T. Goodwin, M. M. Licetti, J. Orlowski, F. Patiño Peña, F. Ratsimbazafy, and D. Sanchez-Navarro. 2022b. "Using ORBIS to Build a Global Database of Firms with State Participation." Policy Research Working Paper 10261, World Bank, Washington, DC.

Dam, L., and M. Koetter. 2012. "Bank Bailouts and Moral Hazard: Evidence from Germany." *Review of Financial Studies* 25 (8): 2343–80.

Dauda, S., G. Pop, and M. Iootty. 2023. "Romania: State-Owned Enterprises Performance and Their Stabilizing Role during the COVID-19 Pandemic." Background paper for this report, World Bank, Washington, DC.

Dewenter, K., and P. Malatesta. 2001. "State-Owned and Privately Owned Firms: An Empirical Analysis of Profitability, Leverage, and Labor Intensity." *American Economic Review* 91 (1): 320–34.

Divakaran, S., H. Halland, G. Lorenzato, P. Rose, and S. Sarmiento-Saher. 2022. *Strategic Investment Funds: Establishment and Operations*. International Development in Focus. Washington, DC: World Bank.

EBRD (European Bank for Reconstruction and Development). 2020. *Life in Transition Survey, Transition Report 2020–2021: The State Strikes Back*. London: EBRD.

Ferro, E., and F. Patiño Peña. 2023. "Private Sector Performance under the Pressure of SOE Competition: The Case of Ecuador." Background paper for this report, World Bank, Washington, DC.

Freund, C., and J. Pesme. 2021. "Five Ways We Can Support Viable but Vulnerable Businesses during COVID-19 Recovery." Unpublished manuscript, World Bank, Washington, DC.

Gelb, A., S. Tordo, H. Halland, N. Arfaa, and G. Smith. 2014. "Sovereign Wealth Funds and Long-Term Development Finance: Risks and Opportunities." Policy Research Working Paper 6776, World Bank, Washington, DC.

Gindling, T., Z. Hasnain, D. Newhouse, and R. Shi. 2020. "Are Public Sector Workers in Developing Countries Overpaid? Evidence from a New Global Dataset." *World Development* 126: 104737.

Hallward-Driemeier, M., R. Aterido, and T. Tran. 2023. "Businesses of the State in Viet Nam: Catalysts or Constraints to Private Sector Development?" Background paper for this report, World Bank, Washington, DC.

Harrison, A., M. Meyer, P. Wang, L. Zhao, and M. Zhao. 2019. "Can a Tiger Change Its Stripes? Reform of Chinese State-Owned Enterprises in the Penumbra of the State." NBER Working Paper 25475, National Bureau of Economic Research, Cambridge, MA.

Herrera Dappe, M., V. Foster, A. Musacchio, T. Ter-Minassian, and B. Turkgulu. 2023. *Off the Books: Understanding and Mitigating the Fiscal Risks of Infrastructure*. Sustainable Infrastructure Series. Washington, DC: World Bank.

Hryckiewicz, A. 2014. "What Do We Know about the Impact of Government Interventions in the Banking Sector? An Assessment of Various Bailout Programs on Bank Behavior." *Journal of Banking and Finance* 46: 246–65.

IEA (International Energy Agency). 2023. *Fossil Fuels Consumption Subsidies 2022*. Paris: International Energy Agency.

IMF (International Monetary Fund). 2019. *Reassessing the Role of State-Owned Enterprises in Central, Eastern, and Southeastern Europe*. IMF European Department Series. Washington, DC: IMF.

IMF (International Monetary Fund). 2020. "State-Owned Enterprises: The Other Government." Chapter 3 in *Fiscal Monitor: Policies to Support People during the COVID-19 Pandemic*, 47–74. Washington, DC: IMF.

IMF (International Monetary Fund). 2021. "State-Owned Enterprises in Middle East, North Africa, and Central Asia: Size, Role, Performance, and Challenges." IMF, Washington, DC.

Isungset, E. 2022. "State Ownership and Climate Change: Can State Ownership of the Economy Reduce Greenhouse Gas Emissions? A Quantitative Study." Master's thesis, Norwegian University of Science and Technology, Department of Sociology and Political Science, Trondheim, Norway.

Jie, J., J. Hou, W. Cangyu, and L. HaiYue. 2021. "COVID-19 Impact on Firm Investment—Evidence from Chinese Publicly Listed Firms." *Journal of Asian Economics* 75: 101320.

Kabaciński, B., J. Kubiak, and K. Szarzec. 2020. "Do State-Owned Enterprises Underperform Compared to Privately-Owned Companies? An Examination of the Largest Polish Enterprises." *Emerging Markets Finance and Trade* 56 (13): 3174–92.

Kikeri, S., and A. F. Kolo. 2005. "Privatization: Trends and Recent Developments." Policy Research Working Paper 3765, World Bank, Washington DC.

Kočenda, E., and J. Svejnar. 2003. "Ownership and Firm Performance after Large-Scale Privatization." William Davidson Institute Working Paper 471a, The William Davidson Institute, University of Michigan Business School, Ann Arbor.

Kopelman, J. L., and H. S. Rosen. 2014. "Are Public Sector Jobs Recession-Proof? Were They Ever?" Working Paper 240, Griswold Center for Economic Policy Studies, Princeton University, Princeton, NJ.

Kornai, J. 1986. "The Soft Budget Constraint." *Kyklos* 39 (1): 3–30.

La Porta, R., and F. Lopez-de-Silanes. 1999. "The Benefits of Privatization: Evidence from Mexico." *Quarterly Journal of Economics* 114 (4): 1193–242.

Laeven, L., and F. Valencia. 2010. "Resolution of Banking Crises: The Good, the Bad, and the Ugly." IMF Working Paper No. 2010/146, International Monetary Fund, Washington, DC.

Le, T., and T. Buck. 2009. "State Ownership and Listed Firm Performance: A Universally Negative Governance Relationship?" *Journal of Management and Governance* 15: 227–48.

Liljeblom, E., B. Maury, and A. Hörhammer. 2020. "Complex State Ownership, Competition, and Firm Performance—Russian Evidence." *International Journal of Emerging Markets* 15 (2): 189–221.

Lipsey, R. G., and K. Lancaster. 1956. "The General Theory of Second Best." *Review of Economic Studies* 24 (1): 11–32.

Marques, L. B., R. Correa, and H. Sapriza. 2018. "Government Support, Regulation, and Risk Taking in the Banking Sector." *Journal of Banking and Finance* 112 (2): 105284.

Martinez Licetti, M., D. Sanchez-Navarro, and J. G. Perrottet. 2020. "Support to Systematically Large Firms in Hard-Hit Sectors. The Case of Airlines State-Support Programs amid COVID-19." Unpublished manuscript, World Bank, Washington, DC.

Mazzucato, M. 2011. "The Entrepreneurial State." *Soundings* 49: 131–42.

Megginson, W. L., D. López, and A. I. Malik. 2021a. "Privatization, State Capitalism and State Ownership of Business in the 21st Century." *Foundations and Trends in Finance* 11 (1–2): 1–153.

Megginson, W. L., D. López, and A. I. Malik. 2021b. "The Rise of State-Owned Investors: Sovereign Wealth Funds and Public Pension Funds." *Annual Review of Financial Economics* 13: 247–70.

Megginson, W. L., and A. I. Malik. 2022. "The Rise of Sovereign Wealth Funds as Global Investors." Background paper for this report, World Bank, Washington, DC.

Megginson, W. L., and J. Netter. 2001. "From State to Market: A Survey of Empirical Studies on Privatization." *Journal of Economic Literature* 39 (2): 321–89.

Meyer, A., and G. Pac. 2013. "Environmental Performance of State-Owned and Privatized Eastern European Energy Utilities." *Energy Economics* 36: 205–14.

Millward, R. 2011. "Public Enterprise in the Modern Western World: An Historical Analysis." *Annals of Public and Cooperative Economics* 82 (4): 375–98.

Montrone, L., N. Ohlendorf, and R. Chandra. 2022. "The Political Economy of Coal in India." In *The Political Economy of Coal: Obstacles to Clean Energy Transitions*, edited by M. Jakob and J. C. Steckel, 137–39. New York: Routledge.

Nellis, J. 2001. "Time to Rethink Privatization in Transition Economies?" In *A Decade of Transition: Achievements and Challenges*, edited by O. Havrylyshyn and M. S. Nsouli. Washington, DC: International Monetary Fund.

Nguyen, B., H. Do, and C. Le. 2021. "How Much State Ownership Do Hybrid Firms Need for Better Performance?" *Small Business Economics* 59: 845–71.

OECD (Organisation for Economic Co-operation and Development). 2004. "Peru: Peer Review of Competition Law and Policy." OECD Country Studies, OECD, Paris.

OECD (Organisation for Economic Co-operation and Development). 2010. "OECD Policy Roundtable: Competition, State Aids and Subsidies." Unpublished manuscript, OECD, Paris.

OECD (Organisation for Economic Co-operation and Development). 2015. *OECD Guidelines on Corporate Governance of State-Owned Enterprises.* Paris: OECD Publishing.

OECD (Organisation for Economic Co-operation and Development). 2022. "Monitoring the Performance of State-Owned Enterprises: Good Practice Guide for Annual Aggregate Reporting." OECD, Paris.

Olsson, M., and J. Tåg. 2021. "What Is the Cost of Privatization for Workers?" IFN Working Paper 1201, Research Institute of Industrial Economics, Stockholm.

Poczter, S. 2016. "The Long-Term Effects of Bank Recapitalization: Evidence from Indonesia." *Journal of Financial Intermediation* 25: 131–53.

Pop, G., and G. Coelho. 2020. "Up in the Air: Airlines and Competition Policy in Times of COVID-19." https://www.pymnts.com/cpi_posts/up-in-the-air-airlines-and-competition-policy-in -times-of-covid-19/.

Pop, G., and D. Connon. 2020. "Industrial Policy Effects and the Case for Competition." Unpublished manuscript, World Bank, Washington, DC.

Prag, A., D. Röttgers, and I. Scherrer. 2018. "State-Owned Enterprises and the Low-Carbon Transition." OECD Environment Working Papers 129, Organisation for Economic Co-operation and Development, Paris.

Rama, M. 1999. "Public Sector Downsizing: An Introduction." *World Bank Economic Review* 13 (1): 1–22.

Ruppert Bulmer, E., K. Pela, A. Eberhard-Ruiz, and J. Montoya. 2021. *Global Perspective on Coal Jobs and Managing Labor Transition out of Coal: Key Issues and Policy Responses.* Washington, DC: World Bank.

Shleifer, A. 1998. "State versus Private Ownership." *Journal of Economic Perspectives* 12 (4): 133–50.

Szarzec, K., B. Totleben, and D. Piątek. 2022. "How Do Politicians Capture a State? Evidence from State-Owned Enterprises." *East European Politics and Societies* 36 (1): 141–72.

Talukdar, D., and C. Meisner. 2001. "Does the Private Sector Help or Hurt the Environment? Evidence from Carbon Dioxide Pollution in Developing Countries." *World Development* 29 (5): 827–40.

Torero, M. 2002. "Peruvian Privatization: Impacts on Firm Performance." IDB Working Paper 186, Inter-American Development Bank, Washington, DC.

Torero, M., E. Schroth, A. Pasco-Font, M. Urquiola, and R. J. Lüders. 2003. "The Impact of Telecommunications Privatization in Peru on the Welfare of Urban Consumers." *Economia* 4 (1): 99–128.

UNCTAD (United Nations Conference on Trade and Development). 2004. "Perú: Informe sobre las necesidades y prioridades en el área de Políticas de la Competencia." United Nations.

Vagliasindi, M. 2023. "The Role of SOEs in Climate Change." Background paper for this report, World Bank, Washington, DC.

Vagliasindi, M., T. Cordella, and J. Clifton. 2023. "Introduction: Revisiting the Role of State-Owned Enterprises in Strategic Sectors." *Journal of Economic Policy Reform* 26 (1): 1–23.

Vickers, J., and G. Yarrow. 1988. *Privatization: An Economic Analysis.* Cambridge, MA: MIT Press.

Wang, Q., M. Liu, and B. Zhan. 2022. "Do State-Owned Enterprises Really Have Better Environmental Performance in China? Environmental Regulation and Corporate Environmental Strategies." *Resources, Conservation and Recycling* 185: 106500.

World Bank. 1995. *Bureaucrats in Business: The Economics and Politics of Government Ownership.* World Bank Policy Research Report. Washington, DC: World Bank.

World Bank. 2014. *Corporate Governance of State-Owned Enterprises. A Toolkit.* Washington, DC: World Bank. https://openknowledge.worldbank.org/server/api/core/bitstreams/f01135d1-9f3c-5b85-9c1c-1a765bda00f5/content.

World Bank. 2020. *State Your Business! An Evaluation of World Bank Group Support to the Reform of State-Owned Enterprises, FY08–18.* Independent Evaluation Group. Washington, DC: World Bank.

World Bank. 2021. "Building SOE Crisis Management and Resilience: Emerging Practices and Lessons Learned during the COVID-19 Crisis." World Bank, Washington, DC.

World Bank. 2022. "Who's the BOSs: Shedding New Light on the State Footprint in Markets." Equitable Growth, Finance and Institutions Notes, World Bank, Washington, DC.

Yu, M. 2013. "State Ownership and Firm Performance: Empirical Evidence from Chinese Listed Companies." *China Journal of Accounting Research* 6 (2): 75–87.

Abbreviations

ADB	Asian Development Bank
ALP	Anticompetitive Laws and Policies
BOS	Businesses of the State (database)
BOSs	businesses of the state
CFE	Federal Electricity Commission (Mexico)
CO_2	carbon dioxide
EBRD	European Bank for Reconstruction and Development
EU	European Union
FDI	foreign direct investment
HHI	Herfindahl-Hirschman Index
IDB	Inter-American Development Bank
IFC	International Finance Corporation
IMF	International Monetary Fund
NACE	Statistical Classification of Economic Activities in the European Community
NPV	net present value
OECD	Organisation for Economic Co-operation and Development
PGE	Polska Grupa Energetyczna (Poland)
PMR	product market regulation
R&D	research and development
SOE	state-owned enterprise
STRI	Services Trade Restrictiveness Index
SWF	sovereign wealth fund
TFP	total factor productivity
TRAINS	Trade Analysis Information Systems

1. The Evolving Business of the State

Introduction

The state is a business owner through various ownership structures across a range of commercial activities. Stylized facts from the World Bank Global Businesses of the State (BOS) database provide new evidence on the state's footprint across sectors and product markets. States have various motivations for establishing and maintaining ownership in markets. These motivations need to be addressed if policy recommendations are to be effective.

- The state's footprint is large and goes beyond that of traditional state-owned enterprises (SOEs). Businesses of the state (BOSs) are large market players, with revenues equivalent to 17 percent of gross domestic product (GDP). They also account for an average of 5 percent of formal employment. This report extends the analysis of their footprint to encompass less visible forms of state ownership, such as minority stakes and indirectly owned firms, including those owned through sovereign wealth funds and special-purpose vehicles (see box 1.1 for definitions of the principal terms used).
- The state's presence in competitive sectors is too large to ignore. It is widespread in competitive markets that the private sector could serve efficiently across manufacturing, wholesale, digital, and transportation sectors. These sectors account for the majority (more than 50 percent) of BOSs in 60 out of the 91 countries covered in the BOS database and across regions, although they are less prominent in Latin America and the Caribbean. The economic rationale for the state to own businesses is less justified in these markets. Moreover, the effectiveness of government ownership is further undermined in low-capacity and low-governance environments. Indeed, governments could adopt other instruments to address market and coordination failures. For example, they could instead improve the investment climate, including removing barriers to entry and improving fair competition, to support the growth of a dynamic private sector.
- There are multiple examples of good justifications and outcomes of BOSs, but examples of bad or ugly justifications and outcomes are common. Some justifications can be good, such as trying to solve market failures that constrain private investment or private service delivery. Some can be bad, such as trying to

Definitions of Key Terms Used in the Report

The following key terms are used throughout this report.

- *Businesses of the state (BOSs)*. The term BOSs is used conceptually to discuss the participation of the state in markets as a direct stakeholder, including firms with minority state ownership starting at 10 percent, as well as its participation in firms that are indirectly owned by the state through another firm with state participation. Both central and subnational governments can participate in BOSs. The terms BOS database or BOS data refer to the World Bank Global Businesses of the State database, which provides empirical measures of BOSs (Dall'Ollio et al. 2022a). The approach is consistent with the Organisation for Economic Co-operation and Development's broad definition of a state-owned enterprise, which refers to any corporate entity recognized as an enterprise by national law in which the state exercises ownership (OECD 2015). See annex 1A. Yet this very broad definition can lead in practice to different accounting of firms in every country.
- *State-owned enterprises (SOEs)*. The term SOE is traditionally used when referring to existing literature and empirical work that use the term and when referring to country-specific SOE policies and reform agendas that are aligned to a country's own definition. These definitions are often limited to firms owned by the central government, with direct state ownership of 50 percent or more (IMF 2021).

Depending on which of the two definitions is used in the report, all other firms are regarded as private firms. The report also differentiates state presence in business by the type of market, as defined in Dall'Olio et al. (2022b):

- *Natural monopoly markets*, activities that exhibit economies of scale or subadditivity cost structures. In these markets, there is a strong economic rationale for state participation and SOEs. Examples include postal services and energy transmission.
- *Partially contestable markets*, economic sectors characterized by some form of market power, externalities, or other market failures. This category also includes markets characterized by public goods, externalities, and asymmetries of information, in which underprovision would persist if only unregulated private firms operated in the market. Examples include banking services, airlines, power generation, and waste management.
- *Competitive markets*, activities in which incumbents and entrants have access to similar information and production technologies and in which the provision of goods and services that are private (that is, rival and excludable) and production activities do not generate significant externalities. Thus, these markets are fully contestable (more likely to behave competitively), and there is no clear economic rationale to justify the specific participation of the state in this type of activities. Examples include manufacturing of food, accommodation industries, and wholesale and retail trade.

play an unduly large role in "strategic" sectors beyond national security purposes, which could be served more efficiently by the private sector. And some can be ugly, such as allowing political patronage or corruption. More transparency and more evidence on the effectiveness of meeting ownership objectives are needed to inform reform priorities.

The New State Footprint

This report leverages for the first time the new World Bank Global BOS database for 91 countries, capturing a broad state footprint across firms and markets. Compared to the traditional definition of SOEs,[1] often characterized as majority directly owned by the central government, the new BOS database expands the universe to businesses in which the state's share is more than 10 percent—whether owned directly or indirectly through another company or owned by a local or central government. These businesses can be operating both domestically and across borders (Dall'Olio et al. 2022a). This expanded recognition of state presence in business and markets blurs the boundaries between BOSs and privately owned enterprises. Traditionally, state participation in markets was captured more systematically in natural monopoly and partially contestable markets, such as utilities, network industries, and the financial sector, and was seen less often in competitive markets, such as manufacturing, hospitality, and retail. Compared with earlier databases on SOEs, the BOS database acknowledges a broader state presence. Its greater country coverage quadruples the number of firms to about 76,000 BOSs identified as having state ownership across 91 countries (see annex 1A).[2] This report presents the most comprehensive picture of the state's current footprint, including after waves of full and partial privatization and the more recent resurgence of state capitalism.

The state's footprint is much larger when considering firms with state participation beyond the traditional SOEs, as revealed by the BOS database (figure 1.1). BOSs are present in more sectors in Europe and Central Asia countries, with several countries having BOSs in more than 50 percent of sectors (defined at the two-digit Statistical Classification of Economic Activities in the European Community—NACE—code). Beyond Europe and Central Asia, the Arab Republic of Egypt, India, Indonesia, South Africa, and Viet Nam stand out as having BOSs in a large share of sectors. Taking into account the new definition of BOSs adds a few economies from Latin America and the Caribbean (Argentina, Brazil, and Colombia), the Middle East and North Africa (Egypt and Morocco), and Sub-Saharan Africa (South Africa and Uganda) where the presence of BOSs is far more extensive than that of traditional SOEs.

The new data show that BOSs are large, key market players that generate substantial revenues for governments. Despite long-standing privatization agendas, the state has a large presence in many countries. The cross-country average of BOSs' revenues relative to GDP is equivalent to 17 percent—a lower bound because revenues are not reported for all BOSs in many countries.[3] In Bhutan, the Russian Federation, the Seychelles, Slovenia, and Viet Nam, BOSs' revenues constitute more than 30 percent of GDP (figure 1.2). On average, BOSs also account for 5 percent of formal jobs—and much more in some countries, such as the Comoros, with 30 percent, and Bosnia and Herzegovina and the Seychelles, with up to 12 percent (figure 1.3). The density of BOSs

FIGURE 1.1 **Sectors with at Least One BOS Firm versus Traditional SOEs in Select Countries, 2019**

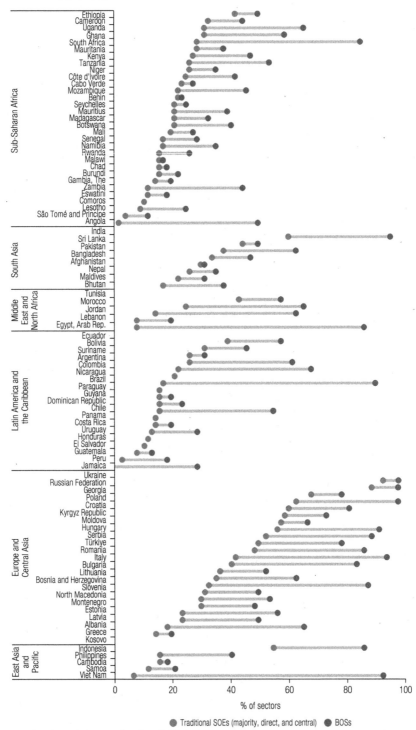

Source: World Bank Global Businesses of the State (BOS) database.

Note: The horizontal axis reports the share of sectors in which firms with state ownership are found out of 77 NACE two-digit code sectors. The blue and red markers use the SOE and BOS definitions of state ownership, respectively. When information on ownership is not available, it is assumed that the BOS firm is centrally owned. BOSs = businesses of the state; SOE = state-owned enterprise.

FIGURE 1.2 BOSs' Revenues as a Percentage of GDP, Select Countries, 2019

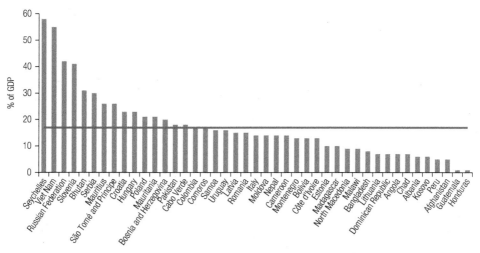

Sources: World Bank Global Businesses of the State (BOS) database and International Labour Organization for 2019 formal employment data.

Note: Includes 43 countries for which there are data available for at least 75 percent of the firms. BOSs = businesses of the state.

FIGURE 1.3 BOSs' Employment as a Percentage of Formal Employment, Select Countries, 2019

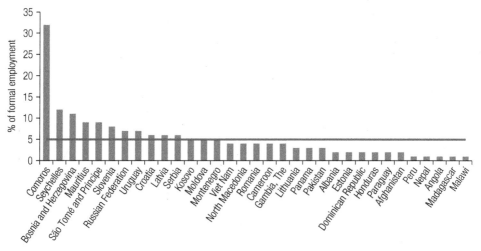

Source: World Bank Global Businesses of the State (BOS) database.

Note: Includes 33 countries for which there are data available for at least 75 percent of the firms. BOSs = businesses of the state.

is also higher in countries with a history of central planning and in high-income countries, including small island countries such as the Seychelles.

Minority ownership, including at the subnational level, prevails for a quarter of the companies in the BOS database. The companies with minority participation are split almost evenly between those with a blocking minority of 25–49.9 percent ownership and

The Evolving Business of the State

those with only minority participation (10–24.9 percent). And, on average, for 30 countries with good data, minority-owned BOSs represent up to 50 percent of revenues and 30 percent of employment generated by all BOSs (figure 1.4). In some economies—such as Eswatini, Madagascar, Mozambique, São Tomé and Príncipe, Slovenia, Türkiye, and Viet Nam—more than 20 percent of firms with state participation have blocking minority stakes.[4] Minority ownership is more frequent in finance, mining, manufacturing, and quarrying. Even with minority participation, the state can intervene and influence decisively, for example, with veto power and "one share, one vote" appointments of board members.

Indirect ownership is often multilayered, which makes quantifying and assessing the true level of state control over these businesses more complex. In the BOS database, the number of firms with state participation increases by about 35 percent when firms indirectly owned by the state, including at the subnational level, are considered as BOSs. In some countries—such as Botswana, Egypt, Jordan, Mauritius, Mozambique, Uruguay, and Viet Nam—more than 60 percent of BOSs have an indirect state presence. And state ownership can originate from several state owners, from line ministries to other central and local government entities. About 8,000 BOSs across 91 countries have more than one owner. Even in countries with centralized management and oversight entities such as Angola or Peru, some entities go beyond their purview. For instance, PETROPERU, the largest fully owned BOS firm in Peru, which operates in the distribution of fuels, does not fall under FONAFE, the institution in charge of monitoring SOEs.

FIGURE 1.4   **Revenues, Employment, and Number of BOSs, by Ownership Level, 2019**

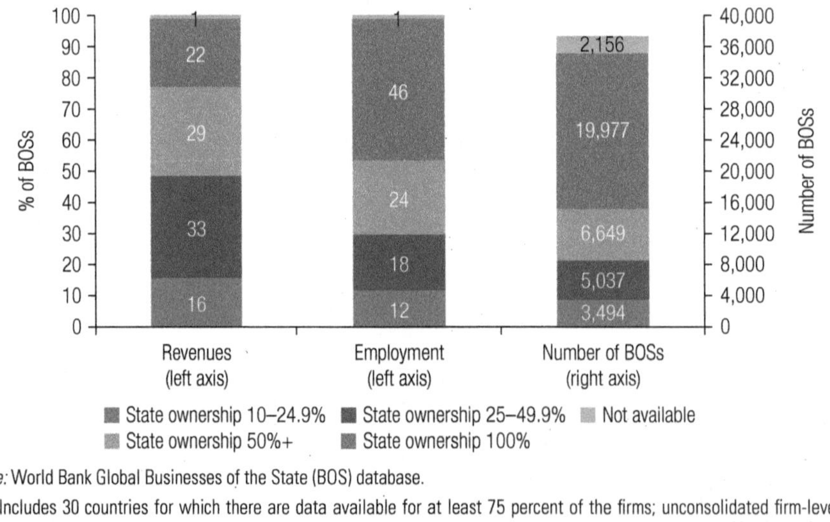

Source: World Bank Global Businesses of the State (BOS) database.

Note: Includes 30 countries for which there are data available for at least 75 percent of the firms; unconsolidated firm-level data. Numbers given in the bars for revenues and employment are the total percentage for each ownership category. Numbers given in the bar for number of BOSs are the total number of BOSs in each category. BOSs = businesses of the state.

The state also takes an indirect stake in firms through sovereign wealth funds (SWFs), creating opportunities for more fiscal discipline but also raising the risks of less transparency. SWFs are currently not included in the BOS database and thus not included in the analytical work in this chapter. Several low- and middle-income countries have SWFs, with the primary objectives of creating intergenerational wealth and protecting and stabilizing fiscal balances from excess volatility in revenues from nonrenewable commodity exports (box 1.2). Among the top 100 SWFs, there are several established by low- and middle-income countries, including Egypt, Ethiopia, Mongolia, Rwanda, and Viet Nam, although 80 percent of these top 100 SWFs are found in high-income and upper-middle-income countries, with Australia, China, the United Arab Emirates, and the United States leading by number of SWFs

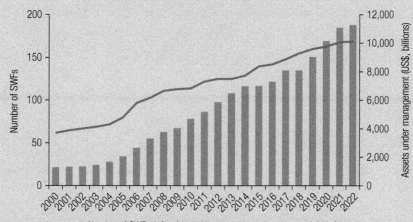

BOX 1.2

The Rise of Sovereign Wealth Funds

Sovereign wealth funds (SWFs) started primarily in countries with significant natural resource exports, including oil and gas. They have various objectives, including financial returns, intergenerational equity, and macroeconomic stabilization (Divakaran et al. 2022; Gelb et al. 2014). SWFs have grown from less than US$1 trillion in assets under management in 2000 to more than US$11 trillion in June 2022; public pension funds exceeded US$23 trillion in May 2022 (figure B1.2.1) (Megginson and Malik 2022). Collectively, these state-owned investors have become the third-largest holders of financial assets globally, after banks and insurance companies.

FIGURE B1.2.1 **Number of Sovereign Wealth Funds and Value of Assets under Management, 2000–22 (June)**

Source: Megginson and Malik 2022, using data from https://globalswf.com/ as of June 2022.
Note: SWFs = sovereign wealth funds.

(Box continues on the following page.)

The Rise of Sovereign Wealth Funds *(continued)*

The number of private firms and BOSs with SWF ownership has increased in the past decade. Between 2010 and 2020, SWF ownership at the 50 percent level grew more than ninefold, from 1,000 to more than 10,000 firms. Using an ownership threshold of 10 percent uncovers an additional 50,000 subsidiaries in 2020 (figure B1.2.2). The median number of subsidiaries owned by SWFs at least doubled over the 10 years, from 20 to 45 subsidiaries (50 percent threshold) and from 89 to 277 subsidiaries (10 percent threshold).

FIGURE B1.2.2 **Distribution of Subsidiary Income over Time, 10 Percent Ownership Threshold, by Income Group, 2010–20**

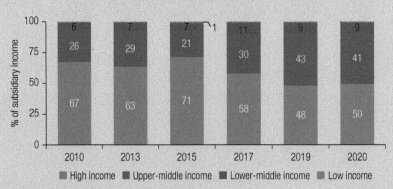

Source: Based on data from https://globalswf.com/ and Orbis.
Note: SWF = sovereign wealth fund.

Most of the increase in the number of businesses of the state with SWF ownership at 10 percent is driven by China and Singapore. By contrast, SWFs in Malaysia and the United Arab Emirates have consolidated their ownership at 50 percent.

SWFs have increased their investment in businesses of the state over time. They owned 446 unique businesses of the state in 2010 and about 2,600 by 2020.

(Megginson, López, and Malik 2021). SWF investments shifted over time from high-income to upper-middle-income economies (box 1.2). Subsidiaries from upper-middle-income economies represented 26 percent of SWF subsidiaries in 2010 and 41 percent in 2020. Over the same period, the share of high-income economies in SWF ownership dropped 17 percentage points. The 68 SWFs with data in Orbis invest primarily in competitive markets. Irrespective of the ownership threshold, more than 50 percent of SWF ownership is in competitive markets.

Since 2000, the bulk of SWF stock purchases have been cross-border transactions (Megginson, López, and Malik 2021). Most countries are investing largely in domestic markets, but SWFs from the Republic of Korea, Kuwait, Qatar, Singapore, Spain, and the United Arab Emirates seem to own predominantly large assets abroad. Other countries with SWF investments abroad include Bahrain, China, Ireland, Kazakhstan, Malaysia, Norway, Saudi Arabia, and the United States. This globalization of BOSs is also closely associated with the rise of China as a global investor (box 1.3).

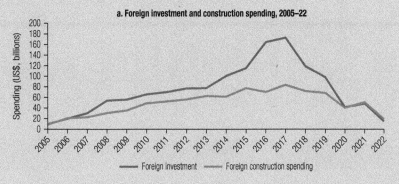

Globalization of BOSs and the Rise of China as a Global Economic Power *(continued)*

FIGURE B1.3.1   **China's Foreign Investment, 2005–22 and 2013–22** *(continued)*

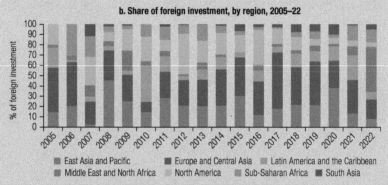

b. Share of foreign investment, by region, 2005–22

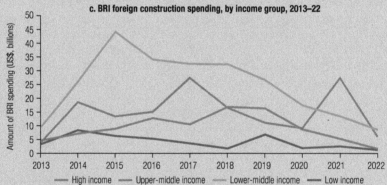

c. BRI foreign construction spending, by income group, 2013–22

d. BRI foreign investment for top 20 recipient countries, by country, 2013–22

Source: China Global Investment Tracker, https://www.aei.org/china-global-investment-tracker/.

Note: BRI = Belt and Road Initiative.

State Presence in Competitive Markets

The state has a large presence in competitive markets. BOSs are widespread in competitive markets and sectors (manufacturing, wholesale, and accommodation) that the private sector can serve efficiently (figures 1.5 and 1.6).[5] The World Bank Global BOS database adopts a novel disaggregated sector taxonomy to classify BOSs on the basis of industries' technological features and market failures (Dall'Olio et al. 2022a). Almost 70 percent of the businesses owned by the state operate in competitive sectors, and in 30 countries with high firm-level data coverage for both revenue and employment, they generate more than 40 percent of total BOS firm revenues and employment (figure 1.7). In Brazil, Costa Rica, Côte d'Ivoire, Jordan, and Senegal, more than 30 percent of BOS firm revenues come from manufacturing activities. In some cases, BOSs even have legal or de facto monopolies in sectors that could be operated under competitive conditions or be fully provided by the private sector (cardboard production in Bolivia, meat production in Botswana, fertilizer provision in The Gambia).

Competitive markets span a wide spectrum of real sectors and are also found within traditionally broadly defined natural monopoly and partially contestable markets, such as network and utility sectors. Among network sectors (such as energy, telecommunications, and transportation), water is a pure case for a natural state monopoly, including for subnational governments. But other sectors, such as transportation, energy, and digital services, have subactivities that the private sector can provide (figure 1.8). For instance, in the digital sectors, computer programming and data processing are fully competitive, whereas wired telecommunications is a natural monopoly.[6] Many BOSs in competitive markets are present not only at the central level but also at the subnational level. This more granular market and geographic classification is important for identifying their presence, distinguishing the policy and reform agenda, and avoiding treating all sectors and BOSs as one size fits all.

Almost a quarter of countries with a high share of BOSs in competitive markets also have low government effectiveness (figure 1.9, top left quadrant). Futhermore, in more corrupt countries, the performance of SOEs, both in profitability and in productivity, is significantly worse relative to that of SOEs in other countries (Baum et al. 2019). Corruption is likely to have a deeper impact on how SOEs operate given the close relationship between the state (bureaucrats, politicians) and the company. The corruption risks associated with BOSs are also heightened because many of these businesses operate in sectors with large economic rents or monopoly power.

FIGURE 1.5 BOSs across Markets and Countries, 2019

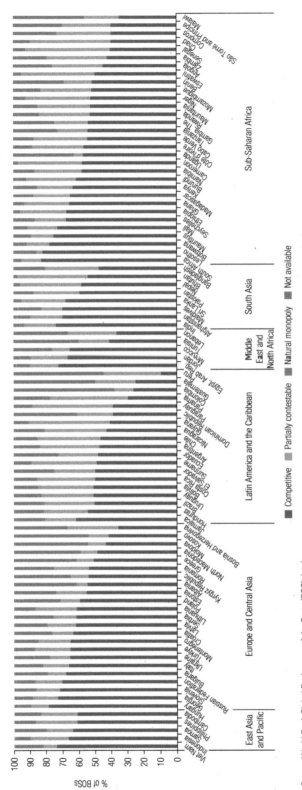

■ Competitive　■ Partially contestable　■ Natural monopoly　■ Not available

Source: World Bank Global Businesses of the State (BOS) database.

Note: BOSs = businesses of the state.

FIGURE 1.6 BOSs, by Sector, Averaged across Countries, 2019

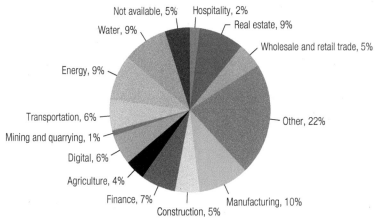

Source: World Bank Global Businesses of the State (BOS) database; 91 countries.
Note: BOSs = businesses of the state.

FIGURE 1.7 Revenues, Employment, and Number of BOSs, by Type of Market, 2019

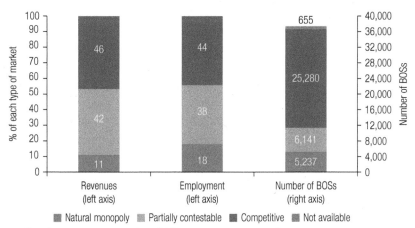

Source: World Bank Global Businesses of the State (BOS) database.
Note: The average across 30 countries with more than 75 percent coverage for revenues and employment variables; unconsolidated firm-level data. Numbers given in the bars for revenues and employment are the total percentage for each market category. Numbers given in the bar for number of BOSs are the total number of BOSs in each category. BOSs = businesses of the state.

Rationale for State Presence in the Economy

The motivations to establish and maintain BOSs persist despite waves of privatization and governance reforms. In a recent Delphi survey, most respondents agreed that guaranteeing affordable access to basic services and goods, development of infrastructure, and the existence of strategic interests are valid justifications for the presence of BOSs in the economy (Vagliasindi, Cordella, and Clifton 2023). Indeed, policy makers and experts justify the presence of BOSs in the economy by assigning them multiple mandates, both economic and noneconomic (box 1.4).

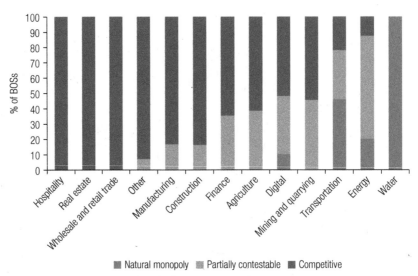

FIGURE 1.8   **BOSs, by Type of Market, Averaged across Countries, 2019**

■ Natural monopoly   ■ Partially contestable   ■ Competitive

Source: World Bank Global Businesses of the State (BOS) database; 91 countries.
Note: BOSs = businesses of the state.

Beyond the economic rationales for BOSs, there are diverse motivations as to why BOSs are formed and participate in economic activity. The economic rationales for the operation of BOSs usually relate to solving market failures (natural monopolies, negative or positive externalities, or public goods). Other motivations include government control over strategic sectors or protecting and advancing legitimate national interests (Bernier, Florio, and Bance 2020). Traditionally, noneconomic objectives can be broadly classified as development policy mandates or as the use of BOSs for political interests. The persistence of BOSs and their popular use as a means to achieve certain mandates are also shaped by the historical context of a country (for example, central planning), despite recent waves of full or partial privatization and governance reforms. BOSs can also play a role during crises through counter-cyclical spending or safeguarding employment levels.

The state footprint in an economy can reflect on the country's stage of development and economic model. It often remains prominent in countries with a history of central planning in their early phase of industrial development. For example, in countries in Eastern Europe and in Viet Nam, the state has receded after waves of privatization but is still present as a minority owner and at the local level. Some countries have justified the use of SOEs to create national and global champions in strategic industries as a means of controlling critical globally integrated supply chains and technologies. China's reliance on and support for state-owned or state-influenced "national champions" in key industrial sectors has prompted many observers to conclude that the country is explicitly adopting a variant of the state capitalism model

FIGURE 1.9 Correlation between Share of BOSs in Competitive Markets and Government Effectiveness, 2019

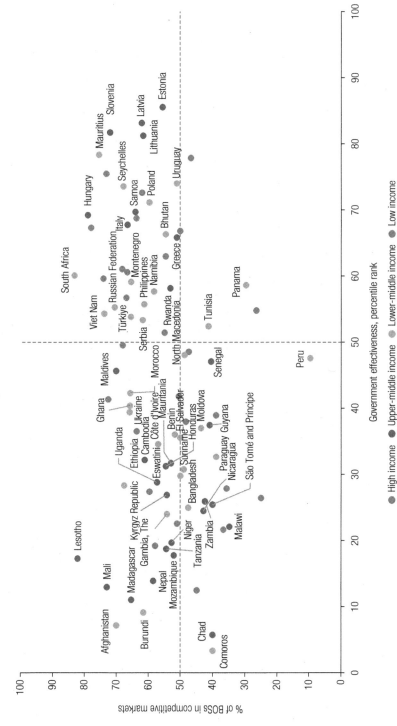

Sources: World Bank Global Businesses of the State (BOS) database and government effectiveness index from the World Bank Worldwide Governance (WGI) Indicators (https://info.worldbank.org /governance/wgi/).

Note: BOSs = businesses of the state.

Economic Rationale for State-Owned Enterprises

In the presence of market failures, some characteristics of goods and services might justify the presence of state-owned enterprises. The following are some key questions to ask when assessing the economic rationale of state-owned enterprises:

- *Public goods.* Is the good or service provided a public good? If the good is nonexcludable (excessive high costs are required for excluding some actors from accessing or using a good or service) and nonrivalrous (use of the good or service does not limit the use or depletes the supply for other actors), the private sector may not provide the goods or services because it cannot charge an individual fee or it is unprofitable to do so. Government provision directly through state-owned enterprises or public administration, indirectly contracting private sector companies (when possible), or jointly contracting (such as through public-private partnerships) are potential solutions to these market failures. Quality and contract enforcement capacity are critical to determine the potential venue of intervention. Defense, street lighting, and research on seed varieties are examples of goods and services with these characteristics.
- *Positive externalities.* Is the sector characterized by positive externalities? In this case, the social returns of providing a good or service exceed the private returns, because the production benefits other members of society. Under this scenario, the private sector either does not have the required profitability to enter the market or could underproduce when operating. One solution in this case is to subsidize goods with positive externalities (Pigovian tax). Some sectors such as rail and road infrastructure, education, and health exemplify these externalities.
- *Negative externalities.* Is the sector characterized by negative externalities? In this case, the total cost of providing a good or service exceeds the private costs and imposes unintended costs on other members of society. Thus, provision by the private sector could result in overproduction, resource depletion, or overexploitation. To mitigate this market failure, the state could impose taxes on and regulate the quantity of goods or services produced. Fisheries, coal mining, and fossil fuels are examples of sectors with these characteristics.
- *Natural monopolies.* Does the market exhibit subadditivity of costs? In this case, the costs are minimized by concentrating production in a single firm. As discussed earlier, this single market player could, in theory, be a private or a public enterprise. Some enabling sectors include segments with natural monopolies such as electricity (transmission), gas, postal services, and high-speed broadband networks.
- *Commercial viability.* Is this activity commercially viable? If it is commercially viable, then the state should not be involved. If the state is still involved in the activity—for example, for revenue generation or "strategic" purposes—then it should make sure that the company does not benefit from any preferential treatment and that no barriers exist to the entry of the private sector (see chapter 3).

Source: World Bank 2021.

that earlier Asian pioneers used successfully in their take-off phases. Other nations, such as Brazil, India, Russia, and Singapore, have also risen to global prominence, with business sectors dominated or heavily influenced by government-controlled companies.

Motivations for having BOSs can vary, and the justifications for these motivations have varying strength and validity. Some justifications can be good, such as trying to solve market failures that constrain private investment or private service delivery. Some can be bad, such as unduly using BOSs in "strategic" sectors beyond national security purposes and using them to ensure global market power and unlevel the playing field— or when the activity would be commercially viable for private companies without government investment. For example, SOEs are being used to secure the provision of critical materials and control global supply chains.[7] Some justifications can be ugly— such as using BOSs as instruments for political patronage whereby elected officials at the national, state, and local levels of government use appointments in BOSs to reward the people who help them to win and maintain office (OECD 2023). It is easier for corrupt politicians to intervene in publicly owned firms—especially when transparency and accountability are weak—and they have an incentive to do so, because they will benefit from the rents without bearing the costs (Boycko, Shleifer, and Vishny 1996).

While there are multiple examples of good justifications and outcomes of BOSs, examples of bad or ugly justifications and outcomes are common. A key challenge is that SOEs often have multiple mandates, which create conflicting incentives for their behavior. At the same time, SOE performance is often not monitored effectively against these objectives because of institutional weaknesses, capacity constraints, and conflicts of interest by the state as regulator, as law enforcer, and simultaneously as owner of SOEs. This report provides new empirical evidence and examples of the positive and harmful impacts of state ownership, illustrating the mechanisms that lead to the "good, the bad, and the ugly" (Laeven and Valencia 2010). More transparency and more evidence of the effectiveness of meeting objectives are needed to inform reform priorities.

An open question remains: Can BOSs play a catalytic role and crowd in private sector investment, particularly in competitive sectors? In a few cases, the presence of the state in competitive sectors can be justified by development goals. But it is crucial that governments consider other policy instruments and reforms (for example, removing market distortions and improving the investment climate, including at the subnational level) that can support the entry and growth of the private sector through other less distortive interventions. The mere absence of the private sector in these markets does not justify the creation of BOSs.

Annex 1A World Bank Global BOS Database

What Counts as a Business with Ownership by the State?

The database's approach is consistent with the Organisation for Economic Co-operation and Development (OECD) definition of a state-owned enterprise:

> Any corporate entity recognized by national law as an enterprise, and in which the state exercises ownership, should be considered as an SOE. ... Also, minority ownership by the state can be considered as covered by the Guidelines if corporate or shareholding structures confer effective controlling influence on the state (e.g. through shareholders' agreements). (OECD 2015)

Here, for a BOS firm, the lower threshold for state ownership is 10 percent, with comparisons made across categories of 10–24.9 percent, 25–49.9 percent, majority participation of 50 percent or more, and full participation of 100 percent. Both direct and indirect ownership links are included, as are holdings by subnational governments. Health and education activities are excluded. The OECD reports about 2,400 self-declared centrally owned SOEs across 38 economies. Comparisons across countries covered by both databases underscore the gaps (see figure 1A.1 for differences in data for select countries). Information on the methodology, sources, and coverage is available in Dall'Olio et al. (2022a).

How Is It Possible to Identify a Business with Ownership by the State?

Similar to a genealogical tree, the database starts from the entities denoted as public authorities according to the type of entity in each country and then recreates all relationships at different degrees (denoted as ownership layers) for all companies, applying the 10 percent ownership threshold at each stage. The public authorities analyzed do not include sovereign wealth funds, international investors (such as BlackRock), or multilateral organizations (such as the International Finance Corporation). See table 1A.1 for a comparison of the World Bank Global BOS database to other SOE databases.

What Sectors Are Included?

The database includes most four-digit Statistical Classification of Economic Activities in the European Community (NACE) sectors, ranging from agriculture, mining and quarrying, and manufacturing to wholesale and services. The financial sector is included. Education, human health and social work, public administration, pension funds, and libraries and cultural patrimony activities, activities of households as employers, and activities of extraterritorial organizations are not included.

FIGURE 1A.1 Total Number of BOSs and SOEs for Select Countries

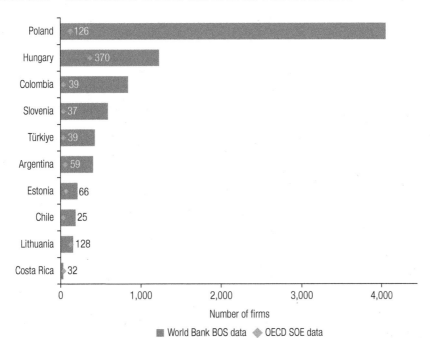

Sources: Based on World Bank Global Businesses of the State (BOS) and Organisation for Economic Co-operation and Development (OECD) data.

Note: For comparison purposes, figure shows countries covered in both the World Bank Global BOS and the OECD databases. BOSs = businesses of the state; SOEs = state-owned enterprises.

Which 91 Countries and Regions Does the Database Currently Cover?

- *East Asia and Pacific.* Cambodia, Indonesia, the Philippines, Samoa, and Viet Nam
- *Europe and Central Asia.* Albania, Bosnia and Herzegovina, Bulgaria, Croatia, Estonia, Georgia, Greece, Hungary, Italy, Kosovo, Kyrgyz Republic, Latvia, Lithuania, Moldova, Montenegro, North Macedonia, Poland, Romania, Russia, Serbia, Slovenia, Türkiye, and Ukraine
- *Latin America and the Caribbean.* Argentina, Bolivia, Brazil, Chile, Colombia, Costa Rica, Dominican Republic, Ecuador, El Salvador, Guatemala, Guyana, Honduras, Jamaica, Nicaragua, Panama, Paraguay, Peru, Suriname, and Uruguay
- *Middle East and North Africa.* Egypt, Jordan, Lebanon, Morocco, and Tunisia
- *South Asia.* Afghanistan, Bangladesh, Bhutan, India, Maldives, Nepal, Pakistan, and Sri Lanka
- *Sub-Saharan Africa.* Angola, Benin, Botswana, Burundi, Cabo Verde, Cameroon, Chad, the Comoros, Côte d'Ivoire, Eswatini, Ethiopia, The Gambia, Ghana, Kenya, Lesotho, Madagascar, Malawi, Mali, Mauritania, Mauritius, Mozambique, Namibia, Niger, Rwanda, São Tomé and Príncipe, South Africa, Senegal, the Seychelles, Tanzania, Uganda, and Zambia.

TABLE 1A.1 World Bank Global BOS Database versus Other SOE Databases

Indicator	World Bank Global BOS database	World Bank (2021 infrastructure data)[a]	IMF[b]	ADB[c]	EBRD[d]	EU[e]	OECD[f]	IDB[g]
Number of countries	91 low- and middle-income countries	19	20	9	25	28 (European Union only)	40	18 (Latin America and Caribbean only)
Number of enterprises captured	87,000+ firms with state participation	135 SOEs	10,000 SOEs	12,742 SOEs	17,600 SOEs	950 SOEs focusing on sectors: electricity, gas, and railways	2,467 SOEs for 39 OECD countries; 55,341 for China	1,019 SOEs
Period covered	2019	2000–18	2014–16	2010–18	2014–16	2008–13	2012, 2015, 2017	2010–16
SOE definition	Unified definition across countries (10%+ ownership), including the full ownership tree; centrally and locally owned SOEs and BOSs	50%+ participation	At least 25% participation	At least 50.01% participation (default of Orbis global ultimate owner)	At least 25% participation	For analysis purposes: at least 20% ownership	As defined by local authorities and survey respondents, including majority (50%+ participation) and minority participation (from 10% to 49%); centrally owned only	As defined by local authorities and survey respondents
Sectors	NACE four-digit sectors; all sectors, including financial sector as well as real sector (for example, agriculture, manufacturing) and services. Excludes health, education, and public administration	Infrastructure assets in power and transportation sectors	Only one-digit sectors (only total values by sector, not firm-level data)	All sectors	Nonfinancial SOEs to prevent distortion	Nonfinancial SOEs	Only one-digit sectors (only total values by sector, not published firm-level data)	Nonfinancial SOEs

(Table continues on the following page.)

Indicator	World Bank Global BOS database	World Bank (2021 infrastructure data)[a]	IMF[b]	ADB[c]	EBRD[d]	EU[e]	OECD[f]	IDB[g]
Focus of analysis	State footprint, breakdown by type of sector, financial indicators, governance indicators, firm-level characteristics, and ownership structure	Financial performance, benchmarked against that of privately owned enterprises	Financial performance, benchmarked against that of privately owned enterprises, ownership structure, and productivity	Financial performance	Financial performance of SOEs	Financial performance of SOEs	Number of firms; total number of workers; sector (digits) of operation	Financial performance of SOEs
Variables	Sector of operation; age of company; revenues; employment, and profit/loss; state participation; level of government (central, subnational), audit status; ownership structure (participation and shareholders)	Accounting financial data; SOE ownership structure and income (netted fiscal transfers)	Revenues; employment; return on assets; corruption (Worldwide Governance Indicators); productivity	Financial data; ownership data	22 indicators of financial performance	% of SOEs in total rail turnover vs. OECD Public Ownership Index in rail; financial performance of SOEs	Number of firms; total number of labor employed; total revenues	Financial performance and netted fiscal transfers
Source	Orbis; EMIS Intelligence, Factiva; government sources	Government sources and company websites; EMIS Intelligence; stock exchanges	Orbis; S&P Capital IQ; surveys of public authorities; external sources	Orbis; external databases	Orbis; government sources; external databases	Orbis, Amadeus databases; government sources; external databases	SOE surveys of authorities (2012, 2015, 2017)	SOE surveys of authorities

Source: Dall'Olio et al. 2022a.

Note: ADB = Asian Development Bank; BOSs = businesses of the state; EBRD = European Bank for Reconstruction and Development; EU = European Union; IDB = Inter-American Development Bank; IMF = International Monetary Fund; NACE = Statistical Classification of Economic Activities in the European Community; OECD = Organisation for Economic Co-operation and Development; SOEs = state-owned enterprises.

a. Herrera Dappe et al. 2022.

b. IMF 2021.

c. Ginting and Naqvi 2020.

d. EBRD 2020.

e. European Commission 2016.

f. OECD 2017.

g. Musaccio and Pineda 2019.

Notes

1. The definition of an SOE varies by country. Majority, direct ownership by the central government is chosen as the benchmark definition because it captures common features in many countries and is the focus of most of the literature on SOEs.

2. BOSs in the Russian Federation represent 36 percent of the database, so Russia is singled out when it distorts the average results.

3. Ideally the measure of BOSs' footprint would be based on value added rather than revenues, but information on inputs is not widely available. "Revenues" are normalized by GDP to get a sense of scale; the actual share of value added in the economy that these firms account for will be smaller.

4. Blocking minority refers to owners with shareholding between 25 and 49 percent.

5. Other databases compile national or regional SOE data but provide limited scope and coverage of countries globally because of the lack of harmonized definition of SOEs across countries and lack of data transparency. Thus, a comprehensive, global cross-country database that identifies SOEs and their financial data has never been compiled. Efforts so far have been limited to certain regions, and coverage of low- and middle-income countries has been lacking. See annex 1A.

6. Similarly, within the energy sector, the transmission and distribution of energy are natural monopolies, whereas the production of electricity can be partially contestable.

7. For example, the central government of China—the world's largest steel-making country—recently established an SOE designed to manage the mining and inflow of iron (Taylor 2022). China also approved the merger of three of China's biggest rare earth metals BOSs, allegedly creating the world's second-largest rare earth minerals producer (Chang 2022). Meanwhile, the government of Canada issued a new policy applying the Investment Canada Act to investments by foreign SOEs in Canada's critical minerals sectors and supply chains. The policy also applies to private investors with close ties to foreign governments (Hersh, Patel, and Wasielewski 2022).

References

Baum, A., C. Hackney, P. Medas, and M. Sy. 2019. "Governance and State-Owned Enterprises: How Costly Is Corruption?" IMF Working Paper WP/19/253, International Monetary Fund, Washington, DC.

Bernier, L., M. Florio, and P. Bance. 2020. *The Routledge Handbook of State-Owned Enterprises.* Abingdon-on-Thames: Routledge.

Boycko, M., A. Shleifer, and R. Vishny. 1996. "A Theory of Privatization." *Economic Journal* 106 (435): 309–19.

Chang, B. 2022. "Analysis: China's Rare Earth Metals Consolidation and Market Power." *Foreign Policy Research Institute* (blog), March 2, 2022. https://www.fpri.org/article/2022/03/chinas-rare-earth-metals-consolidation-and-market-power/.

Dall'Olio, A., T. Goodwin, M. M. Licetti, A. C. Alonso Soria, M. Drozd, J. Orlowski, F. Patino Pena, and D. Sanchez-Navarro. 2022a. "Are All State-Owned Enterprises (SOEs) Equal? A Taxonomy of Economic Activities to Assess SOE Presence in the Economy." Policy Research Working Paper 10262, World Bank, Washington, DC.

Dall'Olio, A., T. Goodwin, M. M. Licetti, J. Orlowski, F. Patino Pena, F. Ratsimbazafy, and D. Sanchez-Navarro. 2022b. "Using ORBIS to Build a Global Database of Firms with State Participation." Policy Research Working Paper 10261, World Bank, Washington, DC.

Divakaran, S., H. Halland, G. Lorenzato, P. Rose, and S. Sarmiento-Saher. 2022. *Strategic Investment Funds: Establishment and Operations.* Washington, DC: World Bank.

EBRD (European Bank for Reconstruction and Development). 2020. *Economic Performance of State-Owned Enterprises in Emerging Economies: A Cross-Country Study.* London: EBRD.

European Commission. 2016. *State-owned Enterprises in the EU: Lessons Learnt and Ways forward in a Post-Crisis Context*. Brussels: European Commission.

Gelb, A., S. Tordo, H. Halland, N. Arfaa, and G. Smith. 2014. "Sovereign Wealth Funds and Long-Term Development Finance: Risks and Opportunities." Policy Research Working Paper 6776, World Bank, Washington, DC.

Ginting, E., and K. Naqvi. 2020. *Reforms, Opportunities, and Challenges for State-Owned Enterprises*. Mandaluyong City, the Philippines: Asian Development Bank.

Herrera Dappe, M., A. Musacchio, C. Pan, Y. V. Semikolenova, B. Turkgulu, and J. Barboza. 2022. "Infrastructure State-Owned Enterprises: A Tale of Inefficiency and Fiscal Dependence." Policy Research Working Paper 9969, World Bank, Washington, DC.

Hersh, C., R. Patel, and K. Wasielewski. 2022. "Canada Restricts Foreign SOE Investment in Critical Minerals Sector and Supply Chains." *Norton Rose Fulbright Canada* (blog), November 3, 2022. https://www.nortonrosefulbright.com/en-ca/knowledge/publications/0cb4e430/canada -restricts-foreign-soe-investment-in-critical-minerals-sector-and-supply-chains.

IMF (International Monetary Fund). 2021. *State-Owned Enterprises in Middle East, North Africa, and Central Asia: Size, Costs, and Challenges*. Washington, DC: IMF.

Laeven, L., and F. Valencia. 2010. "Resolution of Banking Crises: The Good, the Bad, and the Ugly." IMF Working Paper No. 2010/146, International Monetary Fund, Washington, DC.

Megginson, W. L., D. López, and A. I. Malik. 2021. "Privatization, State Capitalism, and State Ownership of Business in the 21st Century." *Foundations and Trends in Finance* 11 (1–2): 1–53.

Megginson, W. L., and A. I. Malik. 2022. "The Rise of Sovereign Wealth Funds as Global Investors." Unpublished working paper, World Bank, Washington, DC.

Musaccio, A., and E. Pineda 2019. *Fixing State-Owned Enterprises: New Policy Solutions to Old Problems*. Washington, DC: Inter-American Development Bank.

OECD (Organisation for Economic Co-operation and Development). 2015. *OECD Guidelines on Corporate Governance of State-Owned Enterprises*. Paris: OECD Publishing.

OECD (Organisation for Economic Co-operation and Development). 2017. *The Size and Sectoral Distribution of State-Owned Enterprises*. Paris: OECD Publishing.

OECD (Organisation for Economic Co-operation and Development). 2023. *Safeguarding State-Owned Enterprises from Undue Influence: Implementing the OECD Guidelines on Anti-Corruption and Integrity in State-Owned Enterprises*. Paris: OECD Publishing.

Taylor, B. 2022. "Chinese Government Steps into Iron Ore Trade." *Recycling Today,* July 20, 2022. https://www.recyclingtoday.com/news/china-iron-ore-cmrg-soe-aluminum-scrap/.

Vagliasindi, M., T. Cordella, and J. Clifton. 2023. "Introduction: Revisiting the Role of State-Owned Enterprises in Strategic Sectors." *Journal of Economic Policy Reform* 26 (1): 1–23.

World Bank. 2021. "CPSD SOE Knowledge Note." World Bank, Washington, DC.

2. State Businesses: Catalysts or Constraints?

Introduction

As an active player in commercial activities, the state competes with private firms, but it also collaborates with the private sector when ownership is joint. This chapter focuses on the economic efficiency of businesses of the state (BOSs) in the real sector. Do they tend to be more, or less, productive than private firms? And what can state presence mean for sector dynamism and investment over time? This chapter examines census data from Brazil, Ecuador, Romania, Türkiye, and Viet Nam as well as panel data from Orbis for 14 European countries.[1] The answers are at the heart of debates over when and where BOSs catalyze or constrain productivity growth and private investment.

State businesses may receive preferential treatment or not be held to the same efficiency standards as private firms. Having the state as full or partial owner could put a firm at an advantage if it receives preferential treatment from regulatory authorities or enjoys preferential access to finance or procurement contracts (IMF 2020; Shleifer and Vishny 1998; World Bank 1995, 2018). BOSs could thus allocate resources away from their most productive uses and dampen innovation and growth. Most literature treats BOSs as homogeneous or looks at a single sector or country. This report is the first to test for these effects across countries, differentiating across types of BOSs and market structures (Dall'Olio et al. 2022a, 2022b).

Three key patterns reinforce the importance of looking not just at the relative performance of firms by ownership but also at their impacts on the broader dynamics of state presence in a sector.

1. The performance of BOSs compared with that of private firms varies across different types of ownership and market structures. Minority-owned firms often perform better than firms with majority state ownership (Brazil, Viet Nam, and 14 European countries). There is also some evidence suggesting that BOSs owned directly have lower sales growth than those owned indirectly. However, rather than sweeping conclusions, analysts should take into account the heterogeneous types of BOSs to understand their performance in specific countries of interest.

2. The presence of BOSs in a sector is associated with a significant misallocation of resources, greater market concentration, and lower rates of firm entry—these are the most significant and worrying effects of BOSs on market dynamism.

3. Despite the state's justification for using BOSs to crowd in or catalyze private investment in competitive markets, there is no significant evidence of this effect in the countries analyzed here. This finding is true in aggregate for a sector and for the average rates of investment of private firms.

Many governments justify the creation of BOSs to address market failures and meet social mandates. However, the ability to deliver these benefits needs to be weighed against the fiscal costs and the adverse impacts on market dynamism and productivity growth. State ownership per se is not the only way to address market failures. The empirical evidence found in this report underlies the importance of reconsidering the state presence in competitive markets and addressing the concerns about governance and preferential treatment of BOSs that may come at the expense of market dynamism.

Mixed Results of State Ownership on BOSs' Performance

Characteristics and Productivity Levels of BOSs versus Private Firms

Across countries, BOSs are larger and employ more workers than private firms in the same two-digit sector. This finding is common in the literature and is true in all five countries with census data and in 14 European countries with panel data (IMF 2020; World Bank 1995). The size premium tends to rise with the extent of state ownership and is most often highest in natural monopoly markets. In Brazil, BOSs in partially contestable and natural monopoly markets are almost twice as large as BOSs in competitive markets. For Türkiye and Viet Nam, the size premium is largest in natural monopoly markets. But, for Ecuador, the size premium is largest in competitive markets.

Labor productivity varies across countries and across types of markets within countries. In Türkiye and Viet Nam, BOSs are more productive, especially those with majority state ownership and those in natural monopoly markets. But, in Romania, BOSs are less productive, particularly in both competitive and natural monopoly markets. In Ecuador, it is worrying that BOSs in competitive markets are much less productive than private firms in the same sector, especially given their greater size. Where data on assets are available, BOSs also tend to have higher capital per worker. With both more labor and more capital, it is not so surprising that total factor productivity varies across countries. Differences in the profiles of BOSs and private firms need to be kept in mind when interpreting results. The sectors and firms in which the state chooses to own or invest are not random; results demonstrate conditional correlations rather than causation.

BOSs are often associated with paying a wage premium consistent with a social contract of providing more and better jobs. One concern is that the public sector sets wages with social goals in mind, decoupling them from productivity; it is also true that many BOSs attract higher-quality and more educated workers. A BOS wage premium is found in almost all countries, ranging from 3 percent to 22 percent. In Brazil, with an employer-employee census of formal workers, the wage premium is 18.5 percent. Controlling for differences in the quality of workers, including individual worker fixed effects to absorb differences in workers who sort into working for BOSs, the premium remains significant, but declines to 4.5 percent. Wages tend to be higher, particularly in minority-owned firms and, even more so, in competitive markets. But, in the other countries, the wage premium is generally highest for wholly and majority-owned BOSs. For minority-owned firms, there is no significant premium. For private firms, the presence of this wage premium can make it hard to attract talent. In the extreme, workers can queue for jobs with BOSs (or the public sector more broadly) if the jobs are seen as more secure and higher paying than in the private sector.

Relative Growth of BOSs and Inefficiencies

In exploring how BOSs may contribute to productivity growth and broader private sector development, much of the literature focuses on whether BOSs grow faster or more slowly than private firms (IMF 2020). However, the presence of BOSs can also impair the reallocation of resources across firms (Fang et al. 2023).[2] BOSs can discourage private firms from entering and hasten their exit. These effects have longer-term implications for growth. This chapter examines three channels for improving productivity growth—the improved relative performance of BOSs over time, the greater reallocation of resources into more productive activities, and the greater net entry of firms—to see whether BOSs and new BOS investments catalyze new investments by private firms. Because concern about the potential distortions of state ownership is greatest in competitive markets, the chapter looks at results overall as well as only in competitive markets.

Overall, while BOSs' sales and employment tend to be bigger than private firms, the relative growth of BOSs is not as striking. Many differences are not statistically significant. And, more tellingly, the patterns are not the same in each country. So it is not possible to make sweeping statements about the growth of BOSs. In part, this heterogeneity can reflect differences in the regulatory environment or the extent to which some BOSs may receive preferential treatment or state aid (chapters 3 and 4).

However, the results underscore that taking the extent and nature of state ownership into account matters. In the four countries with sufficient information to estimate productivity, productivity growth is lower, on average, for BOSs than for private firms, except in Romania. Figures 2.1 and 2.2 illustrate this for Romania and Viet Nam. What is also striking is that in both countries, the results for majority- and minority-owned

FIGURE 2.1
Growth of BOSs Relative to Privately Owned Enterprises in Romania, by Sector, 2011–19

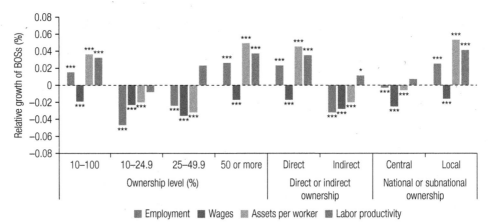

Sources: Dauda, Pop, and Iootty 2023 using World Bank Global Businesses of the State (BOS) database and census data sets.

Note: The regression coefficients are for measures of BOSs on the outcomes of interest, controlling for lagged firm size, age, sector, and year effects. BOSs = businesses of the state.

Significance level: * = 10 percent, ** = 5 percent, *** = 1 percent.

FIGURE 2.2 **Growth of BOSs Relative to Privately Owned Enterprises in Viet Nam, by Type of Ownership, 2007–19**

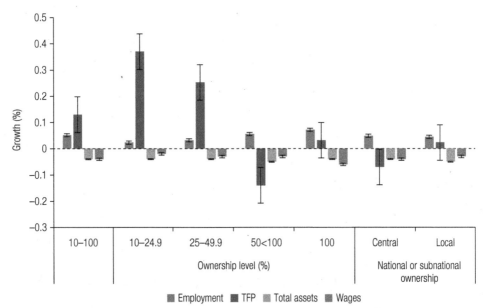

Sources: Hallward-Driemeier, Aterido, and Tran 2023 using World Bank Global Businesses of the State (BOS) database and census data sets.

Note: The error bars provide the 95 percent confidence interval around the estimated effect. If the error bars cross the x-axis, the result is not statistically significant at the 5 percent level. BOSs = businesses of the state; TFP = total factor productivity.

Significance level: * = 10 percent, ** = 5 percent, *** = 1 percent.

BOSs are statistically different from each other. Often the 25 percent threshold is taken as relevant in the literature, as a proxy for control, but the impacts of ownership at the 10–24.9 percent level are often similar to those of 25–49.9 percent ownership. In 9 of the 14 European countries, the effect of government ownership on employment growth is statistically different for BOSs owned directly than for those owned indirectly. In Italy, Lithuania, North Macedonia, and Romania, the effects on employment growth go in opposite directions for firms owned by local governments versus those owned by central governments.

There are some signs that greater shares of private ownership among BOSs provide some market discipline. This is true in Viet Nam, where there is a significant negative relationship between the extent of state ownership and productivity growth (figure 2.2). It is also true in Brazil for employment growth and innovative activities. And it holds for European countries as a whole for productivity growth—but not for all countries.

The patterns are often more striking across market taxonomies, sometimes in conjunction with ownership levels (figure 2.3). In Brazil, the results for employment growth are not significant overall, but they are significant at the 10 percent level for competitive markets (box 2.1). This result is driven by BOSs in competitive markets with minority state ownership. In Romania, employment growth, wage growth, and labor productivity growth are highest and statistically significant for BOSs in natural monopoly markets (figure 2.3).

Figure 2.3 shows the relative performance of BOSs compared to private firms. The height of the bars indicates how much more BOSs hire, are productive, pay wages, etc., compared to the average private firm (more if they are positive; less if they are negative). In Türkiye and Viet Nam, labor productivity, or value added per worker, is higher on average in BOSs than in private firms, particularly in natural monopolies, where sectors can be more capital-intensive. This could reflect some selection issues of which types of firms the state chooses to invest in, but it is also a reminder that not all BOSs are inefficient. However, the growth of labor productivity of BOSs in these countries is lower than that of private firms. Hiring workers faster than the value added is growing will lower productivity growth and lower the efficiency of how resources are allocated.

As Romania is one of the few countries that report data on subsidies at the firm level, box 2.2 discusses the evidence on the extent to which subsidies can explain the relative performance of BOSs in Romania. In Türkiye, employment growth is higher in competitive markets, but productivity growth is lower for BOSs than for private firms, including in competitive and partially contestable markets. In Viet Nam, BOSs in natural monopolies have higher growth of employment and total factor productivity.

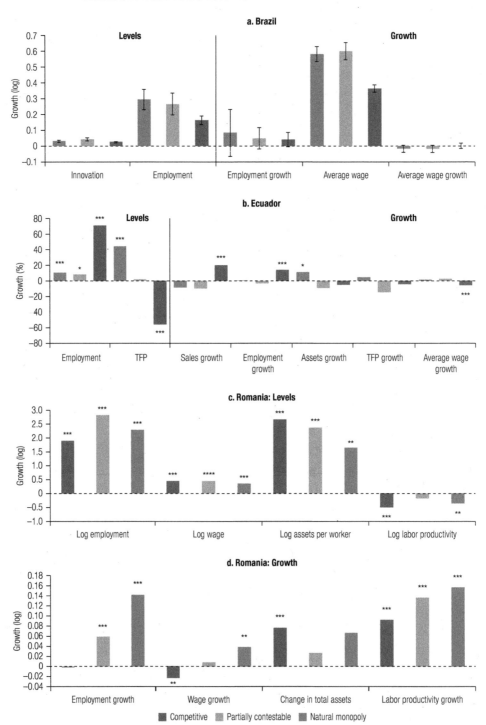

FIGURE 2.3 Performance in Levels and for Growth in Select Countries, by Type of Market, Various Years 2007–19

(Figure continues on the following page.)

The Business of the State

FIGURE 2.3 **Performance in Levels and for Growth in Select Countries, by Type of Market, Various Years 2007–19** *(continued)*

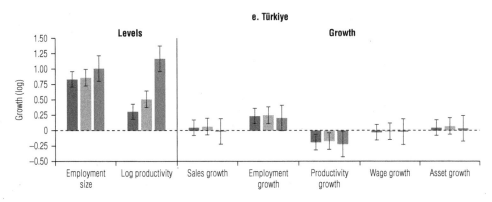

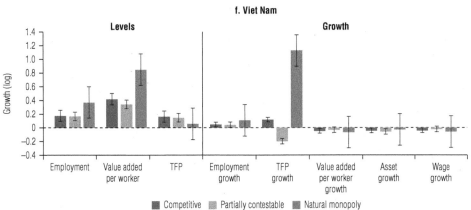

Sources: Cirera, Brolhato, and Martins-Neto 2023 (Brazil); Ferro and Patiño Peña 2023 (Ecuador); Dauda, Pop, and Iootty 2023 (Romania); Akcigit and Cilasun 2023 (Türkiye); and Hallward-Driemeier, Aterido, and Tran 2023 (Viet Nam) using World Bank Global Businesses of the State (BOS) database and census data sets. The years covered vary by country: 2016–19 for Brazil, 2011–19 for Ecuador and Romania, 2015–19 for Türkiye, and 2007–19 for Viet Nam.
Note: The bars are average marginal effects. TFP = total factor productivity.
Significance level: * = 10 percent, ** = 5 percent, *** = 1 percent.

BOX 2.1

Incentives to Innovate

In Brazil and Türkiye, businesses of the state (BOSs) have greater access to both skilled workers and larger markets, which improves their ability and incentives to be more innovative. In Brazil, state-owned firms outperform private firms on two measures of innovation. More than 43 percent of BOSs employ workers in occupations associated with innovation, accounting for an average of 5.7 percent of total firm employment, compared with 3.0 percent and 0.6 percent, respectively, for private firms. Some of the gaps reflect differences in firm size. Firms with state participation

(Box continues on the following page.)

Incentives to Innovate *(continued)*

employ 1,329 workers, on average, and almost 10 percent of them employ technical and scientific occupations highly correlated with investment in research and development (R&D). Private firms without state participation have one-tenth the number of workers with such innovation-related qualifications.

In Brazil's more innovative BOSs, the state participates often as a minority partner, rather than being the majority or full owner: 71 percent of minority-owned BOSs have workers in innovation-related occupations, compared with 46 percent for majority-owned and 22 percent for fully owned BOSs. The intensity of innovation is three times higher for minority-owned BOSs than for wholly state-owned BOSs. The results suggest that the public sector intentionally invests in some key sectors and innovative private companies rather than starting with state ownership and bringing in private partners (productivity data are not available for Brazil).

BOSs in Türkiye are also more likely to have skilled workers and to conduct R&D. They are significantly more likely than private firms to receive patents. So the measures of productivity can reflect the greater skill mix and R&D activities, while leaving open the question of whether BOSs really are strong performers or whether many private firms are fairly weak. Compared with R&D in higher-income countries, R&D activities in private firms in large middle-income countries are indeed lower. And, although Turkish BOSs are more productive than other firms, they have negative productivity growth.

Channeling public resources to firms does not necessarily translate into more innovation. As chapters 1, 3, and 4 show, there are many examples of expensive failures of state-owned firms as national champions, but the converse is also true. In an environment with more limited financial markets and more frictions in the allocation of resources, state assistance can provide the funds and ability to achieve scale that firms otherwise could not achieve. The lower productivity growth of BOSs, despite higher measures of innovation, raises concerns, as does the limited evidence of spillovers to other firms from the innovative activities (Akcigit and Cilasun 2023; Cirera, Brolhato, and Martins-Neto 2023).

Subsidies to Firms in Romania

In Romania, support to firms tends to be geared toward majority-owned businesses of the state (BOSs), and when they receive subsidies the amount tends to be larger, even when all firms are eligible. The average BOS firm is four times more likely to receive government subsidies than the average private firm, irrespective of productivity (figure B2.2.1). The odds of receiving government subsidies are five times higher for majority-owned, direct, and local BOSs than for other firms. The subsidy is also significantly higher for majority state-owned firms. Firms with less than 25 percent state ownership have no statistical advantage.

(Box continues on the following page.)

Subsidies to Firms in Romania *(continued)*

FIGURE B2.2.1 **Probability of a BOS Firm Receiving a Subsidy Relative to a Private Firm in Romania, 2011–19**

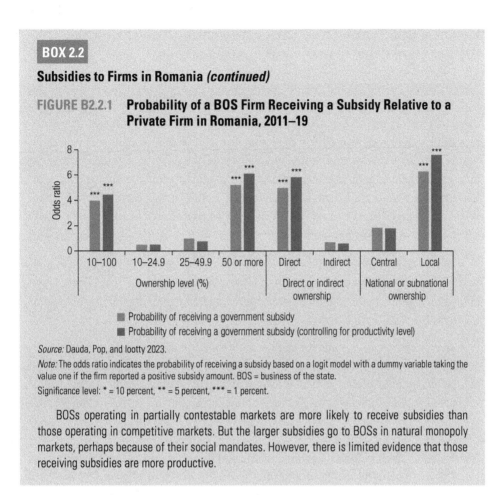

Source: Dauda, Pop, and Iootty 2023.

Note: The odds ratio indicates the probability of receiving a subsidy based on a logit model with a dummy variable taking the value one if the firm reported a positive subsidy amount. BOS = business of the state.

Significance level: * = 10 percent, ** = 5 percent, *** = 1 percent.

BOSs operating in partially contestable markets are more likely to receive subsidies than those operating in competitive markets. But the larger subsidies go to BOSs in natural monopoly markets, perhaps because of their social mandates. However, there is limited evidence that those receiving subsidies are more productive.

BOSs' growth could reflect their preferential access to inputs or markets. When BOS growth is consistently lower than that of private firms, BOSs may not be required to operate at the same standards and performance as private firms to stay in business (Dewenter and Malatesta 2001; La Porta and Lopez-de-Silanes 1999; Le, Park, and Castillejos-Petalcorin 2023; Vickers and Yarrow 1991). Particularly when employment growth is positive and productivity growth is negative, as in Ecuador and Türkiye, the state may distort the allocation of resources when prioritizing employment rather than efficiency gains (Akcigit, Baslandze, and Lotti 2023). To improve the allocation of resources and to raise productivity, labor and capital should be moving to where productivity is growing. For productivity growth, it should be the productive businesses and sectors that are expanding employment. Yet, in Ecuador and Türkiye, the risk with BOSs is that, on average, the inefficient firms are the ones hiring more workers.

Impact of BOS Presence on Sector Dynamism—Lower Firm Entry, Greater Market Concentration, and Misallocation

The effects of state ownership are mixed on measures of firm growth, but the effects on firm entry are striking—and worrying. The greater the state presence is in a sector, the lower the entry of firms in Romania and Türkiye and the lower the share of economic activity accounted for by young firms in Brazil, Ecuador, and Viet Nam (figure 2.4). In Ecuador, Romania, and Viet Nam, the effect is significant for private firms; in Türkiye, it is generally significant for private firms only in competitive sectors. Rather than encouraging entry, the evidence shows that greater state presence in BOSs discourages it. And, as in Viet Nam, in Türkiye rolling back the state's presence encourages the entry of private firms.

The impact on competition is also a concern, with a greater state presence associated with higher market concentration in four of the five countries. The effects are largest in Brazil and Ecuador, the two countries where entry rates are the most sensitive to the presence of BOSs in a sector.

Other measures of dynamism raise additional flags suggesting that a greater state presence can constrain dynamism. In Viet Nam, state presence is associated with less net job creation and less job reallocation, particularly in the private sector. It is also associated with less job creation in Brazil and with misallocation in Ecuador (box 2.3).

FIGURE 2.4   Effect of State Presence on Market Dynamism in Select Countries: Entry and Competition When BOSs Are Present, Various Years 2007–19

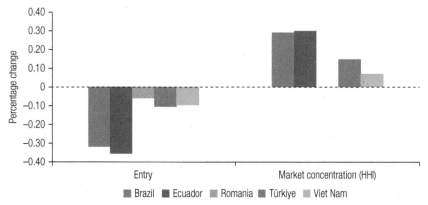

Sources: Cirera, Brolhato, and Martins-Neto 2023 (Brazil); Ferro and Patiño Peña 2023 (Ecuador); Dauda, Pop, and Iootty 2023 (Romania); Akcigit and Cilasun 2023 (Türkiye); and Hallward-Driemeier, Aterido, and Tran 2023 (Viet Nam) using World Bank Global Businesses of the State (BOS) database and census data sets.

Note: Entry is based on the rate of entry of new firms in Romania and Türkiye and on the share of revenues accounted for by young firms (under age five) in Brazil, Ecuador, and Viet Nam. The years covered vary by country: 2016–19 for Brazil, 2011–19 for Ecuador and Romania, 2015–19 for Türkiye, and 2007–19 for Viet Nam. All effects are statistically significant, except the effect of market concentration in Romania was extremely small and not significant and so not graphed here. Coefficients are on the market share of businesses of the state (BOSs) in a two-digit sector for both of the outcomes run separately, controlling for a sector's size over time, and sector, taxonomy, country, and year fixed effects. HHI = Herfindahl-Hirschman Index.

Resource Misallocation in Ecuador

The relationship between the presence of businesses of the state in a sector and a measure of allocative efficiency[a] shows a negative pattern. In sectors in which businesses of the state have a higher share of labor, allocative efficiency is lower. This suggests that the presence of state-owned enterprises may contribute to Ecuador's highly distorted labor markets and the pervasive aggregate productivity effects of labor misallocation.

Source: Ferro and Patiño Peña 2023.
a. From the Olley-Pakes decomposition, the unweighted average of firm-level productivity and the within-industry covariance between firm productivity and firms' shares in economic activity provide a measure of allocative efficiency.

FIGURE 2.5   **Impact of BOS Presence on Market Dynamics in 14 European Countries**

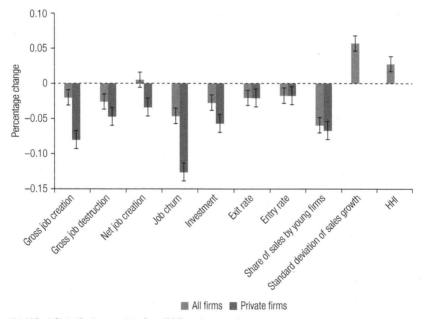

■ All firms ■ Private firms

Sources: World Bank Global Businesses of the State (BOS) database and Orbis.
Note: Coefficients on the market share of BOSs in a two-digit sector for each of the outcomes run separately, controlling for sector's size over time, sector, taxonomy, country, and year fixed effects. The error bars provide the 95 percent confidence interval around the estimated effect. If the error bars cross the x-axis, the result is not statistically significant at the 5 percent level. BOSs = businesses of the state; HHI = Herfindahl-Hirschman Index.

In the 14 European countries, almost all of the measures of dynamism are lower when the presence of the state is greater, but country results can vary (figure 2.5). The impacts are especially large in competitive markets, which is worrying because a larger state presence is associated with less reallocation of capital and workers and less entry and exit.

The effects on market dynamics are more consistent across countries than the effects on the performance of individual firms—yet they do not receive the attention they deserve. The literature often focuses on whether BOSs themselves are efficient or not (for example, Abramov et al. 2017; Kabaciński, Kubiak, and Szarzec 2020; Liljeblom, Maury, and Hörhammer 2020). To be clear, BOSs may not have these dampening effects in all countries. But it is necessary to investigate and monitor their dynamic effects to be sure that they do not. The analysis using panel data includes the effects of changing the extent of state ownership over time. Isolating only at the extreme of state ownership moving to zero—on firms and on workers—helps to understand what effects might be realized with reforms (boxes 2.4 and 2.5). In Viet Nam, greater entry, change in state ownership share among minority BOSs, and exit among majority BOSs are found over time, with mild benefits of increased productivity for privatized firms. But, in both Brazil and Viet Nam, some BOSs provide more and higher-paying jobs and workers bear significant effects of privatization, which can also explain the political resistance to reform.

The analysis so far has been partial equilibrium, but a general equilibrium model can provide insights on the aggregate effects. Such general equilibrium models of the

---

BOX 2.4

Viet Nam's Transition from State to Private Ownership

Viet Nam's transition of firms from state to private ownership displays the following patterns:

- The rate of privatizing state-owned firms is higher for firms with lower shares of state ownership.
- Of firms wholly state owned, more than 80 percent remain so, whereas 10 percent become jointly owned, with the state retaining majority ownership; just over 1 percent come to have only minority ownership, whereas 3.8 percent are privatized and 4.5 percent exit outright.
- The share of private firms that have state ownership is very low: less than 0.1 percent of firms.
- The rate of exit is highest for private firms; among businesses of the state, exit rates are higher the greater is the extent of state ownership.

With just over 300 privatizations, it is possible to do an "event study" to examine the effects on employment and growth of assets in Viet Nam. Comparing firms that were privatized with firms that were not privatized shows no significant difference in rates of employment before privatization. But there is a significant initial decline in employment with privatization and a somewhat lower, but sustained, decline in the years following privatization. This finding is consistent with businesses of the state having higher rates of employment and with privatization weakening the social mandate to provide employment. The growth of total assets also falls after privatization. The effect on productivity after privatization is mildly positive but not significant.

Source: Hallward-Driemeier, Aterido, and Tran 2023.

BOX 2.5

Effects of Privatization on Workers' Employment and Wages in Brazil

Privatization in Brazil reduces workers' income. Workers who are part of a privatization event see their relative wages decline by about 10 percent in the first two years. And privatized firms tend to lay off more educated, older, and longer-tenured individuals (figure B2.5.1). The findings are consistent with the growing literature on the impacts of privatization—for instance, Olsson and Tåg (2021) evaluate the impact of privatization in Sweden from 1997 to 2011 and find that wages declined about 4 percent in the first two years and 9 percent during the third and fourth years. In Brazil, Arnold (2022) evaluates the impact of privatization during the 1990s—the first wave of large privatization in the country. In banking, telecommunications, and electricity state-owned enterprises, workers enjoyed a substantial wage premium, and privatization reduced it. This finding helps to illustrate the possibility of social resistance to reforms or privatization efforts.

FIGURE B2.5.1 **The Effect of Privatization on Brazilian Workers, by Education and Age, 2011–20**

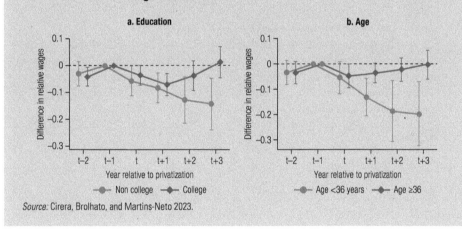

Source: Cirera, Brolhato, and Martins-Neto 2023.

microeconomics of growth emphasize how frictions, constraints, and preferential treatment can hamper the efficient allocation of resources and distort key economic decision-making—with big impacts on long-run growth and prosperity. Cusolito et al. (2022) apply a model of misallocation that looks at frictions in the financial sector to include the role of state-owned enterprises (SOEs) in 24 countries in Europe. They find that an expanded state footprint is associated with lower costs of finance for BOSs, with a resulting increase in their assets and capital intensity. The potential gains from removing frictions in financial markets and closing SOEs that are less productive can deliver productivity gains (see box 2.6).

The greater state presence associated with lower firm entry is already worrying. If BOSs were effective at creating markets, their presence should bring in new firms.

> **BOX 2.6**
>
> ## The Aggregate Costs of Misallocation
>
> Since Hsieh and Klenow's (2009) seminal work, there have been debates as to the extent of misallocation and how best to measure it (Cusolito and Maloney 2018). Applying a general equilibrium model to 24 countries in Europe allows for thought experiments on the potential benefits of reforms. Looking at the period 2010–16, when financial markets were facing distortions and significant state intervention in light of the global financial crisis of 2008–09, Cusolito et al. (2022) conduct an exercise that shows the types of gains that could be realized under various scenarios that assume away frictions and the least-productive state-owned enterprises (SOEs).
>
> Cusolito et al. (2022) estimate that the aggregate potential gains of addressing distortions associated with state ownership could be a 20–80 percent increase in total factor productivity (TFP). A reform that simply removes SOEs from the market could lead to moderate aggregate TFP gains for some countries, whereas other reforms lead to moderate losses. The reason is that, for some countries, SOEs may be more productive, on average, than their private counterparts, and their shutdown would reduce aggregate productivity. And financial market distortions may be severe enough across private firms that reallocating resources would lead to higher inefficiencies. But a targeted reform that shuts down only the less productive state-owned firms could free up more funds that could flow to more productive SOEs and private firms.
>
> This targeted approach can lead to productivity gains for most countries, even with financial market distortions. A targeted approach coupled with fixing financial markets before reallocating resources may be necessary to produce gains in TFP across the board. Under this coupled reform, aggregate TFP would increase between 19 percent and 81 percent for all 25 European countries in the study.
>
> *Source:* Cusolito et al. 2022.

This would be true if BOSs were effective at solving coordination failures or at demonstrating the profitability of engaging in a sector or a location with no activity before (Chang 2002; Mazzucato 2011). An easier test might simply be to see whether, rather than catalyze new firms, investments might expand existing firms.

There is no evidence that BOS presence or new BOS investments trigger new investments from incumbent firms—a remarkably robust nonresult when a key rationale for state ownership is to catalyze private investment. Firms, on average, are not more likely to invest or increase their assets in sectors where the state has a larger presence or where BOS firms are investing. And aggregate assets do not increase in response either to the extent of state presence or to changes in the assets of BOS firms in a sector. The analysis looks at all two-digit sectors (allowing BOSs to spur investments in other BOSs) and at only firms in competitive markets. The regression results show that, on average, there is no significant relationship between increasing BOS presence and private investment. Ecuador and Romania do show increases in the growth of assets of private firms—but only in natural monopoly and partially contestable markets. In Brazil, Türkiye, and Viet Nam, there is no significant effect on investment rates or total asset growth. If the rationale for state ownership in competitive markets is to jump-start growth in these markets, there is little evidence, on average, that it does.

The lack of evidence supporting BOSs as catalyzing new private investment—and the results showing that they even have a constraining effect on firm entry—underscores the importance of revisiting state ownership, particularly in competitive markets. These nonresults do not mean that no market failures limit private investment; they do mean that state ownership is not the most effective way to solve them. Indeed, other regulatory options are discussed in more detail in the following chapters.

Annex 2A The Extent and Nature of the State's Footprint

The countries analyzed in this chapter have different profiles of the presence of BOSs, which allows an examination of broader patterns. Panel census data of firms are needed to look at changes in the presence and dynamics of state ownership, including the impacts on firm entry and the extent of overall misallocation.[3]

This work draws on five countries with different levels of income and from three regions. With Latin America and the Caribbean having some of the biggest increases in firms that meet BOS criteria relative to traditional SOE criteria and Europe and Central Asia having the highest levels of BOSs, two countries were chosen from the former (Brazil and Ecuador) and two from the latter (Romania and Türkiye). Viet Nam has a gross domestic product per capita in purchasing power parity terms comparable to that of Ecuador. Romania had a history of strong state involvement but has undertaken significant steps to reduce the state's footprint since its transition to a market economy in the 1990s. Viet Nam, while still reforming, has a larger state role in the economy. Including Brazil and Türkiye as large G-20 countries where the state is active but not dominant can test where scale matters, including having a sufficient pool of talented workers. In addition, because Europe and Central Asia has the most BOSs and a range of histories with state-led development and privatization efforts, there is a special interest in using Orbis panel data from 14 countries from that region to examine the role of BOSs (Cusolito 2020). To capture dynamics, the BOS indicators were collected for the years 2016–20.[4]

Table 2A.1 summarizes some of the key differences or striking features of each of the five countries examined here.[5] Table 2A.1 summarizes some of the key differences or striking features of each of the five countries examined here, and tables 2A.2 through 2A.7 show BOS distribution for the countries individually and for the region. The analysis is done for Brazil on employment data and for Romania and Viet Nam on the full set of performance measures. For Ecuador and Türkiye, the analysis is only possible using the 0–1 indicator of BOS ownership. Country-specific background papers prepared for this report provide detailed analysis and results; key findings and illustrations of the broader set of relationships are included here.

TABLE 2A.1 Key Characteristics and Trends of BOS Presence in the Five Census Countries

Country and time period covered	Overall trends	Ownership features	Market taxonomy features
Brazil, 2016–20	The number of majority-owned BOSs declines by two-thirds over time.	By 2019, about 40 percent of BOSs are minority-owned by the state.	BOSs are pervasive across sectors; 95 percent of sectors had some BOS firms in 2016 and still 86 percent of sectors by 2020.
Ecuador, 2011–20	The employment share is constant, whereas the revenue share declines (reflecting changing prices for oil). Many of the BOSs surviving until 2019 entered between 2012 and 2016.	The overwhelming share of BOSs are majority owned.	While close to half of all BOSs are in competitive markets, almost a quarter are in natural monopoly and partially contestable sectors, the highest of the five countries studied.
Romania, 2011–20	There is a mild decrease in market and employment shares over time for BOSs surviving until 2019; however, for BOSs in 2019, half were started after 2011.	BOSs in Romania are overwhelmingly majority owned by local governments: 88 percent of BOSs are majority state owned, 80 percent by local governments.	Like Ecuador, there are more BOSs in natural monopoly and partially contestable markets.
Türkiye, 2015–20	There is some increase in the shares of BOS employment and revenues surviving until 2019. Although relatively few in number, the BOSs are large.	Türkiye has many BOSs that are minority as well as majority owned, with most directly owned.	The large majority are in competitive markets. In partially contestable and natural monopolies, ownership is more likely to be minority and indirect.
Viet Nam, 2007–20	There is a significant decline in the market and employment shares of BOSs as the private sector has grown tremendously, reaching 45 percent of total revenues from just over 15 percent and 30 percent of employment from 10 percent (based on all firms in the census). The absolute decline in revenues or employment of BOSs is relatively small.	Viet Nam has a very large share of ownership that is indirect, in both minority and majority BOSs.	The very large majority of BOSs are in competitive sectors. All but 8 of the 96 two-digit sectors have BOSs. Even with the dramatic decline, there has been no complete exit of the state presence in any of the two-digit sectors.
14 European countries, 2016–20	Most countries have a relatively stable share of BOSs in overall employment and revenues. Serbia stands out, with declining shares of BOSs in total revenues.	On average, more than three-quarters of BOSs are majority owned.	Two-thirds of BOSs are in competitive sectors, and just under a fifth are natural monopolies.

Sources: Orbis and census data sets.

Note: In Ecuador, Romania, and Türkiye, BOSs are identified in 2019 and can be traced back in the data. There is thus survivor bias in the identification of BOS firms; the approach omits information on any other BOSs that exited before 2019 and so underestimates the ways in which the state's footprint may have declined. For Brazil, the census contains information about wholly and majority-owned state firms, allowing for variation over time in these firms and in their entry and exit. For minority-owned firms, the data rely on the World Bank Global Businesses of the State (BOS) database for 2019; the approach traces the trends for these surviving firms over time and does not capture the exit of such firms prior to 2019. For Viet Nam, there is information on the percentage of ownership held directly by the local or central government; the exit and privatization of state-owned firms is captured for the whole panel. Information on indirect ownership was not available for the larger set of firms and was not used. BOSs = businesses of the state.

TABLE 2A.2 Distribution of BOSs in Brazil, by Type of Market and Ownership Category, 2019

Percentage

Sector	Minority ownership	Majority ownership
Competitive	19.9	38.9
Partially contestable	9.7	8.2
Natural monopoly	12.4	8.6

Source: World Bank Global Businesses of the State (BOS) database.
Note: Number of businesses of the state (BOSs) = 920.

TABLE 2A.3 Distribution of BOSs in Ecuador, by Type of Market and Ownership Category, 2019

Percentage

Sector	Minority ownership		Majority ownership	
	Direct	Indirect	Direct	Indirect
Competitive	0.3	3.2	41.3	3.5
Partially contestable	0.3	0.0	23.1	0.9
Natural monopoly	0.6	0	26.9	0

Source: World Bank Global Businesses of the State (BOS) database.
Note: Number of businesses of the state (BOSs) = 346.

TABLE 2A.4 Distribution of BOSs in Romania, by Type of Market and Ownership Category, 2019

Percentage

Sector	Minority ownership		Majority ownership	
	Direct	Indirect	Direct	Indirect
Competitive	3.5	6.6	42.1	1.8
Partially contestable	0.6	1.3	19.1	0.6
Natural monopoly	1.0	0.7	22.5	0.2

Source: World Bank Global Businesses of the State (BOS) database.
Note: Number of businesses of the state (BOSs) = 1,416.

TABLE 2A.5 Distribution of BOSs in Türkiye, by Type of Market and Ownership Category, 2019

Percentage

Sector	Minority ownership		Majority ownership	
	Direct	Indirect	Direct	Indirect
Competitive	4.6	12.9	36.5	8.5
Partially contestable	1.3	10.6	6.3	2.9
Natural monopoly	0.2	10.6	2.7	2.9

Source: World Bank Global Businesses of the State (BOS) database.
Note: Number of businesses of the state (BOSs) = 480.

TABLE 2A.6 Distribution of BOSs in Viet Nam, by Type of Market and Ownership Category, 2019

Percentage

Sector	Minority ownership		Majority ownership	
	Direct	Indirect	Direct	Indirect
Competitive	6.7	27.3	26.1	26.1
Partially contestable	0.8	2.5	2.5	2.8
Natural monopoly	0.5	1.3	2.1	1.3

Source: World Bank Global Businesses of the State (BOS) database.
Note: Number of businesses of the state (BOSs) = 5,984.

TABLE 2A.7 Distribution of BOSs in 14 European Countries, on Average, by Type of Market and Ownership Category, 2019

Percentage

Sector	Minority ownership	Majority ownership
Competitive	17.5	47.9
Partially contestable	3.0	12.9
Natural monopoly	1.2	17.6

Source: World Bank Global Businesses of the State (BOS) database.
Note: BOSs = businesses of the state.

Notes

1. The 14 countries analyzed are Bosnia and Herzegovina, Bulgaria, Estonia, Croatia, Italy, Latvia, Lithuania, Montenegro, North Macedonia, Romania, Poland, Romania, Serbia, and Slovenia.

2. State presence is calculated using revenue shares, except for Brazil, which uses employment shares because data on revenues are not available. The background paper for Viet Nam (Hallward-Driemeier, Aterido, and Tran 2023) provides comparisons using both measures.

3. This work underscores the complexity of the agenda and why the effort to collect data does not end here. Currently there are no systematic data on the performance of BOSs in meeting their social mandates. A second dimension of analysis where more data would improve the analysis (and transparency) regards the individual benefits that BOSs receive (see chapter 4).

4. The inclusion reflects the scope of Orbis's coverage. Some firms are captured only after they have been in business for several years. Some of the timing of changes in ownership reflect when Orbis reports the change and not necessarily when it occurred. Over time, Orbis has made greater efforts to record the ownership of firms. It should be noted that having variation in ownership over 4 years is a relatively short panel. The advantages of the longer panels of census data is why those studies get greater emphasis.

5. The background papers provide more descriptive details on the types of ownership and trends over time for each of the countries.

References

Abramov, A., A. Radygin, R. Entov, and M. Chernova. 2017. "State Ownership and Efficiency Characteristics." *Russian Journal of Economics* 3 (2): 129–57.

Akcigit, U., S. Baslandze, and F. Lotti. 2023. "Connecting to Power: Political Connections, Innovation, and Firm Dynamics." *Econometrica* 91 (2): 529–64.

Akcigit, U., and S. M. Cilasun. 2023. "State-Owned Enterprises in Türkiye." Background paper for this report, World Bank, Washington, DC.

Arnold, D. 2022. "The Impact of Privatization of State-Owned Enterprises on Workers." *American Economic Journal: Applied Economics* 14 (4): 343–80.

Chang, H.-J. 2002. *Kicking Away the Ladder: Development Strategy in Historical Perspective.* London: Anthem Press.

Cirera, X., S. Brolhato, and A. Martins-Neto. 2023. "Businesses of the State in Brazil: Employment and Impact on Business Dynamism." Background paper for this report, World Bank, Washington, DC.

Cusolito, A. 2020. "Source Code and Use Instructions for Generating Financial and Ownership Datasets Using Orbis Data." Washington, DC: World Bank.

Cusolito, A., R. Fattal-Jaef, F. Patiño Peña, and A. Singh. 2022. "The Financial Premium and Real Cost of Bureaucrats in Businesses." World Bank, Washington, DC.

Cusolito, A. P., and W. F. Maloney. 2018. Productivity Revisited: Shifting Paradigms in Analysis and Policy. Washington, DC: World Bank.

Dall'Olio, A. M., T. K. Goodwin, M. Martinez Licetti, A. C. Alonso Soria, M. A. Drozd, J. A. K. Orlowski, F. A. Patiño Peña, and D. Sanchez Navarro. 2022a. "Are All State-Owned Enterprises Equal? A Taxonomy of Economic Activities to Assess SOE Presence in the Economy." Policy Research Working Paper 10262, World Bank, Washington, DC.

Dall'Olio, A. M., T. K. Goodwin, M. Martinez Licetti, J. A. K. Orlowski, F. A. Patiño Peña, F. R. Ratsimbazafy, and D. Sanchez Navarro. 2022b. "Using ORBIS to Build a Global Database of Firms with State Participation." Policy Research Working Paper 10261, World Bank, Washington, DC.

Dauda, S., G. Pop, and M. Iootty. 2023. "Does State Ownership Have Limits in Romania? An Assessment of Firm Performance and Market Outcomes before and during the COVID-19 Crisis." Background paper for this report, World Bank, Washington, DC.

Dewenter, K., and P. Malatesta. 2001. "State-Owned and Privately Owned Firms: An Empirical Analysis of Profitability, Leverage, and Labor Intensity." *American Economic Review* 91 (1): 320–34.

Fang, H., M. Li, Z. Wu, and Y. Zhang. 2023. "Reluctant Entrepreneurs: Evidence from China's SOE Reform." NBER Working Paper 31700, National Bureau of Economic Research, Cambridge, MA.

Ferro, E., and F. Patiño Peña. 2023. "Private Sector Performance under the Pressure of SOE Competition: The Case of Ecuador." Background paper for this report, World Bank, Washington, DC.

Hallward-Driemeier, M., R. Aterido, and T. Tran. 2023. "Businesses of the State in Viet Nam: Catalysts or Constraints to Private Sector Development?" Background paper for this report, World Bank, Washington, DC.

Hsieh, C.-T., and P. J. Klenow. 2009. "Misallocation and Manufacturing TFP in China and India." *Quarterly Journal of Economics* 124 (4): 1403–48.

IMF (International Monetary Fund). 2020. "State-Owned Enterprises: The Other Government." *IMF Fiscal Monitor* (April 2020): 47–74.

Kabaciński, B., J. Kubiak, and K. Szarzec. 2020. "Do State-Owned Enterprises Underperform Compared to Privately Owned Companies? An Examination of the Largest Polish Enterprises." *Emerging Markets Finance and Trade* 56 (13): 3174–92.

La Porta, R., and F. Lopez-de-Silanes. 1999. "The Benefits of Privatization: Evidence from Mexico." *Quarterly Journal of Economics* 114 (4): 1193–242.

Le, T., D. Park, and C. Castillejos-Petalcorin. 2023. "Performance Comparison of State-Owned Enterprises versus Private Firms in Selected Emerging Asian Countries." *Journal of Asian Business and Economic Studies* 30 (1): 26–48.

Liljeblom, E., B. Maury, and A. Hörhammer. 2020. "Complex State Ownership, Competition, and Firm Performance: Russian Evidence." *International Journal of Emerging Markets* 15 (2): 189–221.

Mazzucato, M. 2011. "The Entrepreneurial State." *Soundings* 49 (49): 131–42.

Olsson, M., and J. Tåg. 2021. "What Is the Cost of Privatization for Workers?" IFN Working Paper No. 1201, Research Institute of Industrial Economics, Stockholm. http://dx.doi.org/10.2139/ssrn.3134462.

Shleifer, A., and R. W. Vishny. 1998. *The Grabbing Hand: Government Pathologies and Their Cures.* Cambridge, MA: Harvard University Press.

Vickers, J., and G. Yarrow. 1991. "Economic Perspectives on Privatization." *Journal of Economic Perspectives* 5 (2): 111–32.

World Bank. 1995. *Bureaucrats in Business: The Economics and Politics of Government Ownership.* London: Oxford University Press.

World Bank. 2018. "Approach Paper. World Bank Group Support for the Reform of State-Owned Enterprises, 2007–2018: An IEG Evaluation." World Bank, Washington, DC.

3. Crowding Private Firms In—or Out?

Introduction

Policies and regulations that typically apply to most firms and markets—and that determine market outcomes—often do not apply in the same way to businesses of the state (BOSs). BOSs benefit when principles, policies, or regulations give them explicit advantages that unlevel the playing field over private firms. They also have advantages implicitly when policies and regulations that apply to all firms favor them in those markets.

The differences in the treatment and market conditions of BOSs and private firms can lead to two adverse economic outcomes. They can reduce the market-based incentives to improve technical efficiency (productive efficiency effects). They can also distort market outcomes—including prices, quantities, and the ability of rivals to compete—and resource allocations between firms and activities (allocative efficiency effects).

State-owned enterprises (SOEs), in particular, are often responsible for implementing a policy mandate.[1] In some cases, this approach may be a strategy of the state. In others, it may be due to a blurring of responsibilities between the SOE and its supervising entity. The way that SOEs operate in markets—from hiring to production decisions and pricing of products and services—can therefore reflect the implementation of these policy mandates. In many cases, this relationship will involve implicit subsidies to the SOE. For example, if an SOE is used to provide the population with essential goods at below-market prices, it may earn a below-commercial rate of return and will need support to fund its activities. Or it may involve the creation of a monopoly to control prices, quantities, or other market parameters directly. As a secondary effect, the policy mandates of the SOE could affect the incentives it faces for achieving technical efficiency as it moves away from a profit-maximizing objective. This situation can also have implications for performance and therefore create the need for further advantages.

SOEs have greater potential for political capture and a greater likelihood of being used for political patronage. The close relationship between SOEs, governments, and their supervising entities allows the state to use them to achieve political objectives. The resources of SOEs can be used to fund political parties, support electoral campaigns, or gain the support of politically influential individuals. Politicians can win votes by employing workers in an SOE. Politicians can personally profit from arranging patronage jobs in an SOE for their political backers, relatives, and friends. Politicians or local officials can also benefit from influencing the selection of suppliers and contractors or marketing goods in short supply. As with the policy mandate, political capture has the secondary effect of dampening SOE incentives for commercial performance.

The exposure of SOEs to state influence tends to be greatest when ownership rights are exercised by a line ministry and lowest when ownership rights are exercised by a specialized agency that operates at arm's length from the government (Vitale, Moiso, and Wanner 2020). But it is rare to find arm's length specialized agencies responsible for SOE ownership (figure 3.1). In 67 countries with this information, only 4 have this ownership setup. Instead, in more than half of high- and middle-income countries, line ministries most commonly exercise SOE ownership rights. But high-income countries are more likely to have safeguards to ensure that the chief executive officers of SOEs are appointed by board members rather than by public authorities, which reduces the propensity for SOE decision-making to be influenced by government (figure 3.2). Where these safeguards are not in place, the SOE will be more likely to operate with noncommercial objectives (either implicitly or explicitly) and be more prone to political capture.

FIGURE 3.1 Who Exercises the Ownership Rights in SOEs?

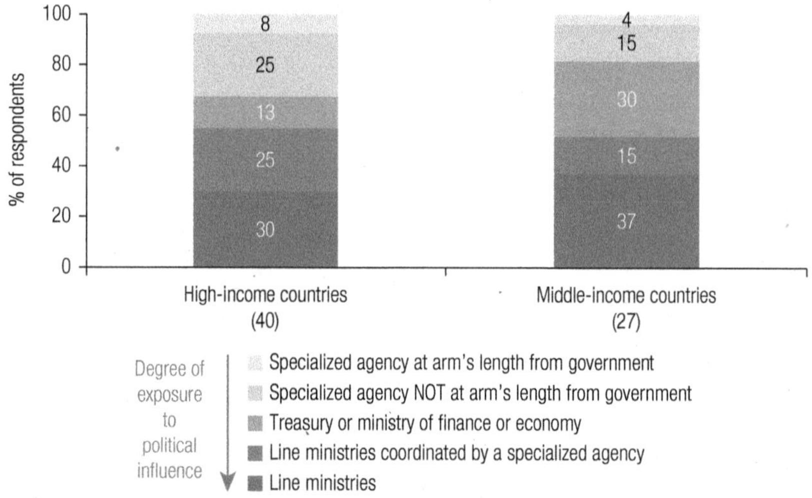

Degree of exposure to political influence ▼

- Specialized agency at arm's length from government
- Specialized agency NOT at arm's length from government
- Treasury or ministry of finance or economy
- Line ministries coordinated by a specialized agency
- Line ministries

Sources: OECD product market regulation (PMR) questionnaires, 2018; OECD and World Bank PMR questionnaires, 2013–22; and data collected by the World Bank on selected PMR questions for eight Middle East and North Africa countries.

Note: High-income countries are Australia, Austria, Belgium, Canada, Chile, Croatia, Cyprus, Czechia, Denmark, Estonia, Finland, France, Germany, Greece, Hungary, Iceland, Ireland, Israel, Italy, Japan, the Republic of Korea, Kuwait, Latvia, Lithuania, Luxembourg, Malta, the Netherlands, New Zealand, Norway, Poland, Portugal, Romania, Saudi Arabia, the Slovak Republic, Slovenia, Spain, Sweden, Switzerland, the United Arab Emirates, and the United Kingdom. Middle-income countries include both upper-middle-income and lower-middle-income countries. Upper-middle-income countries are Albania, Argentina, Belarus, Brazil, Bulgaria, China, Colombia, Costa Rica, Ecuador, Jordan, Kazakhstan, Kosovo, Malaysia, Mexico, Moldova, Montenegro, Peru, the Russian Federation, Serbia, South Africa, and Türkiye. Lower-middle-income countries are Côte d'Ivoire, the Arab Republic of Egypt, Indonesia, Morocco, Tunisia, and Viet Nam. OECD = Organisation for Economic Co-operation and Development; SOEs = state-owned enterprises.

The Business of the State

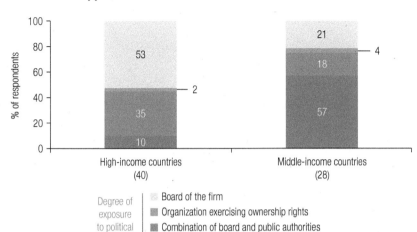

FIGURE 3.2   **Who Appoints the Chief Executive Officers of SOEs?**

High-income countries (40): Public authorities 10, Combination of board and public authorities 35, Organization exercising ownership rights 2, Board of the firm 53

Middle-income countries (28): Combination of board and public authorities 57, Organization exercising ownership rights 18, Board of the firm 21, 4

y-axis: % of respondents

Degree of exposure to political influence
- Board of the firm
- Organization exercising ownership rights
- Combination of board and public authorities
- Public authorities

Sources: OECD product market regulation (PMR) questionnaires, 2018; OECD and World Bank PMR questionnaires, 2013–22; and data collected by the World Bank on selected PMR questions for eight Middle East and North Africa countries.

Note: High-income countries are Australia, Austria, Belgium, Canada, Chile, Croatia, Cyprus, Czechia, Denmark, Estonia, Finland, France, Germany, Greece, Hungary, Iceland, Ireland, Israel, Italy, Japan, the Republic of Korea, Kuwait, Latvia, Lithuania, Luxembourg, Malta, the Netherlands, New Zealand, Norway, Poland, Portugal, Romania, Saudi Arabia, the Slovak Republic, Slovenia, Spain, Sweden, Switzerland, the United Arab Emirates, and the United Kingdom. Middle-income countries include both upper-middle-income and lower-middle-income countries. Upper-middle-income countries are Albania, Argentina, Belarus, Brazil, Bulgaria, China, Colombia, Costa Rica, Ecuador, Jordan, Kazakhstan, Kosovo, Malaysia, Mexico, Moldova, Montenegro, North Macedonia, Peru, the Russian Federation, Serbia, South Africa, and Türkiye. Lower-middle-income countries are Côte d'Ivoire, the Arab Republic of Egypt, Indonesia, Morocco, Tunisia, and Viet Nam. OECD = Organisation for Economic Co-operation and Development; SOEs = state-owned enterprises.

Channels for Granting Advantages to BOSs

As a market regulator, a policy maker, or an enforcer of market rules and laws, the state can provide advantages to BOSs. It can do this through the way that market rules, regulations, and policies are specified "on the books" or in the way those rules, regulations, and policies are implemented or enforced in practice (figure 3.3). There are three main channels through which the state can grant policy and regulatory advantages to BOSs:

- *Channel 1. The state provides explicit advantages to the SOE through preferential treatment.* Principles, policies, or regulations can be applied to an SOE in a way that gives it advantages over private firms, creating an unlevel playing field. These advantages are most relevant in competitive markets.

- *Channel 2. The state provides implicit advantages to the BOS firm through policies and regulations that apply to all firms in the market in which a BOS firm operates.* These rules and policies protect the BOS firm's position in a market or dampen competition in markets with BOSs. These advantages are most relevant in partially contestable markets.

FIGURE 3.3 **Framework of Channels for Granting Advantages to BOSs, with Examples and Primary Effects**

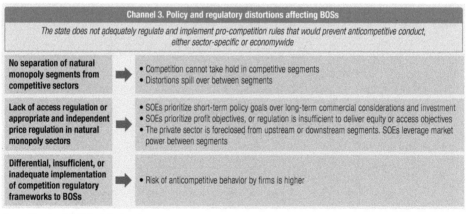

Channel 1. Explicit advantages to SOEs	
The state provides direct advantages to the SOE through preferential treatment	
Requirements for operations of SOEs	• Raises the risk of cross-subsidization between noncommercial and commercial activities, undermining the price mechanism • Alters the incentives to operate efficiently and commercially, distorting pricing mechanisms
Debt advantages	• Artificially lowers costs for the SOE relative to the private sector, leading to resource misallocation • Creates a risk of moral hazard or lower incentives for efficiency
Procurement advantages	• Possibly forecloses the private sector from procurement markets • Increases the price of goods and services for the state
Exemptions from or weak enforcement of laws	• Creates artificially low barriers to entry and lower ongoing costs of regulatory compliance for SOEs than for the private sector, leading to resource misallocation • *Competition law exemptions*: higher risk of anticompetitive behavior by firms • *Financial disclosure, bankruptcy exemptions*: lower transparency and accountability, leading to moral hazard and weaker incentives for performance • *Environmental law exemptions*: greater environmental risks

Channel 2. Implicit advantages to BOSs	
The state provides indirect advantages to the BOSs through policies and regulations that apply to all firms in the market in which a BOSs operates	
Import restrictions	• Protects BOSs from competition from foreign producers • Dampens competition and thus raises prices and reduces quantities
Limits on entry	• Protects BOSs from the threat of new, more efficient firms entering • Dampens competition and thus raises prices and reduces quantities
Price or margin regulation	• Dampens price competition in the BOS market; for example, prevents more efficient firms from undercutting the BOS firm
SOE involvement in regulatory decisions	• Creates the potential for the BOS firm or the regulator to apply regulation in such a way that restricts the private sector from entering the market or that raises the operating costs of competitors

Channel 3. Policy and regulatory distortions affecting BOSs	
The state does not adequately regulate and implement pro-competition rules that would prevent anticompetitive conduct, either sector-specific or economywide	
No separation of natural monopoly segments from competitive sectors	• Competition cannot take hold in competitive segments • Distortions spill over between segments
Lack of access regulation or appropriate and independent price regulation in natural monopoly sectors	• SOEs prioritize short-term policy goals over long-term commercial considerations and investment • SOEs prioritize profit objectives, or regulation is insufficient to deliver equity or access objectives • The private sector is foreclosed from upstream or downstream segments. SOEs leverage market power between segments
Differential, insufficient, or inadequate implementation of competition regulatory frameworks to BOSs	• Risk of anticompetitive behavior by firms is higher

Source: Based on World Bank, forthcoming.

Note: In this figure, SOEs is used when the information is based on laws that provide explicit advantages to SOEs as defined by countries. BOSs is used when all firms in the market are subject to policies and regulations. BOSs = businesses of the state; SOEs = state-owned enterprises.

- *Channel 3. The state does not adequately regulate and implement pro-competition rules that would prevent anticompetitive conduct, either sector-specific or economywide.* This channel is the most relevant for sectors with natural monopolies.

The advantages affecting the market conditions and incentives faced by a BOS firm differ based on the degree of contestability of the economic sector in which the firm operates.

- In competitive or partially contestable markets, actual and potential private competitors can be affected by the advantages provided to the BOS firm. The priority here is to understand whether explicit and implicit advantages crowd out, create an unlevel playing field, or dampen competition with actual and potential competitors (channels 1 and 2). It is important to know whether policies or regulations restrict competition and whether pro-competition policies and regulations will help to boost competition (channel 3). This knowledge is particularly relevant in partially contestable markets, such as network sectors.
- In natural monopoly markets where social welfare is pursued by concentrating production in a single firm, the main policy and regulatory objective of the government should be to prevent the firm from unduly exercising significant market power and to ensure that it invests sufficiently in the good or service. To do so, additional regulations and policies need to be implemented to avoid distortions. The priority here is to know whether the firm is adequately regulated to prevent undue exercise of market power (channel 3). It is also possible to assess whether the BOS firm operates under the same conditions and incentives as a hypothetical private firm in the same position—that is, whether the BOS firm receives explicit advantages (channel 1).

SOEs, in particular, clearly have advantages in middle-income countries (box 3.1). Explicit advantages, implicit advantages, and inadequate protection against anticompetitive firm behavior are evident in 58 countries. Implicit advantages seem to be more common, particularly limits on entry. The most common explicit advantages for SOEs are debt or tax advantages (see chapter 4).

Channel 1: Explicit Advantages to BOSs

Explicit advantages can result from the absence of firm-level principles and policies that should discipline SOEs, as well as from general policies and regulations applied differentially to SOEs and to fully private firms. The first type focuses on operational requirements for SOEs that, if absent, would tilt the playing field against private firms. The second type includes regulatory advantages and economic advantages provided to SOEs. Economic advantages include debt, taxes, procurement processes, and preferential access to finance, land, infrastructure, or other inputs.

When SOEs deliver both commercial and noncommercial services, they should separate those activities to ensure that funds provided to the SOE to fulfill its public service obligations do not cross-subsidize goods or services in another market. This separation is important because cross-subsidizing services can distort market mechanisms in commercial segments and create an unlevel playing field for private firms that do not receive subsidies for noncommercial services. To minimize the risks, countries can put in place frameworks or rules to ensure that these services are separate and thus minimize the risk of cross-subsidies.[2] But most middle-income countries impose

---

BOX 3.1

Advantages of SOEs Identified in a Systematic Review of Core Analytics across the World Bank

A systemic review of core analytics covering 58 middle-income countries finds that almost 90 percent of state-owned enterprises (SOEs) enjoy some type of advantage. Implicit advantages are the most common in the sample. Within this group, limits on entry are prevalent. Explicit advantages are observed in a third of the sample. SOEs commonly face lower tax burdens and can receive financing (such as government guarantees) not available to private companies. Figure B3.1.1 describes the implicit and explicit advantages for SOEs.

Explicit advantages
SOEs can benefit from financial and procurement advantages. For example, in Jamaica SOEs may benefit from public guarantees with the approval of parliament (Public Bodies Management and Accountability Act, Article 5A), and the government regularly subsidizes the debt of SOEs and absorbs their losses (IFC 2022). A joint stock company in Kazakhstan has special rights not afforded to other companies, such as the preemptive right to buy strategic facilities and bankrupt assets, and is exempt from government procurement procedures (IFC 2017).

Implicit advantages
As examples of limits on entry, many SOEs enjoy monopoly rights in network industries.[a] Firms typically acquire many of their inputs—transportation, energy, telecommunications, financial services (that is, network industries)—in local markets. If these upstream markets lack competition, goods and services needed for production are not priced competitively. As a result, firms may be less competitive than their foreign rivals and GDP growth may suffer. Reforms to open key markets to competition have boosted productivity and growth (Kitzmuller and Licetti 2013). Governments typically determine "strategic sectors" that are fully reserved either for SOEs or for joint ventures with limited private ownership of at most 49 percent. In Indonesia, SOEs hold monopoly or quasi-monopoly positions in sectors where competition would be viable, such as energy generation and distribution, seaports, toll roads, and imports of agricultural inputs and cereal grains (IFC 2019). These positions expand to public procurement contracts, as is the case in Bolivia, where only majority-owned SOEs can obtain contracts with the Ministry of Public Works, Services, and Housing for the execution of social inclusion projects in the telecommunications sector (IFC 2021b).

Inadequate protection against anticompetitive firm behavior
Key sectors of the economy are excluded from the Malaysia Competition Commission's antitrust scrutiny, including specific sectors such as telecommunications and energy that are subject to sectoral rules, as well as all enterprises entrusted with operating services of general economic

(Box continues on the following page.)

Advantages of SOEs Identified in a Systematic Review of Core Analytics across the World Bank *(continued)*

FIGURE B3.1.1 **Advantages Identified in a Systematic Review of Core Analytics across the World Bank**

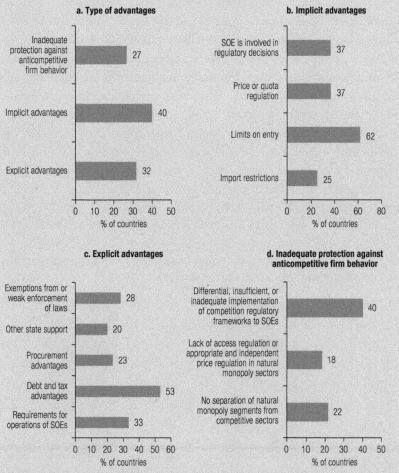

Source: Analysis of 57 World Bank Country Private Sector Diagnostics, 2 Country Economic Memorandums, and 1 Integrated SOE Framework published between 2017 and 2023.

Note: SOE = state-owned enterprise.

interest or having the character of a revenue-producing monopoly.[b] Mozambique's Council of Ministers establishes that SOEs must abide by the competition law; however, the implementation rules are still unclear (IFC 2021a). In Moldova, as in many client countries, the competition authority still lacks sufficient human and material resources to ensure all its attributions, including fully fledged enforcement of competition rules (IFC 2023).

a. Network industries are defined as those industries in which a fixed infrastructure is needed to deliver the goods or services to end users (OECD 2000).
b. Competition Act of Malaysia, Article 3 on application, which excludes activities included in schedules 1 and 2.

no requirement for SOEs to separate their noncommercial from their commercial activities (figure 3.4). Of 28 middle-income and 40 high-income countries with data on separating commercial from noncommercial activities in *all* sectors, only very few (4 percent) are middle-income countries; full separation is more frequent in high-income countries (23 percent). The separation of activities is more frequent in *some* sectors and more prevalent in high-income countries (53 percent) than in middle-income countries (21 percent).[3]

For differential application of policies and regulations, product market regulation (PMR) data for 27 middle-income countries and 39 high-income countries suggest that SOEs commonly receive economic and regulatory advantages, particularly in middle-income countries (figure 3.5). SOEs frequently receive economic advantages, such as access to finance on better terms than private operators. In Belarus, SOEs receive preferential tariffs for electricity and other public utility services. In Ukraine, direct subsidies to SOEs represented about 1.3 percent of gross domestic product in 2015, with direct subsidies to the coal and energy sector alone accounting for about 1 percent of gross domestic product (Pop et al. 2019). Public national air carriers benefit from preferential treatment for fuel prices in Kuwait and time slots in the Arab Republic of Egypt (Arezki et al. 2019, 55).

FIGURE 3.4 Requirements for Separating Commercial and Noncommercial Activities, by Country Income Level

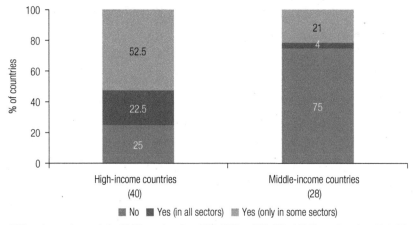

Sources: OECD product market regulation (PMR) questionnaires, 2018; OECD and World Bank PMR questionnaires, 2013–22; and data collected by the World Bank on selected PMR questions for eight Middle East and North Africa countries.

Note: High-income countries are Australia, Austria, Belgium, Canada, Chile, Croatia, Cyprus, Czechia, Denmark, Estonia, Finland, France, Germany, Greece, Hungary, Iceland, Ireland, Israel, Italy, Japan, the Republic of Korea, Kuwait, Latvia, Lithuania, Luxembourg, Malta, the Netherlands, New Zealand, Norway, Poland, Portugal, Romania, Saudi Arabia, the Slovak Republic, Slovenia, Spain, Sweden, Switzerland, the United Arab Emirates, and the United Kingdom. Middle-income countries include both upper-middle-income and lower-middle-income countries. Upper-middle-income countries are Albania, Argentina, Belarus, Brazil, Bulgaria, China, Colombia, Costa Rica, Ecuador, Jordan, Kazakhstan, Kosovo, Malaysia, Mexico, Moldova, Montenegro, North Macedonia, Peru, the Russian Federation, Serbia, South Africa, and Türkiye. Lower-middle-income countries are Côte d'Ivoire, the Arab Republic of Egypt, Indonesia, Morocco, Tunisia, and Viet Nam. OECD = Organisation for Economic Co-operation and Development.

FIGURE 3.5 **Advantages Available to SOEs over Private Firms, by Country Income Level**

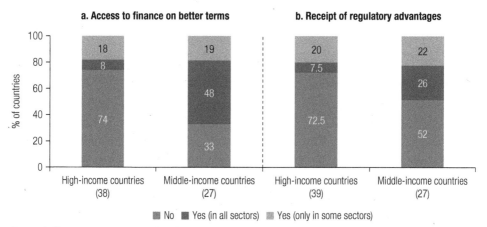

a. Access to finance on better terms
b. Receipt of regulatory advantages

■ No ■ Yes (in all sectors) ▨ Yes (only in some sectors)

Sources: OECD product market regulation (PMR) questionnaires, 2018; OECD and World Bank PMR questionnaires, 2013–22; and data collected by the World Bank on selected PMR questions for eight Middle East and North Africa countries.

Note: High-income countries are Australia, Austria, Belgium, Canada, Chile, Croatia, Cyprus, Czechia, Denmark, Estonia, Finland, France, Germany, Greece, Hungary, Iceland, Ireland, Israel, Italy, Japan, the Republic of Korea, Kuwait, Latvia, Lithuania, Luxembourg, Malta, the Netherlands, New Zealand, Norway, Poland, Portugal, Romania, Saudi Arabia, the Slovak Republic, Slovenia, Spain, Switzerland, the United Arab Emirates, and the United Kingdom. Middle-income countries include both upper-middle-income and lower-middle-income countries. Upper-middle-income countries are Albania, Argentina, Belarus, Brazil, Bulgaria, China, Colombia, Costa Rica, Ecuador, Jordan, Kazakhstan, Kosovo, Malaysia, Mexico, Moldova, Montenegro, North Macedonia, Peru, the Russian Federation, Serbia, South Africa, and Türkiye. Lower-middle-income countries are Côte d'Ivoire, the Arab Republic of Egypt, Indonesia, Morocco, Tunisia, and Viet Nam. Panel a does not include Kuwait or Tunisia. Panel b does not include Albania. OECD = Organisation for Economic Co-operation and Development; SOEs = state-owned enterprises.

Regulatory advantages for SOEs are less common than economic advantages, but they still prevail in many middle-income countries, frequently exempting SOEs from all or some laws and regulations that apply to private firms. Examples include exemptions from economywide commercial and corporate laws in Tunisia, bankruptcy laws in Kuwait, and electricity regulation in Morocco. Egypt, Kuwait, and Tunisia also exempt or exclude SOEs from the competition law. For instance, the competition regulatory frameworks include exemptions granted to certain categories of SOEs, such as utilities. In most countries, SOEs are not incorporated as limited liability companies.

In addition, corporate laws themselves might provide advantages to SOEs or open the door to conflicts of interest, even if unintended. SOEs might be ruled under a separate corporate framework or under the general commercial framework, especially for private firms with a minority state shareholding. Questions remain about the application of bankruptcy law due to the priority of public credits, the nonseizure of certain public assets, and the difficulties of executing decisions against the state. And conflicts of interest for the administrator or even the board might pertain to formal or informal instructions from the state or to their limited responsibility in decision-making.

Channel 2: Implicit Advantages to BOSs

Implicit advantages for BOSs include policies or regulations that restrict entry and reinforce dominance, such as trade and foreign direct investment restrictions, quotas, or outright limits to entry. They also include regulations that dampen rivalry in the market (such as price controls) and policies that raise the risk that BOSs or the regulator will restrict competition, particularly when the market is partially contestable.

Systematic evidence on the presence of implicit advantages for BOSs is scarce. But PMR qualitative data for 24 middle-income and 37 high-income countries suggest that, in middle-income countries, entry is more often restricted through laws and regulations in network industries, where SOEs are fairly common. Middle-income countries, much more often than high-income countries, limit the number of operators in various network industries where competition is viable, including by creating local or national monopolies.

Moreover, ownership rights and regulations are not always separated, increasing the likelihood of an uneven playing field. PMR data for 24 middle-income and 34 high-income countries show that the body that regulates a sector with SOEs is, in almost 40 percent of middle-income countries, not separated from the one that exercises ownership rights in the SOEs. In Egypt, for example, the National Telecommunications Regulatory Authority falls under the authority of the Ministry of Communications and Information Technologies, which also owns 80 percent of the public telecommunications operator. In some cases, the SOE regulates itself. In South Africa, Transnet acts as both the port regulator and the owner-operator of all major commercial ports.

Channel 3: Policy and Regulatory Distortions Favoring BOSs

Some policies and regulations are typically required in natural monopoly sectors to prevent the undue exercise of market power and ensure that the monopoly has incentives to invest. When these regulations are missing or poorly implemented, this situation is likely to lead to high prices, lower access to goods or services, or underinvestment. Although these policies and regulations would be required regardless of firm ownership, key regulatory safeguards may be enacted less frequently or implemented less sufficiently when the natural monopoly is an SOE, partly because of conflicts of interest and soft budget constraints.[4]

The lack of structural separation paired with weak implementation of third-party access regulation can insulate SOE incumbents from competition. Separating natural monopolies from partially contestable markets would allow for competition and restrain the natural monopoly from leveraging its market power in adjacent markets. But, in the electricity and gas sectors, many countries do not have vertical separation between transmission and generation or supply. This is more prevalent in middle-income countries than in high-income ones.

Advantages to BOSs in Competitive Sectors

Combining data on BOS presence with sector information on government policy makes it possible to assess systematically whether governments tilt policies in favor of BOSs. Governments generally intervene indirectly in markets by regulating economic activity. When governments own enterprises or engage in public procurement, they intervene directly in the market, by selling or buying goods or services. Given this dual role, governments may have incentives to tilt policies in favor of the firms they own.

Trade-Related Barriers to Competition

The increased prominence of BOSs in global markets has drawn attention to the potential protection of BOSs through policies and import restrictions that advantage BOSs in exporting activities. Governments may protect BOSs through tariffs, import quotas, and other nontariff barriers.

Some countries have higher ad valorem equivalent tariffs or nontariff measures in sectors with BOSs than in sectors without a BOS presence (maps 3.1 and 3.2). Across all sectors, more than half of the sample countries have higher tariffs in BOS sectors than in private sectors. In Kenya, Namibia, the Seychelles, Tanzania, and Türkiye, sectors with a BOS presence have more than 5 percent higher tariffs, a significant difference. In Ecuador, Paraguay, the Philippines, Tunisia, and Türkiye, sectors with a BOS presence have higher ad valorem equivalent nontariff measures.

MAP 3.1 Tariffs in Sectors with and without BOSs

IBRD 47467 | AUGUST 2023

Sources: Data from the United Nations Conference on Trade and Development Trade Analysis Information Systems (TRAINS) data set and the World Bank Global Businesses of the State (BOS) database. TRAINS data are for 2012–20; BOS data are for 2022.
Note: BOSs = businesses of the state.

MAP 3.2 Ad Valorem Equivalent of Nontariff Barriers in Sectors with and without BOSs

IBRD 47468 | AUGUST 2023

Sources: Data from Kee and Nicita 2022; World Bank Global Businesses of the State (BOS) database. Data cover from the early 1980s until August 2022.
Note: BOSs = businesses of the state.

Some sectors with BOSs have more trade restrictions. The Organisation for Economic Co-operation and Development (OECD) Services Trade Restrictiveness Index (STRI)[5] for telecommunications shows that state ownership in telecommunications is not linked to more service trade restrictions.[6] However, in air transportation, service trade restrictions are higher in countries with a state-owned carrier. Further, in countries with a state-owned carrier that has been privatized, the year of its privatization is correlated with trade restrictiveness: the more recent the privatization, the more restrictive the current policies.

There is also evidence that advantages are conferred to BOSs in export markets.[7] Some trade remedy cases brought against BOSs in the World Bank Trade Remedies Data Portal show that government preferential treatment directly or indirectly supports exports. These policy measures, often referred to as trade remedy actions, are implemented by government authorities against imports likely to have an adverse effect on national production, either through dumping or subsidies.

Domestic Competition Barriers

World Bank Global Businesses of the State (BOS) and Anticompetitive Laws and Policies (ALP) data show that regulatory restrictions on competition are linked to the presence of BOSs in competitive markets. The ALP data collected for this report cover major barriers to competition that relate to regulations restricting entry, reinforcing dominance, facilitating collusion, or protecting vested interests.[8] Overall, regulatory barriers to competition are present in 75 percent of the country-sector pairs in the ALP data. Restrictions are slightly more frequent in sectors with BOSs, with 78 percent of them in BOS sectors. But the presence of BOSs in a sector does not automatically imply regulatory barriers to competition. In 25 percent of the sectors with BOSs, market regulations do not appear to restrict competition in major ways. The findings underline the importance of regulatory reforms to accompany ownership reforms. The findings also suggest that regulatory reforms may be more difficult in BOS sectors, potentially because of strong vested interests and direct links between state enterprises and regulators.

The ALP data demonstrate that BOSs and SOEs benefit from both explicit and implicit advantages in competitive sectors (box 3.2). For example, SOEs are granted exclusive rights, are involved in regulating the sector, or are exempt from economywide laws—all explicit advantages that are not available to private competitors. Implicit advantages that apply to BOSs and private competitors alike are even more prevalent. These advantages affect entry or regulate the conduct of all market players in competitive sectors, including BOSs. In a few cases, explicit and implicit advantages are combined, giving certain SOEs full control over the market.

BOX 3.2

Advantages Identified by Anticompetitive Laws and Policies Data

Explicit advantages

- *Exclusive rights.* Vietnamese law requires the signing of production-sharing contracts for oil and gas exploration and extraction with a state-owned enterprise (SOE) that is also engaged in downstream sectors. Although the participation of SOEs in oil and gas sectors is sometimes required upstream, risks are often borne disproportionately by private investors, giving SOEs involved in downstream sectors an explicit advantage over competitors. In electricity distribution, the provision of services is also reserved for SOEs in some countries.[a]
- *SOE involvement in regulation.* In Ethiopia, an SOE is involved in price regulation and market allocation, while being the sole importer of fertilizer in the country. In Viet Nam, an SOE is one of several market participants in the oil and gas and cement sectors, but it is authorized by law to supervise its competitors. In Angola (cement) and Serbia (intercity buses), SOEs are authorized by law to participate in sector regulation together with private competitors.[b] In these cases, the public authority exercising ownership rights is also the regulator, giving it an outsized influence over policy.[c]
- *Exemptions.* In several countries, SOEs are exempt from economywide laws. In Tunisia, SOEs operating in monopoly sectors are exempt from the competition law. The exemption also covers sectors in which competition is viable, such as the supply of electricity. In Angola, public procurement rules are waived for contracts with SOEs. And, in Pakistan, direct government-to-SOE contracting is permitted. There are also SOE-specific exemptions from bankruptcy laws in several countries, such as Serbia.

(Box continues on the following page.)

Advantages in Network Sectors

Network industries are different from competitive sectors in that firms are inherently more likely to outgrow their rivals. Incumbents in network sectors have strategic advantages over their competitors because of characteristics specific to these industries. Economies of scale, technological bottlenecks, network effects, and scarcities cause firms to be larger and more dominant. Such firms also have incentives to exploit their advantages in adjacent markets and thus become multisectoral.

States can apply a range of policies to contain the market power of network operators and have intervened in network sectors primarily as owners. Policies in network sectors range from participation in markets through BOSs or public procurement to intervention as regulators or referees. In natural monopoly sectors, for instance, firm ownership allows the government to set prices below the monopoly level, thus increasing output and market efficiency. The state can also leave the operation of infrastructure to the private sector and regulate the prices that dominant operators charge. And the state can intervene to unbundle natural monopoly activities from competitive activities, thus opening some market segments to competition.

State ownership and restrictive regulations are correlated in middle-income countries. Whether state ownership, specifically SOE presence, is associated with (the lack of) pro-competition regulation in network sectors can be studied with two measures in the PMR indicators. The first is an index of government involvement in network sectors, which includes information about state ownership, divestment procedures, and special voting rights. The second is an index of the degree to which market regulations inhibit or promote competition. Overall, the link between direct and indirect state intervention in markets is stronger in middle-income countries than in high-income countries (figure 3.6). This difference is strongest in telecommunications, where nearly

FIGURE 3.6 **State Involvement and Restrictive Regulations, by Country Income Level, 2018**

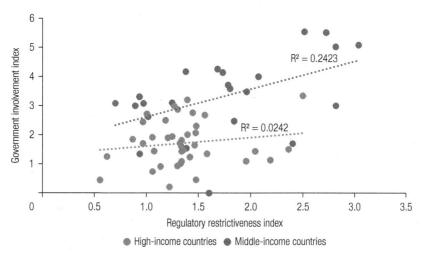

$R^2 = 0.2423$

$R^2 = 0.0242$

● High-income countries ● Middle-income countries

Sources: OECD product market regulation (PMR) questionnaires, 2018; OECD and World Bank PMR questionnaires, 2013–22; and data collected by the World Bank on selected PMR questions for eight Middle East and North Africa countries.

Note: The data cover energy, communications, and transportation in 39 high-income economies and 23 middle-income economies. The maximum value for the regulatory restrictiveness index is 6. The scores on regulatory restrictiveness do not contain information about state ownership. The value for the United States was calculated as an average of the values for the states of New York and Texas. OECD = Organisation for Economic Co-operation and Development.

all middle-income countries cluster around weak state involvement and strong pro-competition regulation or around strong state involvement and weak pro-competition regulation. State involvement and market regulations are also correlated in the energy and transportation sectors, but the differences between high-income and middle-income countries are smaller in these sectors.

Disciplining Anticompetitive Behavior

Authorities have been applying competition laws to BOSs; however, when it comes to SOEs, competition enforcement often focuses on strategic sectors in which governments have an interest in protecting efficient market outcomes. Case studies can help explain how SOEs are treated when they

- Conduct exclusionary behavior that prevents new entry, forces existing rivals from the market, or otherwise diminishes competition through the abuse of a firm's dominant position in the market;
- Engage in anticompetitive agreements with rival or vertically linked firms through collusion or vertical restrains; or
- Attempt to implement mergers or acquisitions that may significantly hinder competition in the market.

To this end, the World Bank collected 224 decisions on each of these categories involving at least one SOE.[9] The majority of cases are about abuses of dominance, and two-thirds of the decisions collected pertain to only four sectors: energy, telecommunications, transportation, and natural resources (figure 3.7). In other words, they cover practices in sectors in which the state would have a special interest in maintaining competitive pressures that foster efficiency and protect consumer welfare because they are key inputs for other markets. Firms typically acquire important inputs—transportation, energy, telecommunications, and financial services—in local markets. Thus, weak competition in upstream markets may cause domestic firms to be less competitive than their foreign rivals.

The case studies confirm that authorities have enforced competition to discipline the behavior of SOEs for collusion, abuses of dominance, and potential negative market effects of mergers and acquisitions or privatizations. They also uncover enforcement and political economy challenges related to the nature of SOEs—including exemptions from competition law, interference from public authorities, and difficulties in collecting fines.

Abuses of Dominance

Abuse of dominance cases involving SOEs often aim at disciplining attempts by vertically integrated public incumbents to limit entry into market segments in which competition is possible. Given the position of SOEs as a monopoly or an incumbent

FIGURE 3.7 **Anticompetitive Conduct, by Type of Conduct, Sector, and Country Income Level**

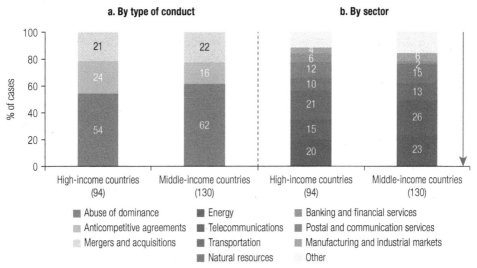

Source: Based on 224 case studies collected from the early 1980s until August 2022 on competition and SOEs.
Note: Numbers in parenthese are number of case studies conducted. In panel b, "Other" includes health, waste management, and lottery and gaming sectors. SOEs = state owned enterprises.

with political support and access to resources, abuse of dominance is the main area of enforcement for SOEs (Moroccan Competition Council 2014). For instance, of 21 abuses of dominance referred to the Competition Tribunal between 1999 and 2016 in South Africa, 13 involved former or current SOEs, with 10 initiated ex officio by the Competition Commission (Healey 2018, 6; Roberts 2017). Denying access to essential facilities and limiting interconnection are common practices across countries and sectors. Such practices include denying access to the wholesale market for broadband internet in France[10] and South Africa,[11] refusing access to the national network of gas pipelines in Italy (AGCM 1999),[12] and limiting access by the railway company to underground or aerial pipelines to crossing railways in Chile.[13] Moreover, price-based abuses, which amount to only about a third of the cases in middle-income countries, focus mostly on abusive or discriminatory pricing and less on predatory pricing and margin squeezes. These practices are often facilitated by regulation, thus confirming the risks of conflicts of interest when it comes to the relationships between SOEs and the authorities.

Anticompetitive Agreements

A comparison of cartels involving SOEs with those involving only private operators shows that, on average, the former are more stable and require longer investigations for competition authorities to issue a decision. Of the almost 939 cartel cases in the World

Crowding Private Firms In—or Out?

61

Bank Anti-Cartel Enforcement database at the global level in the past five years, only 18 involved SOEs.[14] This result is consistent with the case studies analyzed in this chapter, which confirm that SOEs seldom participate in cartels—or that fewer cartels involving SOEs have been investigated than those involving private operators only. Why might this be? SOEs need not obtain market power through a cartel because they often have prominent market positions. And public operators might be reluctant to violate the law, which could explain why a third of the cartel cases involve leniency applications.[15] But nine of these cartels involved bid rigging when SOEs participated in public tenders (building roads or pipelines for gas transmission or providing steel), thus directly hitting the public budget.

Mergers and Acquisitions That May Significantly Hinder Competition in the Market

Exemptions for merger control for SOEs, together with potential interference of public authorities in decision-making, can limit the benefits of market consolidation. PMR data confirm that, in most countries—high-income and middle-income countries alike (85 percent in a sample of 39 high-income countries and 27 middle-income countries)—mergers, equity issues, and restructuring plans of SOEs are cleared by national or subnational governments. The application of public interest clauses may also distort the level playing field in merger control if they prohibit mergers that harm the economic activity of the state-owned domestic players (OECD 2016). In addition, authorities can interfere in decisions, leaving technical considerations on the side. For example, in Colombia in 2001, the president overruled the decision by the Competition Commission blocking the merger between the then-public national airline and a smaller company (Healey 2018).

International experience confirms several outstanding challenges when applying antitrust and merger control to SOEs. Five challenges need to be addressed to leverage competition regulatory and institutional frameworks to level the playing field:

1. Potential conflicts of interest with regulators
2. Difficulties distinguishing BOS decisions in relation to instructions from public authorities and actions based on regulation
3. Difficulties disciplining the anticompetitive behavior of foreign BOSs
4. Need for adapting antitrust tests and analytics to SOEs, given public mandates
5. Prominent use of remedies rather than fines, because half of the antitrust cases against SOEs established violations but did not include fines, especially in middle-income countries, or the fines were low

Complementary mandates to traditional antitrust tools—such as the ability of authorities to advocate for pro-competition principles (that is, competition advocacy)—can help to shape BOSs' behavior. Advocacy can address BOS conduct outside the scope of competition law or when enforcement has been proven unsuccessful or unlikely. Advocacy can also help to identify markets in which the presence of BOSs might be distortive and to design pro-competition processes to phase out BOS presence or bring in private sector participation, through privatization or public-private partnerships.

The International Competition Network—World Bank Competition Advocacy Contest data set confirms the existence of advocacy contest measures targeting SOEs, but they remain limited in number.[16] Of 265 cases gathered from 62 jurisdictions by 2022, only 31 cases focused on competitive neutrality, and only 10 focused specifically on SOEs. Examples of advocacy targeting SOEs, beyond the contest itself, include monitoring recently liberalized markets and complementing enforcement. In Moldova, the electricity market was monitored continuously after privatization of the distribution system operator, and competition authorities eventually recommended unbundling the vertically integrated incumbent to increase competition in partially contestable markets.[17] In China, the competition authorities created a fair competition review mechanism to identify restrictions on competition in regulation that could potentially affect many markets with an SOE presence.

Systematic mechanisms to analyze whether BOSs in commercial markets fulfill a subsidiary role to that of the private sector can focus BOS participation in markets where they are needed. According to the subsidiary principle, if private agents are interested and capable of supplying enough goods and services to meet demand, direct participation of the state might not be needed. Instead, the state may intervene in those markets only by supervising and controlling the behavior of private agents. Although few countries have an explicit mandate to perform this assessment, adopting the subsidiarity principle offers complementarities with competition law.

Notes

1. This chapter differentiates between businesses of the state (BOSs) and state-owned enterprises (SOEs), in line with definitions detailed in box 1.1 of chapter 1. The term BOSs is used conceptually to discuss the participation of the state in markets as an important stakeholder, including firms with minority state ownership starting at 10 percent, as well as participation in firms that are directly as well as indirectly owned by the state through another company. The term SOE is used when referring to existing literature and empirical work that use the term and when referring to country-specific SOE policies and reform agendas that are aligned to a country's own definition. These definitions are often limited to firms owned by the central government, with direct state ownership of 50 percent or more.

2. Such rules should ideally be complemented by a requirement to show a positive rate of return. However, previous competitive neutrality assessments by the World Bank suggest that such a requirement is rare in lower-income countries. And, even when some requirements exist, they are often not laid out in regulations. In Morocco, for example, some contract programs negotiated on a case-by-case basis require a positive net present value (NPV), and a positive NPV is required for a BOS when creating a new subsidiary. But BOSs are not systematically required to achieve a commercial rate of return. In Sri Lanka, the state directs BOSs to make a positive NPV in their investments, but this requirement is not set out in the regulations.

3. Requirements for separation are more common in European countries, although some countries such as Albania, Moldova, North Macedonia, and Norway have no such requirement. In Latin America and the Caribbean, only Mexican BOSs in select sectors are required to separate

commercial from noncommercial activities; in the Middle East and North Africa, many BOSs deliver both commercial and noncommercial services, but no country requires separation between these services. In East Asia and Pacific, China, Indonesia, Japan, the Republic of Korea, and Malaysia have no requirements in any sector.

4. Maskin (1996) provides a detailed explanation of soft budget constraints.

5. The OECD STRI reports on services trade restrictions in 19 major services sectors in 50 countries (38 OECD and 12 non-OECD). The index covers restrictions on foreign entry, movement of people, other discriminatory measures, barriers to competition, and regulatory transparency. The OECD STRI is matched with state ownership data from the OECD PMR and the International Civil Aviation Organization.

6. However, the most restrictive countries have state ownership in the telecommunications sector, suggesting that, although state ownership is not a sufficient condition for protections in the sector, it may be a necessary condition. Indonesia, Kazakhstan, and the Russian Federation have the highest level of restriction in the telecommunications sector, and all have state ownership in the sector.

7. The World Bank Trade Remedy data set covers countervailing and antidumping cases in more than 30 countries. The data set reports on cases from the 1980s through 2019 and includes all investigation actions initiated or measures implemented by countries, including a significant amount of information on the initiating cases (and the timing of their progression), the product or product group involved, the national petitioners and foreign entities targeted, and the resulting measures applied. The time series in the database account for measures that may have been suspended over time.

8. The ALP data cover 10 countries: Angola, Argentina, Ethiopia, Nepal, Pakistan, Peru, the Philippines, Serbia, Türkiye, and Viet Nam. In each of the countries, data have been collected for 14 competitive sectors at the Statistical Classification of Economic Activities in the European Community (NACE) four-digit level based on a review of publicly available primary and secondary regulations. The data have been aggregated into seven sector groups: upstream oil and gas, downstream oil and gas, electricity, cement, fertilizer, air transportation, and road transportation. The data cover laws on the books (de jure) but not their implementation (de facto).

9. The World Bank data set of case studies on competition and SOEs includes 224 decisions of competition authorities in which an SOE was involved in both anticompetitive conduct and economic concentration from the early 1980s until August 2022.

10. Decision 05-D-59, dated November 7, 2005.

11. Case 11/CR/Feb04. In South Africa in 2002, the Competition Commission received a complaint against Telkom from the South African Vans Association and 20 other internet service providers alleging that Telkom was abusing its dominance to exclude (existing and potential) competitors in the downstream market for internet services. The commission and later the Supreme Court of Appeal found that Telkom had abused its dominance by refusing to grant competitors access to an essential facility (in contravention of section 8(b) of the Act) and that it had induced customers not to deal with competitors (contravening 8(d)(i) of the Act).

12. The Italian Competition Authority also found that the method of calculating the charge used allowed the BOS firm to fix the price independently of effective demand for the transport of third parties' gas and was likely to lead to the imposition of unjustifiably burdensome contractual conditions.

13. Ruling No. 76/2008, dated October 14, 2008.

14. The World Bank Anti-Cartel Enforcement Database covers all decisions from competition agencies related to hard-core cartels around 75 jurisdictions worldwide. The database covers the universe of cartels investigated and closed with an official decision by the competition agencies in first instance for both privately owned and state-owned enterprises. In total, 939 cases were mapped between 2017 and 2022 (March) and closed by the competition agencies, including

18 investigations involving SOEs. Out of these cases, 6 involved leniency applications. In 90 percent of the cases, SOEs were sanctioned with fines, which amounted to US$566 million.

15. Leniency programs allow the first cartel member approaching the competition authority with information on a cartel to be exempted from the fine. A well-functioning leniency program can destabilize and deter cartels by creating a permanent threat that any of its members may come forward to the authority in order to avoid the fine. The programs that have proven to be the most successful give complete amnesty to the first cartel member to come forward and reveal the inner workings of the cartel to competition law enforcers. Thus, most competition agencies around the world, including in Brazil, Canada, Chile, China, Colombia, the European Union, India, Korea, Mexico, Türkiye, and the United States, have the ability either to offer total immunity or to reduce significantly the fines for violators that cooperate in their investigations. Miller (2009) finds that the leniency program in the United States reduced the rate of cartel formation by 59 percent and increased the rate of cartel detection by 62 percent.

16. The International Competition Network—World Bank Competition Advocacy Contest database consists of submissions of successful advocacy initiatives from competition authorities, regulators, and public bodies to the International Competition Network—World Bank Group Competition Advocacy Contest from 2014 onward.

17. In addition, the Competition Commission recommended expediting the process of revising the tariff customer agreement and setting obligations for the public retail supplier in order to protect consumers through observance of service quality indicators (supply vs. interruption of electricity, accurate billing).

References

AGCM (Italian Competition Authority). 1999. "Provvedimento n 6926 (A221) SNAM-Tarriffe DI Vettoriamento." *Official Bullettin* 8/1999, February 25, 1999.

Arezki, R, A. Barone, K. Decker, D. Detter, R. Yuting Fan, H. Nguyen, and G. Murciego. 2019. *Reaching New Heights: Promoting Fair Competition in the Middle East and North Africa*. Middle East and North Africa Economic Update, October 2019. Washington, DC: World Bank. https://elibrary.worldbank.org/action/showCitFormats?doi=10.1596%2F978-1-4648-1504-1&mobileUi=0.

Baig, T., A. Mati, D. Coady, and J. Ntamatungiro. 2007. "Domestic Petroleum Product Prices and Subsidies; Recent Developments and Reform Strategies." Working Paper 07/71, International Monetary Fund, Washington DC.

Gillingham, R., and M. Keen. 2012. "Mitigation and Fuel Pricing in Developing Economies." In *Fiscal Policy to Mitigate Climate Change. A Guide for Policymakers*, edited by I. W. H. Parry, R. de Mooij, and M. Keen, ch. 6, 103–32. Washington, DC: International Monetary Fund.

Healey, D. 2018. "Competition Law and State-Owned Enterprises: Enforcement." DAF/COMP/GF (2018)11. Paper prepared in support of a presentation for Session V at the 17th Global Forum on Competition, OECD, Paris, November 29–30, 2018.

IFC (International Finance Corporation). 2017. "Creating Markets in Kazakhstan." IFC, Washington, DC. https://www.ifc.org/en/insights-reports/2017/creating-markets-in-kazakhstan.

IFC (International Finance Corporation). 2019. "Creating Markets in Indonesia: Unlocking the Dynamism of the Indonesian Private Sector." Country Private Sector Diagnostic. IFC, Washington, DC. https://www.ifc.org/content/dam/ifc/doc/mgrt/201910-cpsd-indonesia-v2.pdf.

IFC (International Finance Corporation). 2021a. "Creating Markets in Mozambique: A Study Conducted in Partnership with SIDA." Country Private Sector Diagnostic, IFC, Washington, DC. https://www.ifc.org/en/insights-reports/2021/cpsd-mozambique.

IFC (International Finance Corporation). 2021b. "The Plurinational State of Bolivia: Unlocking Private Sector Potential to Achieve a Sustainable and Inclusive Recovery." IFC, Washington, DC. https://www.ifc.org/en/insights-reports/2021/cpsd-bolivia.

IFC (International Finance Corporation). 2022. "Creating Markets in Jamaica: Country Private Sector Diagnostic." IFC, Washington, DC. https://www.ifc.org/en/insights-reports/2022/cpsd-jamaica.

IFC (International Finance Corporation). 2023. "Creating Markets in Moldova: From a Remittances-Driven Economy to Private Sector–Led Sustainable Growth." Country Private Sector Diagnostic, IFC, Washington, DC. https://www.ifc.org/en/insights-reports/2023/cpsd-moldova.

Kee, H. L., and A. Nicita. 2022. "Trade Fraud and Non-Tariff Measures." *Journal of International Economics* 139 (November): Art. 103637.

Kitzmuller, M., and M. M. Licetti. 2013. "Competition Policy: Encouraging Thriving Markets for Development." ViewPoint Public Policy for the Private Sector Series, No. 331, Finance and Private Sector Development Vice Presidency, World Bank, Washington, DC.

Kpodar, K. R., and P. A. Imam. 2020. "To Pass (or Not to Pass) Through International Fuel Price Changes to Domestic Fuel Prices in Developing Countries: What Are the Drivers?" Working Paper 2020/194, International Monetary Fund, Washington, DC.

Maskin, E. 1996. "Theories of the Soft Budget Constraint." *Japan and the World Economy* 8 (2): 125–33.

Miller, N. H. 2009. "Strategic Leniency and Cartel Enforcement." *American Economic Review* 99 (3): 750–68. https://doi.org/10.1257/aer.99.3.750.

Moroccan Competition Council. 2014. "Special Project: State-Owned Enterprises and Competition." Paper prepared for the International Competition Network Annual Conference, Marrakech, April 23–25, 2014. https://centrocedec.files.wordpress.com/2015/07/soe-and-competition2014.pdf.

OECD (Organisation for Economic Co-operation and Development). 2000. "IV. Regulatory Reform in Network Industries: Past Experience and Current Issues." *OECD Economic Outlook* 67 (1): 151–71.

OECD (Organisation for Economic Co-operation and Development). 2016. "Public Interest Considerations in Merger Control." Background paper prepared by the OECD Secretariat, Paris. DAF/COMP/WP3(2016)3.

Pop, G., M. Licetti, S. F. Gramegna Mesa, and S. Dauda. 2019. "Reducing Market Distortions for a More Prosperous Ukraine: Proposals for Market Regulation, Competition Policy, and Institutional Reform." World Bank, Washington, DC. https://documents1.worldbank.org/curated/en/368301553112891891/pdf/135463-WP-P169603-PUBLIC.pdf.

Roberts, S. 2017. "Assessing the Record on Competition Enforcement against Anti-Competitive Practices and Implications for Inclusive Growth." Working paper, University of Johannesburg. https://doi.org/10.13140/RG.2.2.26699.59686.

Vitale, C., C. Moiso, and I. Wanner. "A Detailed Explanation of the Methodology Used to Build the OECD PMR Indicators." Organisation for Economic Co-operation and Development, Paris.

World Bank. Forthcoming. *Markets and Competition Policy Assessment Toolkit.* Washington, DC: World Bank.

4. Fiscal Impact of Businesses of the State and Principles of State Support

Introduction

The fiscal implications of state ownership are significant. Businesses of the state (BOSs) are often tasked with providing services that generate important benefits (chapter 1). The fiscal costs of BOSs include regular fiscal injections from the budget, in theory to compensate BOSs for their social role. Fiscal risks from BOSs include explicit contingent liabilities—largely debt guarantees—and implicit contingent liabilities, such as when fiscal injections are needed to recapitalize state-owned banks.[1] Liabilities generated by BOSs are a major concern for the overall debt exposure of governments (World Bank 2022a, 2022b).

Even before the recent COVID-19 crisis, many low- and middle-income countries had accumulated debt burdens, pushing them into high risk of debt distress and leading to underinvestment and slow growth. During the financial crisis of 2008, governments channeled resources into the financial sector and other hard-hit sectors to avoid an even worse economic downturn. The COVID-19 pandemic further expanded state support[2] for specific sectors and firms, including BOSs, adding to the financial stress of governments (Freund and Pesme 2021).

Today, countries find themselves with limited fiscal space and greater macroeconomic vulnerability, in part due to state support provided during the pandemic. This chapter examines the fiscal impact of BOSs and illustrates the extent of state support to BOSs as part of the fiscal response to the recent COVID-19 crisis. It provides new evidence on state support and distills policy principles for the design of state support.

- BOSs can pose large fiscal costs and risks. BOSs in many countries have a significant share in public sector balance sheets, reflecting their important role in the economy and in development.[3] Despite the significant fiscal risks posed by BOSs, measuring the scope, performance, and associated risks of BOS portfolios across countries is difficult, given the dearth of publicly available data and the heterogeneity of ownership structures and state support measures.

- Examples of the fiscal impact of state support to BOSs and private firms during past crises show that such support comes with benefits but is also associated with costs and risks. When comparing the benefits of state support to BOSs and private firms, BOSs are more likely to maintain their employment during crises than private firms. The evidence is mixed about whether BOSs maintain investment better than private firms during crises. And there is little evidence that BOSs support growth, although the institutional environment affects whether BOSs have positive or negative impacts on growth. But state support to BOSs and private firms is costly and can exacerbate fiscal pressures; it can also hamper long-term growth by distorting competition, undermining corporate governance, and leading to collusion, corruption, and moral hazard.
- State support to BOSs and private firms needs to be designed and implemented in a way that minimizes costs and mitigates downside risks and potentially distortive impacts. Key policy principles of such state support include having clear objectives and prioritizing support, selecting the least distortive instruments, improving targeting and transparency, and including explicit sunset clauses and exit strategies.

Fiscal Risks Stemming from BOSs

Estimating Fiscal Costs and Risks

In countries where state-owned enterprises (SOEs) represent a large share of economic activity, they can pose risks to public finances (IMF 2021b). The important role of SOEs in those economies is reflected in their substantial portion of public sector balance sheets. SOEs account for the lion's share (66 percent) of publicly financed infrastructure projects in low- and middle-income countries, making up 83 percent of the total financing for infrastructure projects (World Bank 2017).[4] The net liabilities of financial and nonfinancial public sector corporations in public sector balance sheets are equivalent to an estimated 12 percent of GDP in El Salvador, 21 percent in Indonesia, and 33 percent in Kazakhstan (IMF 2020a). For 14 countries in Sub-Saharan Africa, SOE revenues average 7 percent of GDP, SOE assets average about 34 percent of public sector assets, and SOE liabilities average about 20 percent of GDP (figures 4.1 and 4.2) (Harris et al. 2020).

When risks materialize, they often have major and lasting implications for fiscal deficits and debt as well as for the conduct of fiscal policy, and they can lead to economic and financial crises.[5] Of 230 contingent liability episodes during 1990–2014 across 80 low-, middle-, and high-income economies, SOEs were the third most common source of contingent liability—with 32 episodes—that governments were called on to cover (Bova et al. 2016). The fiscal cost was equivalent to 3 percent of

FIGURE 4.1 **SOE Liabilities in Sub-Saharan African Countries and Other Regions**

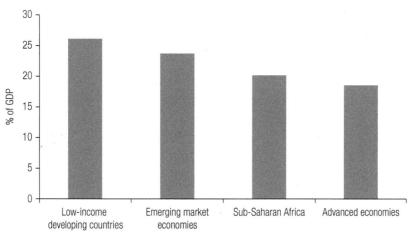

Source: Harris et al. 2020, 2.
Note: Debt comprises loans and debt securities, while other liabilities comprise primarily other accounts payable. Data for anonymized countries are from unpublished sources. SOE = state-owned enterprise.

FIGURE 4.2 **SOE Liabilities in Select Countries in Sub-Saharan Africa**

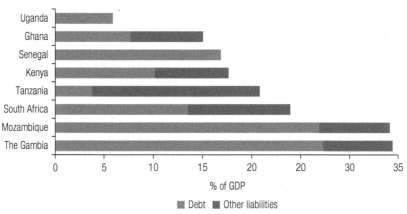

Source: Harris et al. 2020, 2.
Note: Debt comprises loans and debt securities, while other liabilities comprise primarily other accounts payable. Data for anonymized countries are from unpublished sources. SOE = state-owned enterprise.

GDP, on average, reaching as high as 15 percent of GDP in some cases (Bova et al. 2016). For 17 countries in the Middle East and North Africa, including Pakistan (and excluding the Gulf Cooperation Council members), contingent liabilities amounting to 7.7 percent of GDP emanated from explicit or implicit government guarantees to SOEs, the financial sector, pension systems, and obligations under public-private partnerships (figure 4.3 and box 4.1) (Boukezia et al. 2023).

FIGURE 4.3   Budgetary Impact of Contingent Liabilities in Middle East and North African Countries, Cumulative 1990–2018

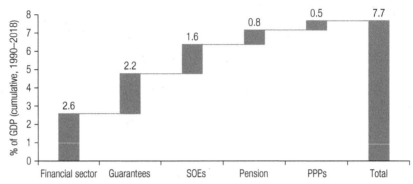

Source: Calculations based on IMF 2020c.

Note: Contingent liability realizations pertaining to SOEs include on-budget support measures and exclude off-budget subsidies. The impact of contingent liability realizations refers to the gross payouts associated with a contingent liability realization, which captures immediate budgetary pressures and excludes any asset recoveries that are associated with the realization. PPPs = public-private partnerships; SOEs = state-owned enterprises.

BOX 4.1

Fiscal Costs and Risks of SOEs in Middle East and North African Countries

Troubled state-owned enterprises (SOEs) can impose fiscal costs from budgetary transfers to compensate loss-making activities, poor dividend performance, nonrepayment of loans, calls on government guarantees, recapitalizations, or asset sales below book value. They frequently receive government support through the tax system, either through formal tax exemptions or through lax tax enforcement. Institutional weaknesses often exacerbate these risks via financial burdens stemming from uncompensated quasi-fiscal activities and poor governance and accountability. In the Middle

FIGURE B4.1.1   Direct Fiscal Support to SOEs as a Percentage of GDP, 2019

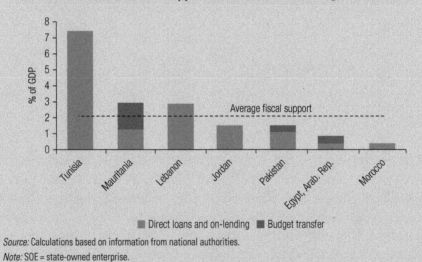

Source: Calculations based on information from national authorities.

Note: SOE = state-owned enterprise.

(Box continues on the following page.)

Fiscal Costs and Risks of SOEs in Middle East and North African Countries
(continued)

FIGURE B4.1.2   **SOE Debt as a Percentage of GDP, 2019**

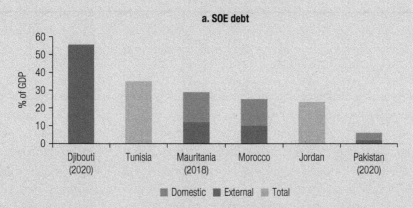

a. SOE debt

Domestic   External   Total

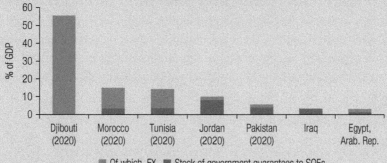

b. Government guarantees to SOEs

Of which, FX   Stock of government guarantees to SOEs

Sources: Calculations based on IMF 2022; World Bank 2021c.
Note: FX = foreign exchange; SOE = state-owned enterprise.

East and North Africa, fiscal costs and risks associated with SOEs are sizable. In 2019 alone, the 17 Middle East and North Africa countries provided, on average, 2.1 percent of gross domestic product in direct budget support to SOEs through transfers, direct loans, and on-lending (figure B4.1.1). In addition, SOEs have received substantial government guaranteed loans, either directly or through state-owned banks (figure B4.1.2), some of which have been called over the years.

SOEs often engage in risky projects on behalf of governments or charge below cost recovery for their services without being fully compensated from the budget. Although these types of activities may improve the fiscal deficit, they often result in SOEs having difficulty meeting their payment obligations to the government, social security funds, other SOEs, or private companies. They also lead to complex cross claims between government and SOEs, hindering transparency and sound fiscal management.

Source: IMF 2021b.

Despite the fiscal risks of BOSs, measuring the scope, performance, and associated risks of BOS portfolios across countries is difficult. Weak institutional capacity, reporting, and oversight mechanisms are key contributors to the scarcity of data. Heterogeneity in ownership and the diversity in sectors where BOSs are present reflect the wide range of government economic and social mandates. In addition, explicit and implicit mandates for BOSs may evolve and become ambiguous over time because of shifts in political and economic dynamics. For example, few countries have a formal state ownership policy that clarifies the state's objectives for its BOS holdings. In the absence of clear objectives, it is difficult to assess their performance, especially with regard to public service delivery and value creation (PwC 2015).

Governance challenges in state ownership can also carry significant risks. For example, central government oversight of BOS borrowing activities is weak in many countries, especially in low-income countries.[6] Because the legal framework is incomplete or is not being implemented, the institutional setup cannot capture liabilities stemming from BOSs, and limited institutional capacity constrains the ability to analyze and publish BOS debt and financial data. Evidence from 13 debt management performance assessments during 2021–22 shows that 11 countries do not have a framework for managing guarantees or on-lending operations, and the 2 countries with provisions have significant compliance gaps (World Bank 2021b). In 9 countries, reporting of borrowing activities to the central government by nonfinancial public sector entities is not enforced. In 10 countries, the requirement to report on nonfinancial public sector debt is not applied; in 12 countries, the legislation is silent on the role of the central government when authorizing nonfinancial public sector bodies to borrow.

Key Transmission Channels of Fiscal Risks

Macrofiscal risks tied to BOSs can emerge from different avenues, both domestic (unfunded mandates, heavy subsidization) and external (shifts in external demand, supply disruptions). They can entail large contingent liabilities and poor oversight, sizable and poorly governed state-owned banks, and negative productivity spillovers (Böwer 2017; Melecky 2021). Cross-BOS ownership structures and connected lending can lead to large payment arrears and systemic risks. Corruption can also pose sizable risks, given the close ties between BOS stakeholders and public officials and the size and scope of BOS services and balance sheets (Transparency International 2017a, 2017b).

Key channels between public finances and BOSs include direct loans (including on-lending), loans across BOSs (for example, from a state-owned development bank to a state-owned utility), loan guarantees, recapitalizations, bailouts, subsidies, transfers, tax waivers, capital spending, dividends, tax receipts, payment arrears, and implicit liabilities (table 4.1). Governments, for example, can impair BOS finances by not fully funding public service obligations or by accumulating payment arrears to BOSs as ways to

TABLE 4.1   Potential Financial Impacts of BOSs' Flows on Public Finances

Type of flow	Potential impact
Receipts	Dividends; guarantee fees; taxes
Outlays	Capital spending; subsidies, transfers; recapitalization, bailouts; tax waivers, arrears
Assets	Capital stock; technology
Liabilities	Loans; guarantees; accumulated losses

Source: Original table for this publication.
Note: BOSs = businesses of the state.

manage fiscal liquidity pressures. Such practices adversely affect BOS and public sector balance sheets and, over time, can erode the delivery of public services. For example, a BOS that has a monopoly can generate substantial revenues for the government, but its overall economic impact can still be negative. If a country's fiscal position is heavily burdened by its BOS sector—say, through large net transfers and backstopping—interest rates for public sector borrowing could rise through a loss of confidence and elevated debt rollover risks. When BOSs are responsible for large capital outlays, they can also have macroeconomic impacts on employment and growth. If BOS policies crowd out the private sector, this crowding out weakens investment, job creation, and economic growth.

Selected country examples provide a sense of the order of magnitude of potential risks and macrofiscal costs:

- Facing a range of issues—such as insolvency, conflicting commercial and socio-economic objectives, and inadequate oversight—SOEs in The Gambia have provided minor revenues in recent years but required significant budget support. At the end of 2020, their total liabilities were estimated at 19 percent of GDP (IMF 2023; World Bank 2021f). Risks from loan guarantees and on-lending have materialized in the past. For example, The Gambia signed a memorandum of understanding in 2018 that converted into capital SOE debt owed to the government (mainly pertaining to on-lent external loans) equal to about 4.5 percent of GDP in 2020 (World Bank 2020b, 2022a).[7]
- In the Kyrgyz Republic, budget subsidies to SOEs roughly equaled their tax and dividend receipts, but energy sector BOSs entailed significant fiscal pressures and risks, given their high debt, large investment needs, and a backlog of reforms. Explicit risks included public investment on-lending equivalent to 16.9 percent of GDP at the end of 2018 (World Bank 2020a, 2021d).
- SOE cross-linkages contributed to Slovenia's 2012–13 crisis, when the banking system dominated by three state-owned banks holding about 63 percent of the total banking sector's equity (IMF 2016b, 2016c), faced widespread bankruptcies that ate up bank capital and resulted in government loss of market access (Böwer 2017).

- For 60 countries, infrastructure SOEs required average annual fiscal injections during 2008–19 of 0.25 percent of GDP to remain afloat, illustrating that government support to SOEs can weaken their fiscal position and increase the risks of sovereign debt distress (World Bank 2023a).

Illustrating the Benefits and Costs of State Support to BOSs

During crises, governments assign unique roles to BOSs and to private firms, usually to stabilize economies. During the global financial crisis and the COVID-19 pandemic, many governments deployed vast fiscal responses that included support for BOSs and private firms to keep people employed and sustain businesses and investment.

Benefits

During a crisis, economies at all income levels use state support to BOSs and private firms alike to mitigate the impacts of the crisis. Governments are under pressure to provide fast relief and short-term stability and to stop the spread of the crisis (Pop and Amador 2020a; Qiang and Pop 2020). Governments resort to BOSs and private firms to provide relief, directing them either to provide emergency goods and services or to function as channels of government support to citizens and firms. They may also use BOSs or private firms to stabilize economies by countercyclically protecting their employment and investment and maintaining the demand for inputs and final goods and services. In addition, they use banks to inject liquidity into the economy. To enable BOSs or private firms to provide relief and function as economic stabilizers, governments often provide them with direct or indirect support.

For past crises, the evidence for whether BOSs support economic stability is mixed. BOSs perform worse in productivity or profitability than firms in the private sector during crises, particularly during the global financial crisis (Beuselinck et al. 2017; Lazzarini and Musachio 2018; Vitoria, Bressan, and Iquiapaza 2020).[8] But they typically are better able than private firms to maintain employment during crises (EBRD 2020; IMF 2019, 2021b; Kopelman and Rosen 2014; Vagliasindi 2022). Still, when BOSs maintain employment during crises, they may crowd out private sector employment during the ensuing recovery. Evidence of the impacts of BOS investment during crises is also mixed (García-Sánchez and Rama 2022; Jaslowitzer, Megginson, and Rapp 2018; Jie et al. 2021; World Bank 2023a).[9] In regard to growth, there is little evidence of whether BOSs support growth, although there is evidence that the institutional environment affects whether BOSs are positive or negative for growth (Coleman and Feler 2014; EBRD 2020; Szarzec, Dombi, and Matuszak 2021).[10]

The World Bank Group Subsidy and State Aid Tracker shows that state support granted to private firms and BOSs during the COVID-19 period involved a wide

FIGURE 4.4 **State Support to Private Firms and BOSs, by Type of Measure, April 2020 to June 2021**

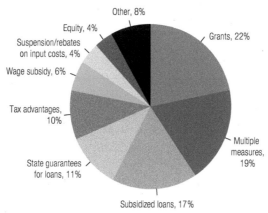

Source: World Bank Subsidy and State Aid Tracker.

Note: The policy tracker includes a sample of announced or approved COVID-19-related measures directed to BOSs. BOSs = businesses of the state.

array of instruments, including subsidized loans, capital increases, deferrals of taxes and fees, direct grants, state guarantees of loans, and deferral in the payment of concession fees, illustrating the fiscal impact of BOSs and the extent of state support to them (figure 4.4).[11]

New evidence comparing BOSs and private firms during the COVID-19 crisis shows that, although all firms lowered employment in 2020, BOSs shed fewer jobs and registered smaller declines in wages than private firms (box 4.2). There is also some evidence that BOSs registered smaller losses in revenue than private firms, but their productivity was the same as or lower than that of private firms.

Costs and Risks

State support to BOSs and private firms—during crises and normal times—comes at a cost and has risks. Such measures are costly and can exacerbate fiscal pressures when tax revenues fall and spending balloons. And they can bring higher inflation that hampers a speedy recovery. In addition to fiscal costs, other risks are associated with state support to BOSs or private firms. State support can create inefficiencies in resource allocation and market distortions, unleveling the playing field. It can also undermine corporate governance and foster corruption, moral hazard, and waste. If emergency state support is not withdrawn promptly after a crisis and if there is no clear exit strategy, state support can weaken incentives for a healthy recovery. The potential risks for anticompetitive behavior, corruption, and moral hazard due to state support arise when directed to both BOSs and private firms.[12]

New Evidence on the Role of BOSs during the COVID-19 Crisis

New empirical evidence on the COVID-19 period that was compiled for this report indicates that businesses of the state (BOSs) maintained employment and wages in Brazil (Brolhato, Cirera, and Martins-Neto 2023); Ecuador (Ferro and Patiño Peña 2023); Estonia, Latvia, Montenegro, Poland, Serbia, and Slovenia (this report); Romania (Dauda, Pop, and Iootty 2023); and Türkiye (Akcigit and Cilasun 2023). The results hold when considering employment and wage trends for all BOSs compared with those of private firms and when considering BOSs operating in competitive sectors compared with private firms. The latter finding suggests that natural monopoly sectors are not driving the effect and that this trend may come at the cost of crowding out private sector employment and reducing allocative inefficiency during recovery periods.

For Türkiye (Akcigit and Cilasun 2023) and Europe and Central Asia countries (this report), the evidence is mixed for access to credit and investment behavior of BOSs compared with those of private firms during 2020. Of 14 Europe and Central Asia countries, BOSs have higher rates of asset growth in 5 countries, whereas the difference is positive but not statistically significant in 6 others. In Türkiye, when short-term and long-term credit growth of BOSs and private firms in 2019–20 are compared, BOS short-term credit growth was significantly lower, but there is no significant difference between long-term credit growth for private firms.

In Romania (Dauda, Pop, and Iootty 2023), BOSs registered smaller losses in revenues than private firms. This revenue effect is more prominent for BOSs operating in competitive sectors than for private firms in those sectors. The result is driven by majority-owned BOSs (including BOSs with 25.0–49.9 percent state ownership), directly owned BOSs, and local BOSs, suggesting that these categories of firms may have been less vulnerable to the pandemic effects in Romania.

In Ecuador (Ferro and Patiño Peña 2023), total factor productivity was lower for both BOSs and private firms during 2020. Total factor productivity growth was 41 percentage points lower for BOSs in competitive sectors than for private firms in those sectors. Although BOSs became less productive during the pandemic, workers employed in these firms were cushioned, as worker compensation grew. This finding suggests that, during economic downturns, BOSs are potentially less efficient (and more distortive) in competitive sectors.

In terms of fiscal cost, in high-income countries such as Australia, Germany, Japan, and the United Kingdom, support to firms during the COVID-19 pandemic accounted for more than 10 percent of GDP. In lower-middle-income and low-income countries, additional spending amounted to 3.4 percent of GDP, and equity, loans, and guarantees amounted to about 1 percent of GDP (figure 4.5) (IMF 2021a). The International Monetary Fund estimated in May 2020 that support by countries to their firms in the form of loans, equity, and guarantees totaled US$4.6 trillion (IMF 2020b). For example, the European Commission implemented a State Aid Temporary Framework for support directed to firms mirroring the framework implemented during the global financial crisis.[13] Between March 2020 and September 2021, the European Commission

FIGURE 4.5 **Discretionary Fiscal Responses to the COVID-19 Crisis, by Country Income Level, 2020–21**

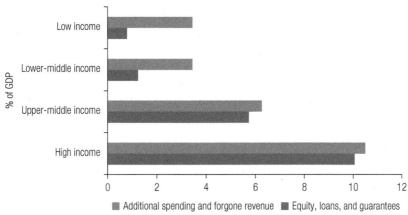

Source: IMF 2021a.

Note: Based on data for available countries, including 15 lower-middle-income and 5 low-income countries.

approved more than 650 measures providing more than €3 trillion in state support to firms. Measures included creating new BOSs and granting state support to BOSs and private firms through cash transfers, tax reductions, payment deferrals, and access to finance. This extensive state support, increased state ownership, and control of BOSs can amplify fiscal risks (OECD 2020a).

Besides fiscal costs, other risks are associated with state support to BOSs or private firms—during periods of crisis or normal times. State support affects the way firms interact with their competitors and reduces competition and economic efficiency. First, when resources are channeled to inefficient BOSs or private firms, state support may prolong their life span and help them to gain market share, while more productive peers face pressure to shrink and eventually exit the market. Second, support may distort their incentives to invest in productivity-enhancing activities, given the expectation that the state would provide additional support to failing BOSs and private firms in the future (soft budget constraints). Third, state support might help a single BOS or private firm (or a group of BOSs or private firms) consolidate its market power or even take over (existing and potential) competitors. Through these channels, state support can distort the market selection process, which in turn may hamper productivity growth while generating allocative, technical, and dynamic inefficiencies (box 4.3). In the long run, these distortions could reduce market competitiveness (see also Pop and Connon 2020).

The type of state support affects the level of distortions. Using the example of state support during the COVID-19 period, the World Bank Subsidy and State Aid Tracker shows that state support targeted BOSs and private firms alike, but BOS support was

Does State Support during Crises Distort Competition?

There is limited evidence on whether support during crises is more or less distortive than during noncrisis periods. For the global financial crisis, many studies review the effectiveness of liquidity injections in improving credit conditions, but there is limited evidence of the support's distortions in markets. For example, studies find that the US Troubled Asset Relief Program had limited impact on the activities of firms or local economic conditions (Berger and Roman 2015; Sheng 2019).[a] But research also finds that the program allowed banks to obtain competitive advantages (Berger and Roman 2015), with politically connected banks being more likely to receive capital injections (Duchin and Sosyura 2012).

For the responses to the COVID-19 pandemic, data are limited on the actual disbursement of support to firms, and it is hard to assess the possible competitive distortions with precision. The European Commission published a study suggesting that state support disbursed during the crisis had a limited effect on competition because support measures implemented by member states were proportionate to the economic damage suffered (Mathieu Collin et al. 2022). But the analysis did not cover sector or firm distortions. For COVID-19, fiscal measures to firms provide limited information about how beneficiaries were selected. Because the schemes were largely horizontal, covering all sectors (except financial services), the actual distribution could be expected to be demand determined and directed to sectors that suffered most. But World Bank (2021e) finds that 20 percent of firms that were not affected by COVID-19 reported receiving public support, compared with 26–29 percent of firms that were affected.

a. The same result was found when studying the effects of subsidies for small and medium enterprises following the Great East Japan Earthquake of 2011. Kashiwagi (2019) finds that, although subsidies were effective in the retail sector, they made no significant difference in the manufacturing and service sectors.

more likely to distort markets (box 4.4). BOSs were less likely to receive deferrals of fees, costs, taxes, and payments, which are less distortionary than other measures. BOSs were more likely to receive equity injections, which can be stickier than measures such as grants or loans, particularly if they are not linked to performance targets are not limited in time and are not accompanied by sunset clauses.

In the provision of state support, there is always the potential for corruption. However, irrespective of the type of firm ownership, this risk is more acute during crises, given the large scale of fiscal stimulus being disbursed in a short period and with limited oversight. The resources allocated to crisis emergency response and recovery can offer significant opportunities for illicit gains, given the need for speed and flexibility.[14] Although BOSs face corruption risks similar to those of private companies, the risks are compounded by the scale of assets they control, the considerable value of public contracts, and their proximity to governments. During a crisis, this privileged position also may put some BOSs in a position to secure preferential support when bailouts are decided and funds are limited. BOS procurement is vulnerable to corruption and collusion during crises, as it is in normal times. Crises exacerbate the corruption risk,

BOX 4.4

Support to BOSs and Private Firms during COVID-19

Governments most frequently purchased equity in businesses of the state (BOSs) as part of their support (32 percent of schemes), which can be more distortionary in the long term. Private firms, by contrast, received a wider variety of less distortionary measures, such as grants (about 22 percent of schemes) (figures B4.4.1 and B4.4.2). Capital injections, share purchases, and debt alleviation were typically directed to BOSs with high state ownership. Loans and grants more often targeted BOSs with lower state ownership, with levels similar to those of private firms (figure B4.4.3). Some countries created new BOSs during the COVID-19 crisis.

FIGURE B4.4.1 **State Support to BOSs, by Type of Measure, April 2020 to June 2021**

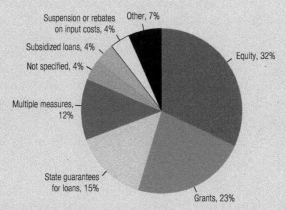

Source: World Bank Subsidy and State Aid Tracker.
Note: BOSs = businesses of the state.

FIGURE B4.4.2 **State Support to Private Firms, by Type of Measure, April 2020 to June 2021**

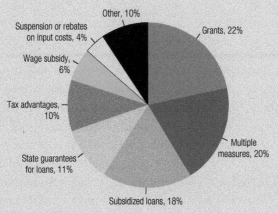

Source: World Bank Subsidy and State Aid Tracker.

(Box continues on the following page.)

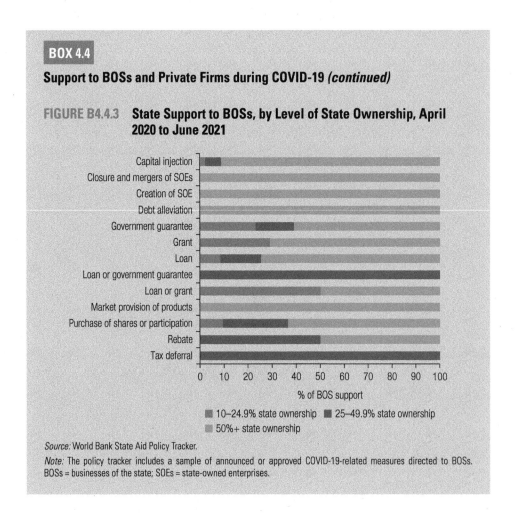

BOX 4.4

Support to BOSs and Private Firms during COVID-19 *(continued)*

FIGURE B4.4.3 **State Support to BOSs, by Level of State Ownership, April 2020 to June 2021**

Source: World Bank State Aid Policy Tracker.

Note: The policy tracker includes a sample of announced or approved COVID-19-related measures directed to BOSs. BOSs = businesses of the state; SOEs = state-owned enterprises.

particularly when oversight and accountability measures are limited during an emergency response or when coupled with weak institutional frameworks.

State support can create moral hazards because it can raise expectations of future support, which may weaken market discipline. For example, recipients may take on more risk in the future if past support during crises leads them to believe that they will be bailed out in the event of a crisis. Particularly in the case of recapitalizations of banks, bailouts may encourage risk-taking behavior.[15] Several studies find that bailouts result in higher risk taking.[16] If state support is targeted toward larger firms that are deemed essential for systemic stability, they may have more access than smaller firms to other support. There is also concern that state support disbursed during the crisis may lead to "zombie firms," which are economically unviable but continue to operate thanks to government support. So state support should not be available to firms that were failing or had structural issues before a crisis.[17]

Principles of State Support

State support represents a significant amount of fiscal resources with a large opportunity cost, requiring a careful weighing of benefits against risks. Based on the implementation of state support during previous crises for which relatively good data are available, key policy principles for the design of state support to BOSs and private firms—especially during crisis periods—include the need to undertake the following:[18]

- *Prioritize competing demands.* With scarce public resources, governments need to consider if support to BOSs and private firms is feasible. Given limited budgetary resources, such support may result in fewer resources for other critical areas, such as health care.
- *Clarify objectives.* Support to BOSs and to private firms must have clear objectives. If the mandate is to provide public services or critical goods and services, BOSs must be properly funded to fulfill their objectives in the same way as private firms.
- *Ensure proportional support and competitive neutrality.* BOSs should not be overcompensated to meet specific objectives, because doing so could result in market distortions, especially when BOSs compete with private peers in the same market. Governments should avoid soft budgeting and create separate budgets for assigning temporary and special public policies for BOSs. Competitive neutrality should be embedded in BOS governance and operations and be an overall requirement for targeting state support to maximize the effectiveness of public interventions given limited fiscal space and to minimize market distortions. It is important to identify BOSs' commercial and noncommercial activities through separation of accounts, careful methodologies for calculating compensation for public service obligations, and requirements to earn market-consistent rates of return in line with those of the private sector under similar market conditions.
- *Minimize selectivity and maintain incentives.* Governments should consider clear criteria for the design and disbursement of state support to minimize distortions, applicable in the same way to BOSs and private firms. At the same time, state support needs to incentivize the recipient of that support to meet stated objectives. For example, if the aim of the support is to protect jobs, the support can be tied to rules for maintaining a certain level of employment during times of crisis.
- *Select the least distortive instruments.* The level of distortion introduced by state support depends on the instrument. Governments should design support measures and associated instruments considering the objective pursued in conjunction with the risk of distortions. For example, deferrals (of taxes, contributions, interest, or payments) are less distortionary than other measures. In general, one-off and time-limited subsidy measures are less likely to have harmful effects. A loan typically leads to less distortion than a grant because it will ultimately need to be paid back by the beneficiary (table 4.2). The risk taken by

TABLE 4.2 Distortions of Different State Support Instruments

Type of financial support	Competition distortions	Moral hazard	Additional transaction costs required for unwinding
Deferrals (of taxes, contributions, payments for inputs)	Low	Low	Not required
Guarantees			
Loans	High	High	
Grants			
Equity (or asset purchase)			Required

Source: Original table for this publication.

the state in guaranteeing loans can be capped at a certain percentage, and a minimum premium can be required. Recapitalizations can generate market inefficiencies and are a sticky form of support. When situations require distortive measures, such as recapitalizations,[19] governments can also provide incentives for private sector buy-in to limit competitive distortions. For example, equity injections can be combined with bankruptcy proceedings.

- *Target support based on viability and exposure to financial distress.* Targeting beneficiaries, whether BOSs or private firms, is equally important to ensure that support measures are effective (table 4.3). State support to BOSs can be more distortive if BOSs in competitive and partially contestable markets are targeted and if targeting is based on select firms rather than clear objectives.

- *Set sunset clauses, and articulate exit strategies.* Support to BOSs should embed clear phasing-out mechanisms to prevent long-term sticky support that distorts markets. Sunset clauses for support can also minimize the cost of the intervention for taxpayers if they are transparent about the timing and process for terminating support, which may include reversing equity participation stemming from bailouts and BOS exits. If state support includes restrictions on long-term state ownership, an exit plan should detail how government will divest the company over a specified period.

Transparency can reduce distortions to competition, prevent misuse of public funds, and inform fiscal risk analysis (IMF 2016a; OECD 2016; Polackova Brixi and Schick 2002; World Bank 2023b). For example, during crisis periods, public awareness of state support facilitates take-up by businesses and reduces distortions when firms would otherwise miss out on needed relief, particularly in rural areas. Data on beneficiaries and levels of support can limit the ability to target support unfairly or to politically connected firms. Transparency can be combined with anticorruption monitoring and enforcement stipulations. Transparency measures are critical for strengthening public financial management of BOSs and include identifying BOS-related fiscal risks and mitigation measures as part of state ownership policies. Governments should require BOSs to publish financial statements and all support

TABLE 4.3 Targeting and Required Interventions, by Level of Financial Distress

Type of BOSs or private firms	Support needed	Instrument
Viable and not facing financial distress	No targeted support needed to address financial distress, but general development policies may still be relevant to achieve certain objectives	General business environment policies and regulations that are competitively neutral (including, for instance, through the proper separation of BOSs' commercial and noncommercial functions, requirements for BOSs to earn market-conforming rates of return) and provide regular access to finance. Adequate compensation for BOSs (and private firms) if entrusted with emergency public service delivery (particularly in competitive markets).
Viable but facing financial distress	Targeted support to solve liquidity problems	Support through grants and loans. Pre-insolvency procedures may also be needed.
Viable but insolvent	Debt restructuring (possibly followed by targeted support)	Debt restructuring procedures that benefit BOSs or private firms and lenders.
Nonviable and insolvent	Liquidation	Insolvency procedures that reduce the cost of bankruptcy and protect public sector balance sheets. Application to BOSs as well as divestiture, as required.

Source: Adapted from World Bank 2021e.

Note: The principles in this table can apply to BOSs and to private firms. BOSs = businesses of the state.

given to various beneficiaries, both private and state owned. Information should be provided on the roles of state-owned banks and commercial banks in allocating credit. Transparency and clear communication of support measures also help to manage business expectations and build public support.

Notes

1. Contingent liabilities can be either explicit (that is, legally grounded, such as government loan guarantees) or implicit, with a public expectation of government responsibility that is not established in law (for example, bailing out troubled subnational governments or state-owned enterprises). Different contingent liabilities frequently are realized in tandem, either because they are caused by the same underlying shock or because the realization of one risk triggers that of another, for instance, if the financial troubles of a BOS firm put its lenders into difficulty.

2. State support can take different forms. Such support to BOSs and private firms can include access to credit through grants, loans, or guarantees and indirect support through payment deferrals and tax relief, cash transfers, fee reductions, or wage subsidies. Governments can also provide support through equity and debt finance, especially if companies are deemed strategically important.

3. Public sector balance sheets combine all of the accumulated assets and liabilities that governments control, including public corporations, natural resources, and pension liabilities, and account for the entirety of what the state owns and owes.

4. State-owned banks often play an important role in the financial sector—for example, the Bhutan Development Bank accounts for 25 percent of total assets of the banking system, and Uruguay's Banco de La Republica Oriental Del accounts for 43 percent. Some state-owned banks account for a significant share of their markets—for example, the Viet Nam Bank for Social Policies provides 60 percent of all the country's micro loans, and Mexico's Fideicomisos Instituidos en Relación con la Agricultura accounts for 67 percent of total lending to the agriculture sector (World Bank 2018).

5. For example, given their dominance in network and primary sectors, BOSs are vulnerable to climate change risks, including decarbonization transition risks, that can affect public finances through dividend and asset losses (see chapter 5).

6. Most standard statistics and definitions of debt focus on the nonfinancial public sector debt, which would include BOSs and exclude state-owned banks.

7. In the past, two SOEs did not have the resources to repay their credits, and the government made payments on behalf of those two SOEs.

8. In the case of the European Union, the European Commission (2016) finds that, although the profitability and productivity of BOSs tend to be lower than those of private firms, the difference in performance between BOSs and private companies became smaller (or statistically insignificant) during the global financial crisis, suggesting that BOSs were potentially stabilizing during the crisis.

9. Jaslowitzer, Megginson, and Rapp (2018) find that state ownership is associated with stability-seeking investment policies. García-Sánchez and Rama (2022) find that BOSs in Spain outperformed other firms during the global financial crisis in their ability to cooperate with partners on innovation. However, Jie et al. (2021) find that investment fell more for BOSs than for other listed firms during the COVID-19 crisis, suggesting that they may have exacerbated the impacts of the crisis. Bortolloti, Fotak, and Wolfe (2022) find that government ownership did not mitigate research and development investment during crises. Further, the World Bank (2023a) finds that, although infrastructure BOSs that faced a negative shock received additional fiscal injections equal to 3.5 percent of average assets, average capital expenditure declined by 40 percent of average assets the year after the shock.

10. EBRD (2020) finds that the presence of state-owned banks had a positive impact on income growth and other outcomes after the crisis in the Caucasus, Central and Eastern Europe, and Türkiye. Coleman and Feler (2014) find similar results in Brazil. Szarzec, Dombi, and Matuszak (2021) investigate the effect of BOSs on economic growth in 30 European countries in the period of 2010–16 and find that BOSs are per se neither positive nor negative for growth but that their impact on growth depends on the country's institutions. With good (bad) institutions, the effect of BOSs is more beneficial (detrimental), turning significantly positive (negative) in the right tail (left tail) of the sample distribution of institutional quality.

11. The World Bank State Aid Tracker presents the state support schemes implemented by governments across all continents in the context of the COVID-19 pandemic. The tracker includes a sample of 1,075 approved COVID-19-related measures in 167 countries from April 2020 up to June 2021 based on criteria that would qualify them as subsidies according to the World Trade Organization definition. A subsidy is a financial contribution by a government or public body conferring a benefit to its recipients, which are firms (not individuals or households). According to the World Trade Organization Agreement on Subsidies and Countervailing Measures, Article 1 subsidies may include grants, tax exemptions, capital injections, loan guarantees, accelerated depreciation allowances, and other in-kind benefits (https://www.wto.org/english/docs_e /legal_e/24-scm_01_e.htm). In the European Union context, state aid is defined as "any aid granted by a Member State or through State resources in any form whatsoever which distorts or threatens to distort competition by favoring certain undertakings or the production of certain goods shall, insofar as it affects trade between Member States, be incompatible with the internal market" (Article 107 (1) of the Treaty on the Functioning of the European Union). The tracker includes approved schemes but does not include data on the disbursement of funds at the recipient level. Data included in the tracker were collected through a desk research exercise using publicly available information from countries' ministries of finance (annual budget information for 2020/21; published lists of COVID-19-related measures and press releases), the European Commission, the European Free Trade Association, the International Monetary Fund, and other organizations, such as KPMG, Deloitte, White and Case, and Ernst and Young. They were updated regularly

during April 2020–June 2021. Overall, data from all the regions covered were publicly available and accessible, with some exceptions in a few countries from the Middle East and North Africa and East Asia and Pacific regions.

12. The role of state-owned financial institutions in a crisis warrants particular attention, separate from that of BOSs in the real sector (Gutierrez and Kliatskova 2021).

13. Although the 2008 and 2020 frameworks were similar regarding the type of aid (grants and soft loans) and the conditions for granting them (existence of a ceiling on the amount of subsidy per company), the framework adopted during the 2008 crisis focused mainly on the financial sector—the 2020 framework largely concerned the real economy.

14. For example, an analysis of US congresspersons regarding the Emergency Economic Stabilization Act in October 2008 revealed that "higher campaign contributions from the financial industry increase the likelihood of supporting the Emergency Economic Stabilization Act" (Mian, Sufi, and Trebbi 2010, 1967). In the health care sector, approximately US$2 trillion of procurement expenditures are lost to corruption globally per year, and rapid processes during crises likely exacerbate these losses. Single-source procurement, implemented by many countries during the COVID-19 crisis, created not only risks of corruption, but also risks of collusive behavior among all types of firms (United Nations 2021).

15. See, for example, OECD (2010, 34): "The financial crisis of 2008 is an extreme instance of the damage wrought by the existence of a soft budget constraint. One ingredient that contributed to excessive risk taking by banks was the implicit government guarantee they felt to be enjoying (and that they indeed were enjoying, as has been revealed by the various, costly rescue plans). The damage caused by the excessive risk taking was not caused by the granting of aid, but by the expectation that aid would be granted should the need arise."

16. Dam and Koetter (2012) focus on German bailouts in which banks received capital injections from their responsible banking association's insurance fund. Those authors find that a higher probability of bailout increases banks' risk taking significantly, consistent with increased moral hazard. Hryckiewicz (2014) investigates the effects of bailouts on bank risk using data on banks rescued during 23 systemic banking crises in 23 countries, finding that bailouts increase bank risk significantly and that blanket guarantees, nationalizations, and asset management companies contribute the most to increased risk. Using a sample for 53 countries, Brandao-Marques, Correa, and Sapriza (2018) also find that more government support is associated with more risk taking. In the case of the East Asia financial crisis, Poczter (2016) finds that recapitalization of banks in Indonesia increased the long-term risk taking of banks.

17. Under the European Union COVID-19 Temporary State Aid Framework, aid could be granted only to undertakings that were not already in financial distress before the start of the pandemic. Indeed, this was the case for the Portuguese €1.2 billion rescue loan in favor of a Portuguese airline (https://ec.europa.eu/commission/presscorner/detail/en/ip_20_1029).

18. This section builds on recommendations regarding the design of support and literature on the level of distortion of different support measures, including Blanchard, Philippon, and Pisani-Ferry (2020); Copenhagen Economics (2020); European Commission (2022); Freund and Pesme (2021); Manuilova, Burdescu, and Bilous (2022); Motta and Peitz (2020); ODI (2020); OECD (2009, 2020a, 2020b, 2020c); Pop and Amador (2020b); Qiang and Pop (2020); Vitale et al. (2020); and World Bank (2021a).

19. Criteria for recapitalization measures should include (a) evidence that the viability of the company would be at risk without state intervention; (b) proof that no other measures were available to raise capital; (c) recapitalization measures that are limited in time; (d) establishment of appropriate remuneration; and (e) adoption of structural or behavioral commitments, notably in the form of prohibitions on misuse of financial support.

References

Akcigit, U., and S. Cilasun. 2023. "State-Owned Enterprises in Türkiye." Background paper for this report, World Bank, Washington, DC.

Berger, A., and R. Roman. 2015. "Did TARP Banks Get Competitive Advantages?" *Journal of Financial and Quantitative Analysis* 50 (6): 1199–36.

Beuselinck, C., L. Cao, M. Deloof, and X. Xia. 2017. "The Value of Government Ownership during the Global Financial Crisis." *Journal of Corporate Finance* 42 (February): 481–93.

Blanchard, O., T. Philippon, and J. Pisani-Ferry. 2020. "A New Policy Toolkit Is Needed as Countries Exit COVID-19 Lockdowns." PIIE Policy Brief 20-8, Peterson Institute for International Economics, Washington, DC.

Bortolloti, B., V. Fotak, and B. Wolfe. 2022. "Government Share Ownership and Innovation: Evidence from European Listed Firms." BAFFI CAREFIN Centre Research Paper 2018-72, Centre on Economics, Finance, and Regulation, Milan.

Boukezia, R., J. Charaoui, J. Frank, M. Harb, M. Queyranne, N. Reyes, P. F. Ryan, and A. F. Tieman. 2023. "Managing Fiscal Risks in the Middle East and North Africa." IMF Departmental Paper DP/2023/005, International Monetary Fund, Washington, DC. https://www.imf.org/en /Publications/Departmental-Papers-Policy-Papers/Issues/2023/06/08/Managing-Fiscal-Risks -in-the-Middle-East-and-North-Africa-529220.

Bova, E., M. Ruiz-Arranz, F. Toscani, and H. E. Ture. 2016. "The Fiscal Costs of Contingent Liabilities: A New Dataset." IMF Working Paper WP/16/14, International Monetary Fund, Washington, DC.

Böwer, U. 2017. "State-Owned Enterprises in Emerging Europe: The Good, the Bad, and the Ugly." IMF Working Paper WP/17/221, International Monetary Fund, Washington, DC.

Brandao-Marques, L., R. Correa, and H. Sapriza. 2018. "Government Support, Regulation, and Risk Taking in the Banking Sector." *Journal of Banking & Finance* 112 (2): 105284.

Brolhato, S., X. Cirera, and A. Martins-Neto. 2023. "The Impact of State-Owned Enterprises in Brazil." Background paper for this report, World Bank, Washington, DC.

Coleman, N., and L. Feler. 2014. "Bank Ownership, Lending, and Local Economic Performance during the 2008–2010 Financial Crisis." International Finance Discussion Paper 1099, Board of Governors of the Federal Reserve System, Washington, DC.

Copenhagen Economics. 2020. "The Economics of State Aid in Times of Crisis: How Large Is the Damage?" Copenhagen Economics, Copenhagen. https://copenhageneconomics.com/publication /the-economics-of-state-aid-in-times-of-crisis-how-large-is-the-damage/.

Dam, L., and M. Koetter. 2012. "Bank Bailouts and Moral Hazard: Evidence from Germany." *Review of Financial Studies* 25 (8): 2343–80.

Dauda, S., G. Pop, and M. Iootty. 2023. "Romania: State-Owned Enterprises Performance and Their Stabilizing Role during the COVID-19 Pandemic." Background paper for this report, World Bank, Washington, DC.

Duchin, R., and D. Sosyura. 2012. "The Politics of Government Investment." *Journal of Financial Economics* 106 (1): 24–48.

EBRD (European Bank for Reconstruction and Development). 2020. *Life in Transition Survey, Transition Report 2020–2021: The State Strikes Back.* London: EBRD.

European Commission. 2016. "State-Owned Enterprises in the EU: Lessons Learnt and Ways Forward in a Post-Crisis Context." Institutional Paper 31, July 2016, European Commission, Brussels. https://economy-finance.ec.europa.eu/publications/state-owned-enterprises-eu-lessons-learnt -and-ways-forward-post-crisis-context_en.

European Commission. 2022. "State Aid: Commission Amends the Temporary Crisis Framework." European Commission, Brussels.

Ferro, E., and F. Patiño Peña. 2023. "Private Sector Performance under the Pressure of SOE Competition: The Case of Ecuador." Background paper for this report, World Bank, Washington, DC.

Freund, C., and J. Pesme. 2021. "Five Ways We Can Support Viable but Vulnerable Businesses during COVID-19 Recovery." *Voices* (blog), April 14, 2021. https://blogs.worldbank.org/voices/five -ways-we-can-support-viable-vulnerable-businesses-during-covid-19-recovery.

García-Sánchez, A., and R. Rama. 2022. "Cooperative Innovation and Crises: Foreign Subsidiaries, State-Owned Enterprises, and Domestic Private Firms." *Science and Public Policy* 49 (6): 915–27.

Gutierrez, E., and T. Kliatskova. 2021. *National Development Financial Institutions: Trends, Crisis Response Activities, and Lessons Learned.* Washington, DC: World Bank.

Harris, J., B. Imbert, P. Medas, J. Ralyea, and A. Singh. 2020. "Government Support to State-Owned Enterprises: Options for Sub-Saharan Africa." Special Series on COVID-19, International Monetary Fund, Washington, DC. https://www.imf.org/-/media/Files/Publications/covid19 -special-notes/enspecial-series-on-covid19government-support-to-stateowned-enterprises -options-for-subsaharan-afric.ashx.

Hryckiewicz, A. 2014. "What Do We Know about the Impact of Government Interventions in the Banking Sector? An Assessment of Various Bailout Programs on Bank Behavior." *Journal of Banking & Finance* 46 (September): 246–65.

IMF (International Monetary Fund). 2016a. "Analyzing and Managing Fiscal Risks—Best Practices." Informal Session Brief, IMF, Washington, DC. https://www.imf.org/external/np/pp/eng/2016 /050416.pdf.

IMF (International Monetary Fund). 2016b. "Slovenia 2016 Article IV Consultation – Staff Report." IMF Country Report 16/122, IMF, Washington, DC.

IMF (International Monetary Fund). 2016c. "Slovenia—Financial Sector Development Issues and Prospects." IMF Country Report 16/345, IMF, Washington, DC.

IMF (International Monetary Fund). 2019. "Reassessing the Role of State-Owned Enterprises in Central, Eastern, and Southeastern Europe." IMF, Washington, DC.

IMF (International Monetary Fund). 2020a. "Overview of the Public Sector Balance Sheet Database." IMF, Washington, DC.

IMF (International Monetary Fund). 2020b. "Tracking the $9 Trillion Global Fiscal Support to Fight COVID-19." *IMF Chart of the Week* (blog), May 20, 2020. https://www.imf.org/en/Blogs/Articles /2020/05/20/tracking-the-9-trillion-global-fiscal-support-to-fight-covid-19.

IMF (International Monetary Fund). 2020c. *World Economic Outlook: A Long and Difficult Ascent* (October 2020). Washington, DC: IMF.

IMF (International Monetary Fund). 2021a. "IMF Fiscal Monitor Database of Country Fiscal Measures in Response to the COVID-19 Pandemic." IMF, Washington, DC. https://www.imf .org/en/Topics/imf-and-covid19/Fiscal-Policies-Database-in-Response-to-COVID-19.

IMF (International Monetary Fund). 2021b. "State-Owned Enterprises in Middle East, North Africa, and Central Asia: Size, Role, Performance, and Challenges." Departmental Paper 2021/019, IMF, Washington, DC.

IMF (International Monetary Fund). 2022. *Regional Economic Outlook: Middle East and Central Asia.* Washington, DC: IMF, October 2022.

IMF (International Monetary Fund). 2023. "The Gambia: Sixth Review under the Extended Credit Facility Arrangement, Request for a Waiver of Nonobservance of a Performance Criterion, and Financing Assurances Review—Debt Sustainability Analysis." IMF Staff Country Report 23/216, IMF, Washington, DC.

Jaslowitzer, P., W. Megginson, and M. S. Rapp. 2018. "State Ownership and Corporate Investment." University of Marburg, Marburg, Denmark, August 22, 2018.

Jie, J., J. Hou, C. Wang, and H. Y. Liu. 2021. "COVID-19 Impact on Firm Investment: Evidence from Chinese Publicly Listed Firms." *Journal of Asian Economics* 75 (C): 101320.

Kashiwagi, Y. 2019. "Postdisaster Subsidies for Small and Medium Firms: Insights for Effective Targeting." ADB Economics Working Paper Series 597, Asian Development Bank, Mandaluyong City, Philippines.

Kopelman, J. L., and H. S. Rosen. 2014. "Are Public Sector Jobs Recession-Proof? Were They Ever?" Griswold Center for Economic Policy Studies, Princeton University, Princeton, NJ, October 2014.

Lazzarini, S. G., and A. Musachio. 2018. "State Ownership Reinvented? Explaining Performance Differences between State-Owned and Private Firms." *Corporate Governance: An International Review* 26 (4): 255–72.

Manuilova, N., R. Burdescu, and A. Bilous. 2022. "State-Owned Enterprises during a Crisis: Assets or Liabilities?" *Governance for Development* (blog), April 6, 2022. https://blogs.worldbank.org /governance/state-owned-enterprises-during-crisis-assets-or-liabilities.

Mathieu Collin, A., G. Cannas, K. van de Casteele, and S. Ferraro. 2022. "Competition State Aid Brief: Issue 1/2022—February 2022." European Commission, Brussels.

Melecky, M. 2021. *Hidden Debt: Solutions to Avert the Next Financial Crisis in South Asia*. South Asia Development Matters. Washington, DC: World Bank.

Mian, A., A. Sufi, and F. Trebbi. 2010. "The Political Economy of the US Mortgage Default Crisis." *American Economic Review* 100 (5): 1967–98.

Motta, M., and M. Peitz. 2020. "State Aid Policies in Response to the COVID-19 Shock: Observations and Guiding Principles." *Intereconomics* 55 (4): 219–22.

ODI (Overseas Development Institute). 2020. "Covid-19 Economic Recovery: Fiscal Stimulus Choices for Lower-Income Countries." ODI, London.

OECD (Organisation for Economic Co-operation and Development). 2009. *The Financial Crisis: Reform and Exit Strategies*. Paris: OECD Publishing.

OECD (Organisation for Economic Co-operation and Development). 2010. *Policy Roundtables: Competition, State Aids, and Subsidies*. Paris: OECD Publishing.

OECD (Organisation for Economic Co-operation and Development). 2016. *Risk Management by State-Owned Enterprises and Their Ownership*. Corporate Governance. Paris: OECD Publishing. https://doi.org/10.1787/9789264262249-en.

OECD (Organisation for Economic Co-operation and Development). 2020a. "The COVID-19 Crisis and State Ownership in the Economy: Issues and Policy Considerations." OECD COVID-HUB Policy Brief, OECD Publishing, Paris. https://www.oecd.org/coronavirus/policy-responses/the -covid-19-crisis-and-state-ownership-in-the-economy-issues-and-policy-considerations -ce417c46/#section-d1e79.

OECD (Organisation for Economic Co-operation and Development). 2020b. *OECD Policy Responses to Coronavirus (COVID-19): Equity Injections and Unforeseen State Ownership of Enterprises during the COVID-19 Crisis*. Paris: OECD Publishing.

OECD (Organisation for Economic Co-operation and Development). 2020c. *OECD Policy Responses to Coronavirus (COVID-19): Government Support and the COVID-19 Pandemic*. Paris: OECD Publishing.

Polackova Brixi, H., and A. Schick. 2002. *Government at Risk: Contingent Liabilities and Fiscal Risks*. Washington, DC: World Bank and Oxford University Press. https://elibrary.worldbank.org/doi /abs/10.1596/978-0-8213-4835-2.

Poczter, S. 2016. "The Long-Term Effects of Bank Recapitalization: Evidence from Indonesia." *Journal of Financial Intermediation* 25 (January): 131–53.

Pop, G., and A. Amador. 2020a. "State Aid and COVID-19: Support Now, but Bear in Mind Long-Term Effects." World Bank, Washington, DC.

Pop, G., and A. Amador. 2020b. "To Aid and How to Aid: Policy Options to Preserve Markets." *European State Aid Law Quarterly* 19 (2): 127–36.

Pop, G., and D. Connon. 2020. *Industrial Policy Effects and the Case for Competition, Equitable Growth, Finance, and Institutions Insight.* Washington, DC: World Bank.

PwC (Pricewaterhouse Coopers). 2015. "State-Owned Enterprises: Catalysts for Public Value Creation?" PwC, London. https://www.pwc.com/gr/en/publications/assets/state-owned-enterprises -catalysts-for-public-value-creation.pdf.

Qiang, Z., and G. Pop. 2020. "State-Owned Enterprises and COVID-19." *Private Sector Development* (blog), July 28, 2020. https://blogs.worldbank.org/psd/state-owned-enterprises-and-covid-19.

Sheng, J. 2019. "The Real Effects of Government Intervention: Firm-Level Evidence from TARP." Paper prepared for the 2019 American Economic Association annual meeting, Atlanta, GA, January 4–6, 2019.

Szarzec, K., A. Dombi, and P. Matuszak. 2021. "State-Owned Enterprises and Economic Growth: Evidence from the Post-Lehman Period." *Economic Modelling* 99 (June): 105490.

Transparency International. 2017a. "Preventing Corruption in State-Owned Enterprises." Press release, November 28, 2017, Transparency International, Berlin. https://www.transparency.org /en/news/how-to-prevent-corruption-in-state-owned-enterprises.

Transparency International. 2017b. "Transparency International Launches 10 Anticorruption Principles for State-Owned Enterprises." Press release, November 28, 2017, Transparency International, Berlin. https://www.transparency.org/en/press/transparency-international-launches -10-anti-corruption-principles-for-soes.

United Nations. 2021. "Corruption and COVID-19: Challenges in Crisis Response and Recovery." United Nations, New York.

Vagliasindi, M. 2022. "SOEs as a Stabilizer in Period of Crisis: Lessons from the Global Financial Crisis." Unpublished working paper, World Bank, Washington, DC.

Vitale, C., J. Strasky, A. Elgouacem, T. Kozluk, and C. Abate. 2020. "State Ownership Will Gain Importance as a Result of COVID-19." *VoxEU*, July 7, 2020.

Vitoria, R., A. Bressan, and R. Iquiapaza. 2020. "Do State-Owned Enterprises in Brazil Require a Risk Premium Factor?" *Brazilian Business Review* 17 (5): 488–505.

World Bank. 2017. "Who Sponsors Infrastructure Projects? Disentangling Public and Private Contributions." Public-Private Infrastructure Advisory Facility (PPIAF), World Bank, Washington, DC. https://ppi.worldbank.org/content/dam/PPI/documents/SPIReport_2017_small _interactive.pdf.

World Bank. 2018. *2017 Survey of National Development Banks.* Washington, DC: World Bank. http:// documents.worldbank.org/curated/en/977821525438071799/2017-Survey-of-National -development-banks.

World Bank. 2020a. "Kyrgyz Public Expenditure Review (PER)." World Bank, Washington, DC.

World Bank. 2020b. "The Gambia Economic Update: Preserving the Gains." World Bank, Washington, DC.

World Bank. 2021a. *Building SOE Crisis Management and Resilience: Emerging Practices and Lessons Learned during the COVID-19 Crisis.* Washington, DC: World Bank.

World Bank. 2021b. *Debt Management Performance Assessment.* Washington, DC: World Bank. https://documents.worldbank.org/en/publication/documents-reports/documentdetail /526391628746190611/debt-management-performance-assessment-methodology-2021 -edition.

World Bank. 2021c. *International Debt Statistics 2021*. Washington, DC: World Bank.

World Bank. 2021d. "Kyrgyz Republic: iSOEF Assessment." World Bank, Washington, DC. https://cfrr.worldbank.org/sites/default/files/2022-03/Kyrgyz-Republic-Integrated-State-Owned-Enterprises-Framework-iSOEF-Assessment.pdf.

World Bank. 2021e. "Supporting Firms in Restructuring and Recovery." Equitable Growth, Finance, and Institutions Insight, World Bank, Washington, DC.

World Bank. 2021f. "The Gambia Integrated State-Owned Enterprises Framework (iSOEF) Assessment." World Bank, Washington, DC. http://hdl.handle.net/10986/37376.

World Bank. 2022a. *Global Economic Prospects 2022*. Washington, DC: World Bank.

World Bank. 2022b. *World Development Report 2022: Finance for an Equitable Recovery*. Washington, DC: World Bank.

World Bank. 2023a. *Off the Books: Understanding and Mitigating the Fiscal Risks of Infrastructure*. Washington, DC: World Bank.

World Bank. 2023b. "World Bank Debt and Fiscal Risks Toolkit." World Bank, Washington, DC. https://www.worldbank.org/en/programs/debt-toolkit/fiscal-risk.

5. Businesses of the State and Climate Action

Introduction

Governments have comparative advantages in underwriting investments to advance the climate agenda, coordinating multiple actors around the common goal of decarbonization, and ensuring that the costs and benefits of a green transition are distributed equitably across society so that economic growth and poverty are tackled alongside environmental crises. The state can also choose to provide direct support for research and development (R&D) to create and scale up new low-carbon technologies, instead of providing tax incentives or imposing regulations. Any state intervention should be considered in the context of a menu of policy options that can achieve the same objective more efficiently and without deterring private investment. For example, restrictive regulations in these markets can slow the green transition by inhibiting private investment, innovation, and technology adoption. The presence of many businesses of the state (BOSs)—often operating in protected markets with nonfinancial mandates or benefiting from explicit or implicit advantages—can deter the private sector from engaging in climate action. Yet climate finance flows to developing countries should increase by a factor of 4–8 times (World Bank 2022a), in particular from private sector sources towards low- and lower-middle income countries where current private mobilization rates are low (OECD 2022).

For these reasons, it is essential to identify the state's footprint through BOSs in high-emitting sectors and in sectors vulnerable to climate change and to design reforms to scale up climate action. It is also critical to understand how market regulations and market structures can influence and potentially deter both private investment in climate action and the mobilization of private climate finance.

- The new World Bank Global Businesses of the State (BOS) database unveils the extensive presence of the state across many potentially high-emitting sectors as well as sectors that are vulnerable to climate change. Current estimates focused on traditionally defined state-owned enterprises (SOEs) in fossil fuel–dominated economies show that SOEs are responsible for one-sixth of global greenhouse gas emissions, mostly driven by SOE emissions in the energy sector (Benoit 2019a, 2019b; Benoit et al. 2022). This share is likely an underestimate: the presence of BOSs in other high-emitting sectors (such as manufacturing, cement, and steel) has not been captured consistently largely because of a lack of data.

The share of BOSs in sectors that are at risk of experiencing the negative effects of climate change is also large, underscoring the vulnerability of these BOSs, the sectors in which they operate, and the importance of investing in their resilience, especially in infrastructure and network industries.

- The need to scale up finance for climate adaptation and mitigation is growing, particularly in credit-constrained low- and middle-income countries. Most BOSs in these sectors are less creditworthy than their sector's revenue leaders and use state resources to boost their credit rating. So, when BOSs are present in sectors that call for large investments in climate action, their low profitability and creditworthiness impair their ability to engage in climate adaptation and mitigation. Such firms also add to governments' financial burden when state guarantees notch up their creditworthiness. For these reasons, more efforts are needed to incentivize private capital to invest in adaptation and mitigation.

- Regulatory reforms are needed to encourage more private investment and to scale up climate action. BOSs in competitive markets are the least justified. They often operate in protected markets or benefit from explicit and implicit advantages, deterring the green transition. This chapter provides a deep dive into the cement industry, a hard-to-abate sector characterized by dominant market players, including BOSs, an unlevel playing field, and anticompetitive behavior—all of which can slow investment in new technologies and a low-carbon transition. The focus on the energy sector illustrates how regulatory reforms are still needed to support the entry of private players and speed the transition toward renewable energy and the diffusion of green technologies.

State Presence in High-Emitting Sectors and in Sectors Vulnerable to Climate Change

BOSs in Potentially High-Emitting Sectors

The state is an owner across high-emitting sectors,[1] including many sectors outside power generation and sectors in fully competitive markets. It is likely responsible for a greater share of greenhouse gas emissions than assumed. To date, most estimates focus on the emissions in power generation, where BOSs hold about 50 percent of global generation capacity. New data on the state footprint across sectors and types of markets reveal the presence of BOSs in other high-emitting sectors too.

Globally, about one-fifth of BOSs in the World Bank BOS database operate in high-emitting sectors, underlining their role as a major source of greenhouse gas emissions. Of the 76,400 BOS firms with state ownership of at least 10 percent in the BOS database across 91 countries, 18 percent are in high-emitting sectors. This does not imply that they emit more emissions than their privately owned peers, but it does suggest that BOSs contribute to greenhouse gas emissions outside the power sector more than previously assumed. Because the BOS database does not include information on the consumption of energy (fuels) or on the sectoral emissions of greenhouse gases, high-emitting sectors are defined in broad categories, such as mining, oil, gas, and chemicals (including petrochemicals, fertilizers, plastics); manufacturing (including pulp and paper, cement, steel, aluminum); transportation (rail cargo and passenger, air, freight and logistics, sea and water transportation); agriculture (including cattle farming, rice growing, logging); and power generation.[2]

However, the degree to which some sectors are effectively high emitters depends on the resources used and technology actually applied by the respective companies in the sector. For instance, the extent to which the power generation sector is a high-emitting sector very much depends on the country's mix of fuels, because countries endowed with hydropower and renewable energy will be much less polluting than countries where fossil fuels dominate. An examination of the power sector provides more granularity on the country specifics of electricity supply and the mix of renewable and fossil fuels. Similar considerations apply in the case of (1) agriculture and land use, with the application of climate smart technologies playing an important role in the level of green house gas emissions; (2) emission from buildings, with the type of construction material used and the introduction of a green building certification system focused on making buildings more resource-efficient having a strong impact on greenhouse gas emissions; or (3) transportation, with the mode of transportation (for example, road, railways, air, freight, and logistics) and the degree of electrification or reliance on heavy fuels playing a key role in determining the level of emissions.

Slightly more than half of BOSs in high-emission sectors are in competitive markets—growing rice, raising dairy cattle, manufacturing cement, casting steel and iron, and so on—with a weaker economic rationale for state participation (figure 5.1)

FIGURE 5.1   **Share of BOSs in Potentially High-Emitting Sectors, 2019**

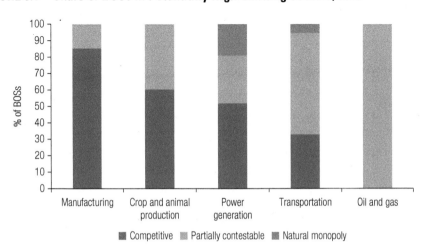

Source: World Bank Global Businesses of the State (BOS) database.
Note: Distribution of businesses of the state (BOSs) in potentially high-emitting sectors, by type of market for 14,000 firms.

(Dall'Olio et al. 2022). Although power generation is still the single most important high-emitting sector in which BOSs are active, transportation and crop and animal production have substantial shares. Power generation has the most BOSs (42 percent), followed by crop and animal production (23 percent), transportation (21 percent), manufacturing (12 percent), and extraction (2 percent).

The state footprint of BOSs in high-emitting sectors is heterogeneous across countries, and a closer assessment of emissions (depending on fuels used in the production process) is needed to draw policy implications. For at least 12 countries, BOSs in high-emitting sectors account for more than 50 percent of all BOSs in the country, by revenues (figures 5.2 and 5.3). The relative importance of high-emitting sectors ranges from 68 percent of BOS revenues in the Dominican Republic to 8 percent in the Comoros. Likewise, the presence of BOSs across the potentially high-emitting sectors varies, with more than half of BOSs in high-emitting sectors in power generation in eight countries, for example. Some of these firms may already have transitioned to renewable energy sources, whereas others still rely on fossil fuel. In Viet Nam (a country dependent largely on fossil fuel power generation) and the Kyrgyz Republic (a country dependent largely on the hydropower sector), only about 13 percent of BOSs in high-emitting sectors are active in power generation. These countries have significantly higher shares of high-emitting BOSs in manufacturing (Viet Nam) and crop and animal production (the Kyrgyz Republic).

The literature presents very limited systematic empirical evidence on the relationship between enterprise ownership and greenhouse gas emissions. And the limited evidence is inconclusive—leaving open whether BOSs are *leaders* or *laggers* in climate action. Yet the emerging evidence indicates the importance of several enabling factors regardless of ownership. These factors include sound institutions and regulations, foreign direct investment, and well-functioning domestic capital markets (Isungset 2022; Talukdar and Meisner 2001).

BOSs in Sectors Most Vulnerable to Climate Change

The presence of BOSs in sectors at risk of experiencing the negative effects of climate change is more pronounced than their presence in high-emitting sectors, underscoring their vulnerability. Of the 76,400 BOSs with state ownership of at least 10 percent in the 2019 World Bank BOS database, 44 percent operate in sectors likely to experience the effects of climate change—such as floods or storms impairing transmission lines or droughts reducing the capacity of hydropower plants (figure 5.4).[3] These sectors include water supply, treatment, and collection (12 percent); followed by power production, transmission, and distribution; most means of transportation; construction; agricultural production and subsequent processing; finance (including insurance); tourism; information and communication technologies; and selected segments of manufacturing and wholesale or trade. In about 75 percent of International Development

FIGURE 5.2 **Share of BOSs in Potentially High-Emitting Sectors, by Region and Country, 2019**

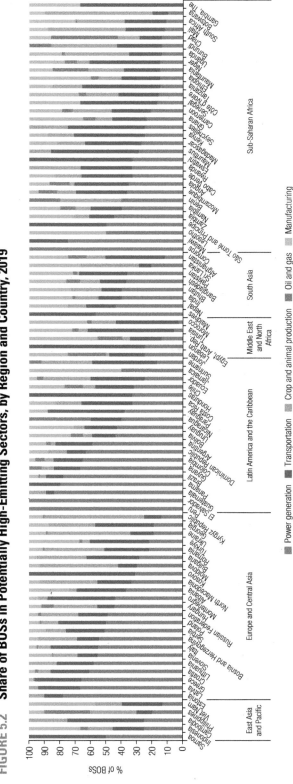

■ Power generation ■ Transportation ■ Crop and animal production ■ Oil and gas ■ Manufacturing

Source: World Bank Global Businesses of the State (BOS) database.

Note: Distribution of businesses of the state (BOSs) in potentially high-emitting sectors, by country, for 14,000 firms. Because of a general lack of systematic firm-level data on greenhouse gas emissions, this report could not assess in greater detail the impact of ownership on the intensity of greenhouse gas emissions of firms. The level of emissions will differ by country, depending, to a large extent, on the energy mix.

FIGURE 5.3
Distribution of BOSs across High-Emitting Sectors, by Share of Revenues, Employment, and Number of Firms, 2019

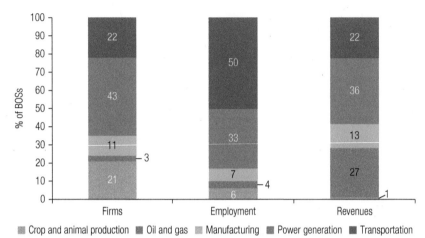

Source: World Bank Global Businesses of the State (BOS) database.
Note: Numbers given in the bars are the total percentage for each sector. BOSs = businesses of the state.

FIGURE 5.4 **Share of BOSs in Sectors Vulnerable to the Negative Effects of Climate Change, 2019**

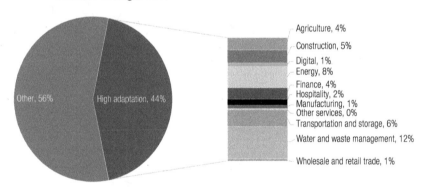

Source: World Bank Global Businesses of the State (BOS) database.
Note: BOSs = businesses of the state.

Association countries (25 of 33), more than 50 percent of BOSs are in sectors with high adaptation needs (figure 5.5).

With such high exposure of BOSs to the effects of climate change, the risks extend beyond mere infrastructure damage to fiscal and debt sustainability. These risks can impair a country's economy and financial standing through a range of channels (box 5.1). Such fiscal risks pose a particular threat to low-income countries, because of the 36 low-income countries, 16 countries are either in debt distress or have a high risk of debt distress. Understanding the climate risk exposure of their BOSs is thus vital.[4]

FIGURE 5.5

Countries with a Large Share of BOSs in Highly Climate-Vulnerable Sectors, 2019

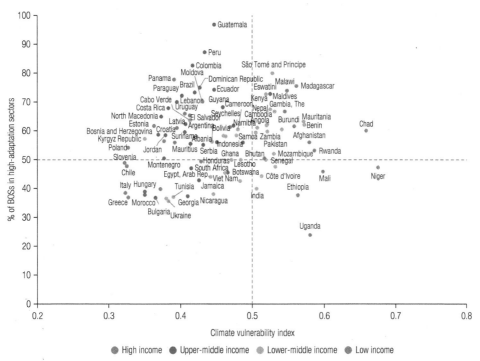

Sources: World Bank Global Businesses of the State (BOS) database. The climate vulnerability index source is from ND-GAIN (https://gain.nd.edu/our-work/country-index/rankings/), downloaded June 20, 2023.

BOX 5.1

How the Exposure of BOSs to Climate Risks Can Have an Economic Impact

The channels of climate-related risk transmission overlap, and the interplay of likely and recurring events and sources of risks and sectors could become a vicious cycle. For instance, the materialization of climate physical and transition risks could lead to a higher probability of loan default by firms, including businesses of the state (BOSs). Many of the guarantees on which BOS finance relies may have to be called.

And contingent liabilities could become more likely with climate change, leading to a gradual deterioration of a country's public finance conditions. For example, guarantees provided to BOSs or minimum revenue guarantees under public-private partnerships could be activated under pressure from climate physical and climate transition risks. These events would lower the credit rating of BOSs and further tighten their lending conditions.

Disaster-related contingent liabilities could pose a significant risk to public finance frameworks, not only reducing the fiscal space of the government to invest in adaptation but also jeopardizing its debt sustainability as pending contingent liabilities increase the risk of default.

Thus, taking the lead in the transition to decarbonization and adaptation of state-owned enterprise holdings (and other state assets) should strengthen investor confidence, leading to a reduction in prevailing interest rates and facilitating a crowding in of private sector investment.

Sources: Baum et al. 2020; Dunz and Power 2021; Gamper et al. 2017; Kling et al. 2021.

Difficulties in Mobilizing Climate Finance Action for BOSs

Outside Australia, Europe, and the United States, only 36 percent of climate finance comes from the private sector—in Sub-Saharan Africa, only 12 percent comes from the private sector, with the remaining 88 percent coming from public sources. This points to the importance of mobilizing private funds for low- and middle-income countries (Boehm et al. 2021; CPI 2021; IEGCF 2020). Private climate finance—and having fair and transparent competition rules and market structures—can attract private investors.

Global climate finance—that is, mitigation and adaptation finance together—almost doubled in the last decade, with a cumulative US$4.8 trillion in climate finance committed over 2011–20, or US$480 billion a year, on average, during this time. Climate finance reached US$632 billion on a 2019/20 biennial average and is expected to continue to grow.[5] Despite a cumulative average annual growth rate of 7 percent over the last 10 years, climate finance is not increasing enough to meet a 1.5°C global warming scenario, which would require climate investment to increase at least seven times by the end of this decade as well as to align all other financial flows with Paris Agreement objectives. Three-quarters (75 percent) of climate finance was concentrated in East Asia and Pacific (led primarily by China), North America, and Western Europe, with very limited finance reaching low- and middle-income countries. Voluntary actions and domestic policies to reduce emissions in East Asia and Pacifc, North America, and Western Europe have provided a significant push for climate finance in those regions. For example, China has set mandatory targets to reduce its national energy intensity, which has contributed to an increase in investment in China's manufacturing capability in solar (Naran et al. 2022).

Adaptation finance is particularly underfunded, both in general and by BOSs. Finance for climate adaptation increased by 53 percent, from US$30 billion in 2017/18 to US$46 billion in 2019/20. Despite exhibiting a cumulative annual growth rate of 16.7 percent over the last 10 years, total adaptation finance remains far below the scale necessary to respond to existing and future climate change. The United Nations Environment Programme's *Adaptation Gap Report 2022* estimates that annual adaptation costs in low- and middle-income economies will be in the range of US$155 billion to US$330 billion by 2030 (UNEP 2022a, 2022b). Multilateral and national development finance institutions continued to deliver most of the public finance for adaptation (together 69 percent or US$31 billion of the US$46 billion total). BOS investments in adaptation are marginal, at only US$119 million globally (biennial average 2019/20) (box 5.2). Although this is a steep increase from US$11 million in 2019, it constitutes only 0.3 percent of global adaptation finance in 2019/20 and only 11 percent of what private corporations and investors invested in adaptation in 2019/20 (CPI 2021).

The weak financial capacity of many BOSs impairs their ability to engage in climate action. Large global leaders across the high-emitting sectors can also access more internal resources to support their investment in mitigation than the average BOS firm.

Why Firms Lag in Adaptation Investments

The general underinvestment in adaptation is surprising, given that the Global Commission on Adaptation found that the overall rate of return on investments in improved resilience is very high, with benefit-cost ratios ranging from 2:1 to 10:1. One reason adaptation still does not receive the attention it should is that most decisions do not internalize the impacts of climate change. Firms deciding whether to invest in climate adaptation should consider the many ways that climate puts expected outcomes at risk. Examples of such investments include fortification of their assets—for example, bridges or ports; utilities deciding whether to build a new power plant; agricultural producers deciding to switch to drought-resistant crops; or firms deciding to diversify their supply chain to buffer remote effects of climate change transmitted via supply chains. Research has identified several barriers to attracting the volume of private finance needed to advance most developing countries' adaptation agendas. They fall into three broad categories: (1) lack of country-level climate risk and vulnerability data and information services that can be used to guide investment decision-making; (2) limited clarity on the government's capital investment gaps to achieve adaptation goals, and/or on where private investment is needed; and (3) low perceived or actual returns on investment.

Sources: CPI 2021; Global Commission on Adaptation 2019, 2022; Li 2022; Tall et al. 2021.

Profits of companies are an important indicator as to whether they can afford to invest in climate action because part of a company's profits can usually be applied toward new equity investments or be used to service additional debt. However, average profits of global leaders are 29 to 185 times higher than those of the highest revenue-generating BOSs.[6] The average equity of global leaders (that is, assets in excess of external claims on assets, some of which may be available to serve as additional collateral) is 24 to 218 times higher than that of the top tier of BOSs.

Most BOSs are less creditworthy than their sector's revenue leaders and use state guarantees to boost their credit rating. If a BOS firm—for example, a utility—is creditworthy, it will be able to raise commercial finance; but BOSs tend to have low creditworthiness. Baseline credit assessments for 89 electricity BOSs in middle- and high-income countries show that 65 percent are rated as "investment grade" and 35 percent as "junk" (table 5.1).[7] This analysis likely overestimates the average credit rating of BOSs: ratings of electricity BOSs in low-income countries are likely even lower because most of them lack an international credit rating. If electricity BOSs lack a credit rating or have only a "junk" rating, below Baa3 or BBB−, they have very limited prospects to access capital markets. And, if they do have access, loan conditions and terms will be onerous, increasing their cost of capital and pushing future climate mitigation actions out of (financial) reach. In this sample, the credit ratings of 67 out of 89 BOSs were boosted by state guarantees, by an average of 1.85 notches. Without state support, BOSs might face challenges in accessing capital at affordable rates, delaying their climate mitigation and adaptation investments.

TABLE 5.1 Baseline Credit Assessments for 89 State-Owned Electricity Enterprises

Moody's rating	Long-term prospects	% of firms
Investment grade		
Aaa	Highest quality; lowest credit risk	1
Aa1/Aa2/Aa3	High quality; very low credit risk	0
A1/A2/A3	Upper-medium grade; low credit risk	11
Baa1/Baa2/Baa3	Medium grade; some speculative elements; moderate credit risk	53
Junk grade		
Ba1/Ba2/Ba3	Speculative elements; significant credit risk	25
B1/B2/B3	Speculative; high credit risk	8
Caa1	Poor quality; very high credit risk	2
Total		100

Sources: Adapted from Prag, Röttgers, and Scherrer 2018; Moody's.

Note: This compilation excludes many electricity businesses of the state—including in lower-income countries—that lack an international credit rating, any prospect of access to capital markets, or any significant capacity to invest in climate mitigation.

Climate Action, BOSs, and Market Reforms: Cement and Energy

Regulatory reforms are needed to accelerate private sector climate action in high-emitting sectors and to scale up climate finance in industries critical for the green transition. Governments have advantages in underwriting the scale of investments to advance the climate agenda, coordinating multiple actors around the common goal of decarbonization, and ensuring that the costs and benefits of a green transition are distributed equitably across society so that poverty is tackled alongside environmental crises. The state can also support R&D to develop and scale up new low-carbon technologies. But the presence of BOSs in competitive markets can deter private sector climate action, innovation, and technology adoption. In other markets, many BOSs are incumbents and benefit from a dominant market position, slowing the green transition and dampening private participation.

Cement

BOSs in competitive markets, and their implicit and explicit advantages, can undermine the green transition. When BOSs receive preferential treatment or dominate the market, they may deter private sector investors from engaging. BOSs can also weaken the productivity and competitiveness of the value chain when they are dominant market players upstream or downstream. These market distortions can lower the private sector's readiness to innovate and invest in low-carbon technologies. And regulatory restrictions on competition that benefit BOSs may limit the ability of proper market forces to reduce emissions by shifting market shares to "cleaner and more productive" market players.

The case of the cement industry shows how market regulation and anticompetitive behaviors can undermine the low-carbon transition. With its long and diverse supply chain, cement is central to the construction industry. With growing global population, increasing urbanization, and rapid infrastructure development in many emerging, low-income, and middle-income economies, the demand for cement is projected to grow between 12 percent and 23 percent by 2050 (IEA 2018).

Among all industries, cement is the second-highest emitter of greenhouse gas emissions. It emits about a quarter of industry's carbon dioxide (CO_2) emissions and between 5 percent and 8 percent of global CO_2 emissions (Andrew 2019; Czigler et al. 2020; Ellis et al. 2020; Lehne and Preston 2018). It generates the most emissions per revenue dollar, and its emissions intensity is highest among hard-to-abate industries, producing about 6.9 kilograms of CO_2 per revenue dollar, almost five times that of iron and steel and nine times that of oil and gas (Czigler et al. 2020). The cement industry is a hard-to-abate sector because most of its emissions are generated directly by the chemical production process.[8] A marginal abatement approach by trying to improve efficiency or similar measures will therefore not work, calling for more substantial investments in R&D to yield the required greenhouse gas emission reductions.

Global cement BOSs are among the key market players. The *Global Cement Report*, listing about 2,300 integrated and clinker grinding plants outside China, shows that BOSs (with a state holding of at least 10 percent) account for about 13 percent of all integrated and grinding cement plants (CemNet.com 2022) (see box 5.3). Larger shares of BOS plants are in the East Asia and Pacific and Middle East and North Africa regions and in middle-income countries. About 2 percent of the plants are owned either wholly or partly by foreign BOSs in various regions, particularly by Chinese and South African BOSs. Globally, BOSs are also among the key players in the cement market: 4 of the top 10 global cement producers by installed production capacity are BOSs, and BOSs among the top 110 cement producers in 2020/21 accounted for close to 40 percent of the installed production capacity of the top 110 producers and about 27 percent of installed production capacity of all cement producers (figure 5.6).[9]

BOSs tend to be less productive and to emit more CO_2 per revenue dollar than their private peers. Because of their weak financial health, they have limited ability to adopt climate mitigation technologies.[10] The top global cement BOSs are less productive and have lower profit margins than their private peers, but they have higher CO_2 emissions intensity than that of their private counterparts (figure 5.7).

The well-documented high concentration and dominance of large players in the cement industry are largely due to structural features. The cement industry in many economies is characterized by high levels of market concentration and relatively low competition (Kirchberger and Beirne 2021; World Bank 2016). In about 40 percent of countries, just one firm accounts for more than 50 percent of the country's total cement capacity (Kirchberger and Beirne 2021). The concentration is high mainly because of

BOX 5.3

State Presence in the Cement Industry in China

China is the main producer of cement, accounting for about 57 percent of global cement production in 2020. As in most countries, the industry is highly concentrated. The top 10 cement companies accounted for about 57 percent of the market in 2020 (FitchRatings 2021a).

Businesses of the state (BOSs) have a significant presence in China's cement industry, even after waves of market consolidation. In 2002, about 72.7 percent of the 4,626 cement firms were owned by national, provincial, and local governments (Ligthart 2003). In 2019, out of the 3,363 cement firms, the top five companies in clinker production capacity are BOSs, accounting for about 46 percent of the total clinker production capacity in China (Thomas 2021, supplemented with desk research).

BOSs in China are also significant emitters of carbon dioxide (CO_2). Of the 15 cement firms in the 2021 "China Listed Companies Carbon Emission Ranking" covering 100 high-carbon-emitting companies listed on A-shares and Hong Kong, China's stock exchanges, 10 are entities in which national and provincial governments hold ownership stakes of 10 percent or more, emitting 782 metric tons of CO_2 in 2020. Their emissions represented about 64 percent of the industry's CO_2 emissions and about 12.4 percent of China's total emissions in 2020. These top 10 high-carbon-emitting cement BOSs are also less productive,[a] and their average emissions intensity—CO_2 per revenue dollar—is twice that of average private non-Chinese counterparts (figure B5.3.1)

FIGURE B5.3.1   Performance of the Top 10 Non-Chinese Cement Privately Owned Enterprises and the Top 10 Chinese BOSs, 2020–21

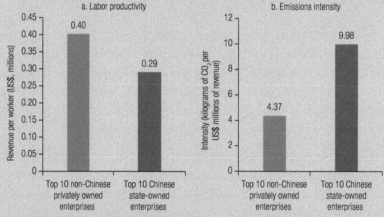

Source: Based on desk research (as of January 24, 2023).
Note: BOSs = businesses of the state; CO_2 = carbon dioxide.

a. This measure of productive efficiency (revenue per worker) has some shortcomings in general, but in the cement industry, it has the additional drawback that the price of cement is often distorted by regulation and anticompetitive practices.

FIGURE 5.6 **Share of Production and Capacity of BOSs in the Top 110 Global Cement Producers, by Installed Capacity and Ownership Level, 2020–21**

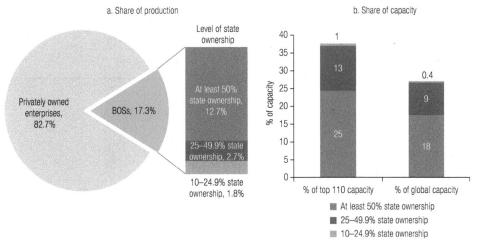

a. Share of production

b. Share of capacity

Sources: Calculations using data from company annual reports, financial statements, sustainability reports and websites, and CemNet.com 2022.

Note: BOSs = businesses of the state; SOEs = state-owned enterprises.

high barriers to market entry, high initial capital investments to reach sufficient economies of scale, spatial location due to high transportation and storage costs, and access to key raw materials and markets. The industry has vertically integrated supply chains and often a captive clientele. These structural features—in addition to the behavioral characteristics of the industry, such as multimarket contacts and the presence of influential producer associations—are also why the industry is susceptible to collusive conduct characterized by pervasive economic cartels.

Cement BOSs also benefit from regulations that limit their competition with privately owned incumbents. Regulatory restrictions on competition in the cement manufacturing industry appear to be related to the presence of BOSs in the industry. In 6 of the 10 countries currently covered by the data set, BOSs benefit from explicit advantages, such as involvement in policy making (Pakistan) and exemption from public procurement laws (Angola, Pakistan), as well as from implicit advantages, such as when entry into the manufacture of cement is allowed by official initiatives only (Argentina).[11] Cement prices are regulated in Ethiopia, and foreign direct investment is restricted in Angola. In Angola, cement BOSs are involved in regulating entry, and they benefit from regulations that limit their competition with privately owned incumbents. In some of these countries, BOSs are dominant market players (controlling about 40 percent of production capacity in Viet Nam and 30 percent in Angola).

FIGURE 5.7 Performance of Privately Owned Enterprises Relative to BOSs among the Top 110 Global Cement Producers, by Installed Production Capacity, 2021

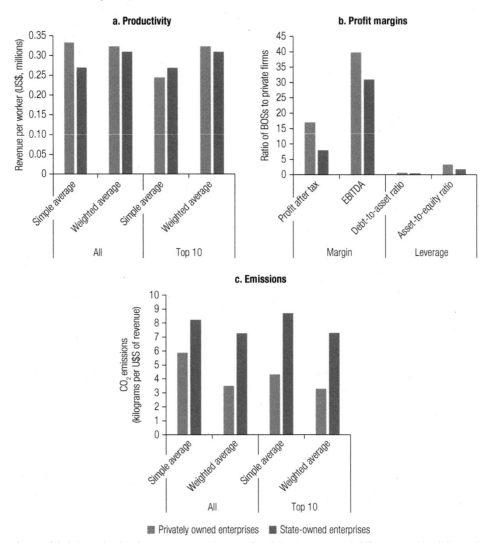

Sources: Calculations using data from company annual reports, financial statements, sustainability reports and websites, and CemNet.com 2022.

Note: Data include scope 1 and scope 2 carbon dioxide (CO$_2$) emissions. BOSs = businesses of the state; EBITDA = earnings before interest, taxes, depreciation, and amortization.

The market power of cement producers can influence their response to climate mitigation actions. Cement prices in Sub-Saharan Africa tend to be significantly higher than in other regions (Kirchberger and Beirne 2021; World Bank 2016). Although higher profits may enable firms to afford climate-mitigating technologies, inefficient and less innovative producers can remain in operation, thus limiting the

The Business of the State

creation and adoption of innovative solutions for climate actions (box 5.4). Cartels have been linked with deteriorating allocative, productive, and dynamic efficiency (Günster, Carree, and van Dijk 2012). Although quantity-restricting cartels could tame production and contribute to climate goals in carbon-intensive industries, such as cement, the main goal of all economic cartels is higher profits. Thus, the market share rules of cement cartels can induce "overproduction" because cartel members would find it more profitable to sell more in their local market, as in the case of the Norwegian cement industry cartel, which may harm climate abatement efforts (Röller and Steen 2006).

Energy

Government interventions in contestable and natural monopoly sectors can unlevel the playing field between BOSs and private operators and disincentivize private participation and climate action in these markets. Of 89 public utilities in Organisation for Economic Co-operation and Development countries, 67 obtained implicit or explicit state guarantees boosting their credit ratings and giving them a comparative advantage over private operators (Prag, Röttgers, and Scherrer 2018). In China, the share of solar power plants invested in and held by the private sector plummeted from more than 70 percent of total capacity in 2018 to less than 40 percent by the end of 2019, a result of the decision to phase out subsidies for solar photovoltaic (World Bank 2022b).

Government fossil fuel support remains a barrier to achieving global climate goals. Globally, fossil fuel subsidies amounted to about US$5.9 trillion (6.8 percent of gross domestic product) in 2020 and are expected to increase to 7.4 percent of gross domestic product in 2025 as the share of fuel consumption in emerging markets (where price

---

BOX 5.4

Climate Action and Anticompetitive Behavior in Competitive Markets

Although cartels generally involve agreements to fix prices and markets, they also may involve agreements to delay the adoption of green technology. For instance, the European Commission in July 2021 fined five automakers—BMW, Daimler, and Volkswagen group (Audi, Porsche, and Volkswagen)—for breaching its antitrust rules by limiting competition in emissions cleaning for new diesel passenger cars, although they had superior cleaning technology. For hard-to-abate sectors, it may be more effective to achieve sustainability goals if competition laws allow for legitimate collaborations among competitors on green initiatives (OECD 2020). However, regulators must be watchful of "cartel greenwashing" under sustainability initiatives. For example, the European Union Consumer Detergents cartel engaged in price fixing and market sharing when implementing an initiative via its trade association to improve the environmental performance of detergent products (European Commission 2011).

gaps are generally larger) continues to climb (Damania et al. 2023; Parry, Black, and Vernon 2021). Moreover, global fossil fuel subsidies in 2020 alone were 23 percent higher than the total global investment in climate finance during 2011–20. Immediate action to remove dependence on fossil fuel, including subsidies, would free up resources for more sustainable investments, create much-needed fiscal space, improve incentives for investments in renewable energy, result in environmental benefits (including reduced greenhouse gas emissions), and lead to eventual stability in energy sources (Black et al. 2023; CPI 2022).

Governments also intervene in the energy sector through BOSs, which are important investors in high-carbon fossil fuel technologies. The BOS share of energy investment in global energy investment was 36 percent in 2019, down from nearly 40 percent in 2015 (figure 5.8, panel a). However, BOSs still play an outsized role in low- and middle-income countries, accounting for about 60 percent of energy investment (figure 5.8, panel b), a much higher percentage compared with 10 percent in high-income economies. BOSs invest substantially in fossil fuel power generation. Half of their investments in energy were in fossil fuel generation in 2019, up from 43 percent in 2015.

In some instances, BOSs have encouraged renewable energy investment in high-income economies such as Sweden and Switzerland (Prag, Röttgers, and Scherrer 2018).[12] The energy sector offers commercially feasible low-carbon solutions, regardless of ownership structure. Such investments may reflect the purposeful use of BOSs by governments in these economies to promote a "green agenda" and the possibility of preferential access by BOSs to finance, especially for risky and long-term renewable energy projects (Prag, Röttgers, and Scherrer 2018). A regression analysis of 46 Organisation for Economic Co-operation and Development and other G-20 firms during 2000–14 shows a statistically significant positive relationship between state ownership of electricity generation and renewable energy investment (Prag, Röttgers,

FIGURE 5.8 **Share of Investments by BOSs in the Energy Sector**

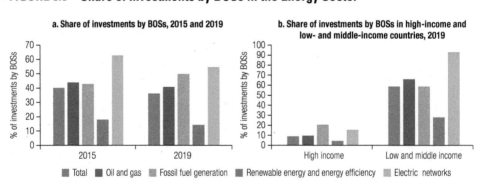

Source: Elaborated using International Energy Agency data (https://www.iea.org/data-and-statistics/data-sets).
Note: BOSs = businesses of the state.

The Business of the State

and Scherrer 2018). However, higher market concentration is found to hamper investment in renewable energy.

Across the world, the private sector has been the major driver of investment in renewable energy generation, in particular initially, when small-scale solar and on-shore wind offered investment opportunities that were attractive for private investors because of their modular design, limited complexity, and smaller scale. The private sector has contributed about 40 percent of new generation capacity in low- and middle-income countries since 1990. Until 2010, coal was the dominant technology for the private energy generation projects of independent power producers, but renewable energy sources have since increased (figure 5.9). About 68 percent of total wind capacity and 78 percent of solar capacity added during 1990–2016 were funded by the private sector, compared to 45 percent of thermal capacity.

Continuing emphasis on fossil fuel (especially coal) electricity may reflect the desire of governments to maintain the value of sunk-cost investments, leading to so-called carbon lock-in. Firms with many carbon-intensive thermal power assets, regardless of ownership, have a commercial incentive to avoid investing in renewable generating capacity—and potentially to oppose policy support or even shun renewable energy investment. The more fossil fuel power plants a company owns and the higher their combined net present value, the more it stands to lose from energy policies that support and promote the market entry of producers of renewable electricity. Incumbent energy generators in fossil fuel—many of them BOSs—oppose such policies in an effort to protect the value of their assets (Prag, Röttgers, and Scherrer 2021). South Africa initially attracted private investors to renewables;

FIGURE 5.9 **Public and Private Investments in the Energy Sector, by Type of Energy Generation, 1990–2016**

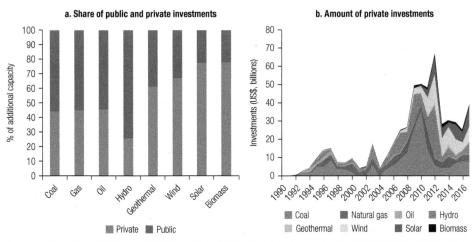

Sources: Foster and Rana 2019; based on World Bank Private Participation in Infrastructure database, 2017; Utility Data Institute World Electric Power Plants database, 2017.

however, because of obstructions by the state-owned utility, the renewable energy agenda was not as successful as it could have been (box 5.5). Episodes of policy reversals in the renewable energy sector have occurred in Mexico as well.

Employment in fossil fuel power generation is another reason for the continued engagement of BOSs in this sector. Several economies with participation of BOSs in high-emitting sectors have high investment in coal mining, and an early decommissioning of coal plants can have major adverse impacts on jobs and poverty, particularly in poor coal-dependent communities (box 5.6). The total number of workers currently engaged in the coal mining sector is 4.7 million globally. The economies with the largest

BOX 5.5

Businesses of the State and Private Investment in Renewable Energy Generation: The Cases of Mexico and South Africa

Mexico's first three clean energy auctions, held in 2016–17, were seen as an unqualified success, bringing major new solar and wind developers into the market and delivering stunningly low prices as much as 29 percent below previous prices for solar and 35 percent for wind (IRENA 2017). The changes were intended to benefit the Federal Electricity Commission (CFE), Mexico's fossil fuel–dependent state-owned electric utility, by prioritizing CFE at the expense of private power contracts and permits. The amendments would modify dispatch rules to benefit power plants owned by CFE. Power produced by CFE plants (including thermal plants) would be fed into the power grid first, displacing lower-cost renewable energy from private producers. Under the proposed changes, CFE would no longer be required to purchase energy for basic supply via auctions. Instead, it would be able to buy from its own power plants, even if the energy generated was more expensive. The amendment would also require the revision and potential termination of certain power purchase agreements. Existing power purchase agreements between CFE and independent power producers would be reviewed and could potentially be terminated or renegotiated. These new provisions and regulations will possibly reduce new private generation projects in Mexico.

South Africa successfully implemented well-designed renewable energy competitive tenders, but incumbent energy businesses of the state obstructed efforts to allow grid access to low-cost, low-carbon renewable energy. Under the Renewable Energy Independent Power Producer Procurement Program, South Africa carried out four rounds of competitive bidding between 2011 and 2015 to facilitate private investment in grid-connected renewable energy generation. Competition was fierce, with more than 300 submissions, resulting in significant price drops from US\$345/MWh in 2011 (IRENA 2017) to US\$64/MWh in 2015 (Eberhard and Kåberger 2016). Projects awarded under the latest bidding round indicate that both solar photovoltaic energy and wind energy are now 40–50 percent cheaper than energy from Eskom's new coal-fired plants (Montrone, Ohlendorf, and Chandra 2022). In 2015, they were also among the lowest-priced grid-connected renewable energy projects in the world. To ensure that these lost costs are passed through to the consumer, an intergovernmental framework agreement was signed. But Eskom reportedly refused to sign the winning bidders' purchase agreement. This obstruction of government policy is fueling calls for Eskom to be restructured, with various parties arguing that the utility's conflict of interest is due to its vertically integrated model and that its obstructive behavior threatens the survival of the independent power producer program in South Africa.

Poland's Coal Mining Reforms and Jobs

In Poland, the reduction in coal mining jobs from about 260,000 in 1990 to 110,000 at present "generated persistent economic challenges in mining communities," including about 40 percent long-term unemployment and even higher unemployment among workers above the age of 45 (Ruppert Bulmer et al. 2021, 68). Separation assistance for redundant Polish miners during 1998–2002 amounted to 0.75 percent of gross domestic product (Ruppert Bulmer et al. 2021). In response to these declines, policies have been implemented to restructure the mining industry, for example, through SRK, the Mine Restructuring Company, to bolster the competitiveness of the sector, and to reduce unemployment among former coal workers. These policies to address the social and economic consequences of mine closures include early retirement, and dedicated welfare allowances, paired with one-time bonuses for workers who found a new job or through special allowances that enabled mines to cover the mining companies' expenditures associated with pension payments to former employees (Śniegocki et al. 2022).

numbers of employment in coal mining include China (3.2 million jobs), India (416,000), Indonesia (240,000), the Russian Federation (150,000), Poland (110,000), and South Africa, Ukraine, and Viet Nam, each with about 75,000–110,000 coal mining jobs, excluding employment in the sector value chain beyond mining (Ruppert Bulmer et al. 2021; Springer, Shi, and Kudrimoti 2022). Even if the power generation is not state dominated, heavy investment in thermal generation may sustain an extensive fossil fuel supply chain that is state dominated, extensive, and resistant to downsizing. For example, although electricity generation in India is only 16 percent state owned, this activity is at the nexus of important state-owned monopolies.[13] In Indonesia, where about three-quarters of coal production is purchased by the wholly state-owned electricity company (PLN), which owns 73 percent of installed generation capacity (FitchRatings 2021b), coal pays more than most other sectors, and coal jobs are highly concentrated in two regions. In South Africa, the wholly state-owned monopoly electricity company (Eskom) relies on coal, whose production provides jobs (Ruppert Bulmer et al. 2021).[14]

Over the last decade, 2.4 million coal mining jobs have been lost worldwide in net terms, reflecting coal phase-out in some countries, expansion in others, and sector productivity gains in most. Countries that have transitioned away from coal production—so-called advanced transitioners—experienced coal mining job losses long before the recent contraction in the last decade. Looking back to the 1980s, coal mining employment was over 416,000 in Poland, 365,000 in Germany, and 172,000 in the United Kingdom; in these countries, governments took phase-out measures to close mines, which translated into lower employment numbers. Today, the United Kingdom employs fewer than 1,000 workers in the sector, Germany's coal mining employment is under 15,000, and in Poland, where mining activities are ongoing, total coal mining employment is about 93,000. Given the importance of coal mining in many countries and potential job losses induced by an energy transition away from coal, it is of crucial importance for governments to develop clear road maps to phase out coal and protect workers, their families, communities, and the environment. It is equally important for government to also support investments in energy efficiency and low-carbon, renewable energy.

In addition to introducing some sort of carbon pricing mechanism, to decarbonize the energy sector many countries will have to liberalize markets, pursue ambitious BOS reforms, and create level playing fields between private and state-owned actors. Enabling a shift toward increased investment in renewables implies allowing third parties to access the transmission and distribution networks often owned and controlled by state-owned utilities. Such access needs to be granted at regulated tariffs so that private investors in renewables can sell directly to eligible customers without discrimination. Doing so will lead to the creation of open wholesale and balancing markets that will make investment market driven, not government driven. It will require adjusting the market structure, unbundling state-owned utilities, and establishing an independent regulator.

Annex 5A Fossil Fuel Power Systems in Select Low- and Middle-Income Countries

SOEs are dominant in fossil fuel power generation, largely because of their strong involvement in coal generation. Data for a few countries with a large share of fossil fuel generation confirm that technology is a key driver of ownership. With 70 percent of installed capacity, SOEs are dominant in fossil fuel power generation. They are even more dominant in coal-fueled power plants, where they account for 84 percent of total installed capacity. Even more striking is their dominance in hydro and nuclear power, where their role grows to 94 percent (Vagliasindi 2023). By contrast, the private sector owns about 80 percent of the nonconventional installed capacity of renewable energy.

In countries dominated by coal production, such as Poland and South Africa, SOEs have contributed the bulk of installed capacity in fossil fuel power generation (figure 5A.1). The private sector portfolio is more balanced toward a combination of fossil fuel and renewable energy in Poland and is almost exclusively clean in South Africa. In Pakistan and Türkiye, SOEs hold a higher share of installed generation capacity in renewable energy (hydropower) than the private sector, which generates power largely from fossil fuels in both countries.

The potential competitive issues reported in this chapter may be due to the much larger size and dominance of the electricity incumbent in the market (figure 5A.2). For instance, in South Africa, the vertically integrated power company Eskom dominates the power market with a 90 percent market share. In Pakistan, the Pakistan Water and Power Development Authority is a government-owned public utility with a market share close to 40 percent, although it does not manage thermal power. In Türkiye, the state-owned Electricity Generation Inc. (EÜAŞ), despite having a much lower 20 percent market share,

Installed Generation Capacity in Select Countries, by Fuel and Ownership, 2021

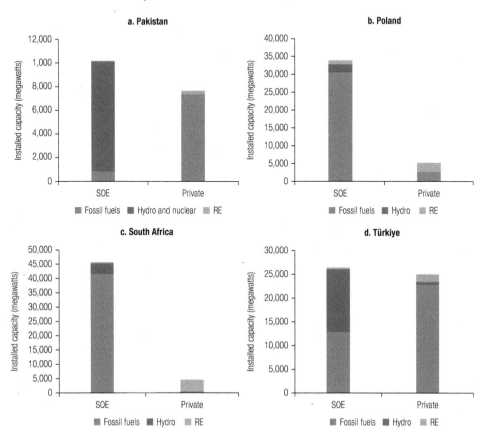

Source: Preliminary estimates provided by Vagliasindi 2023, based on World Resources Institute Global Power Plant database.
Note: RE = renewable energy; SOE = state-owned enterprise.

FIGURE 5A.2 **Market Share Held by the Electricity Incumbent in Select Countries, 2021**

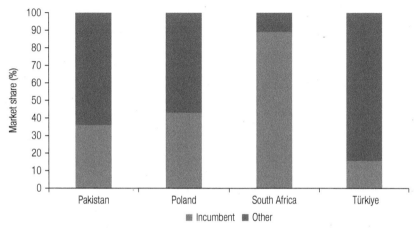

Source: Preliminary estimates provided by Vagliasindi 2023, based on World Resources Institute Global Power Plant database.

still ranks first in terms of production capacity. In Poland, four companies control most of the electric power market: Polska Grupa Energetyczna (PGE)—Tauron Polska Energia, Energa, and Enea—holds a market share of 40 percent. Poland's transmission grid is owned and operated by state-owned Polskie Sieci Elektroenergetyczne (PSE). In October 2020, PGE published a new strategy by 2030 and a transformation plan aimed at achieving climate neutrality of the group in 2050. The key directions of PGE's development will be offshore and onshore wind energy, photovoltaics, grid infrastructure, and low-emission heating and energy services. The area of divestment and limitation of activity will include coal energy and hard coal trade.

Notes

1. High-emitting sectors were identified using the World Greenhouse Gas Emissions in 2019 by sector and converted into Statistical Classification of Economic Activities in the European Community (NACE) code. This research was also supported by relevant literature. Some of the sources used include Climate Watch (2023); Ge, Friedrich, and Vigna (2020); Ritchie (2020); and Ritchie, Roser, and Rosado (2020).

2. The high-emitting sectors in which BOSs are located include extraction of crude petroleum; extraction of natural gas; growing of rice; raising of dairy cattle; raising of other cattle and buffaloes; raising of swine or pigs; raising of poultry; logging; manufacture of pulp; manufacture of paper and paperboard; manufacture of corrugated paper, paperboard, and containers of paper and paperboard; manufacture of household and sanitary goods and of toilet requisites; manufacture of paper stationery; manufacture of wallpaper; manufacture of other articles of paper and paperboard; manufacture of coke oven products; manufacture of refined petroleum products; manufacture of other inorganic basic chemicals; manufacture of other organic basic chemicals; manufacture of fertilizers and nitrogen compounds; manufacture of plastics in primary forms; manufacture of synthetic rubber in primary forms; manufacture of cement; manufacture of basic iron and steel and of ferro-alloys; manufacture of tubes, pipes, hollow profiles, and related fittings of steel; aluminum production; casting of iron; casting of steel; production of electricity; manufacture of gas; passenger rail transportation; interurban, freight rail transportation; urban and suburban passenger land transportation; taxi operation; other passenger land transportation; freight transportation by road; sea and coastal passenger water transportation; sea and coastal freight water transportation; inland passenger water transportation; inland freight water transportation; passenger air transportation; and freight air transportation.

3. The sectors prone to the negative effects of climate change were identified using the risk classification by sectors and converted into NACE code. The risk classification was corroborated with results from the literature, including Arent et al. (2014); Baum et al. (2020), Benoit (2019a, 2019b); Cho (2019); Dunz and Power (2021); EPA (n.d.); Kling et al. (2021); and Richmond et al. (2021).

4. The World Bank Group and the International Monetary Fund work with low-income countries to produce regular debt sustainability analyses, which are structured examinations of low- and middle-income-country debt based on the Debt Sustainability Framework. The data are sourced from https://www.worldbank.org/en/programs/debt-toolkit/dsa#:~:text=The%20World%20Bank%20Group%20and,on%20the%20Debt%20Sustainability%20Framework.

5. Based on currently available information, Climate Policy Initiative estimates suggest that the 2021 flow of climate finance amounted to between US$850 billion and US$940 billion, representing a 28 percent to 42 percent increase from 2019/20 averages, reaching an all-time high (CPI 2021).

6. Based on a comparison of 31 revenue leaders in electricity, oil and gas, iron and steel, and cement, including 8 with substantial state ownership (such as Baowu Steel, CNBM, Électricité de France, KEPCO, and Saudi Aramco), with 491 BOSs in these sectors from 27 emerging market or low- and middle-income economies.

7. A stand-alone benefit-cost analysis provides a comprehensive assessment of an enterprise's ability to service debt using its own balance sheet resources, without recourse to *additional* government or other external assistance. The benefit-cost analyses in this compilation already take regular *ongoing subsidies* from the government into account.

8. In the cement industry, 60 percent of the CO_2 emissions are due to the underlying chemical process (calcination) and cannot be abated, unless cement is replaced by other construction material (laminated wood). Of the remaining 40 percent of emissions, about 10 percent can be abated by improving energy efficiency and a further 10 percent can be abated by burning waste (plastics). The cement sector's main abatement potential would be realized through new technologies, cement substitutes, circular economy business models, and carbon capture (Czigler et al. 2020).

   Generally, the cement sector is considered a hard-to-abate sector. The consensus that efficiency improvements may only generate up to 10–20 percent abatement suggests that significant carbon reductions may only come from substantial investment in R&D. Even among the top 10 global cement producers, which are in a better position to undertake such investments, their sustainability strategies suggest that their emission mitigation efforts mostly involve tinkering at the margin, such as improving energy efficiency, although some strategies involve structural innovation (such as developing alternative raw materials to reduce the rate of clinker incorporation, developing alternative fuel sources including biomass, and investing in carbon capture R&D). Among the top 10, these mitigation strategies seem to be common among both privately owned firms and BOSs.

9. The top 110 global cement producers by installed production capacity are headquartered in 47 countries; together, they account for 72 percent of global capacity. Out of the top 110, 19 firms are BOSs from 14 countries and 4 of the top 10 are BOSs.

10. Even among the top 110 global cement producers for which a concerted effort was made to obtain actual emissions data, a sizable number of the top companies do not disclose their emissions levels in sustainability or annual reports. Stronger and more concerted efforts are required to collect and analyze greenhouse gas emissions data to understand better how market and ownership structures affect the climate agenda.

11. The 10 countries covered are Argentina, Angola, Ethiopia, Nepal, Pakistan, Peru, the Philippines, Serbia, Türkiye, and Viet Nam.

12. Between 2000 and 2014, unlisted SOEs and governments increased their yearly capacity additions of renewables (excluding large hydro and nuclear) from 0.63 gigawatt to almost 34 gigawatts, boosting their share in the market for new renewables from 9 percent to 23 percent (Prag, Röttgers, and Scherrer 2018).

13. For example, although India now gets 74 percent of its electricity from coal-fired plants, only 16 percent of electricity generation capacity is state owned. But coal is mined by a quasi-monopolist "public sector undertaking"—Coal India Limited—and transported via railways managed by the Ministry of Railways and operated by the Indian Railways, a public sector undertaking. Bharat Heavy Electricals Limited, an engineering and manufacturing public sector undertaking under the Ministry of Heavy Industries, manufactures products for the power sector, such as turbines and boilers for thermal power plants and transmission lines (Montrone, Ohlendorf, and Chandra 2022).

14. In the province that provides 93 percent of coal jobs, coal jobs represent 11–26 percent of employment in four municipalities. Compared with national averages, coal jobs are more likely to provide protections, a pension, and unionization.

References

Andrew, R. 2019. "Global CO$_2$ Emissions from Cement Production, 1928–2018." *Earth System Science Data* 11 (4): 1675–710.

Arent, D. J., R. S. J. Tol, E. Faust, J. P. Hella, S. Kumar, K. M. Strzepek, F. L. Tóth, and D. Yan. 2014. "Key Economic Sectors and Services." In *Climate Change 2014: Impacts, Adaptation, and Vulnerability. Part A: Global and Sectoral Aspects. Contribution of Working Group II to the Fifth Assessment Report of the Intergovernmental Panel on Climate Change.* Cambridge, UK: Cambridge University Press.

Baum, A., P. Medas, A. Soler, and M. Sy. 2020. "Managing Fiscal Risks from State-Owned Enterprises." IMF Working Paper 2020/213, International Monetary Fund, Washington, DC.

Benoit, P. 2019a. "Engaging State-Owned Enterprises in Climate Action." Center on Global Energy Policy, Columbia University, New York. https://www.energypolicy.columbia.edu/research/report/engaging -state-owned-enterprises-climate-action#_ednref68.

Benoit, P. 2019b. "State-Owned Enterprises." *Journal of International Affairs* 73 (1): 135–44.

Benoit, P., A. Clark, M. Schwarz, and A. Dibley. 2022. "Decarbonization in State-Owned Power Companies: Lessons from a Comparative Analysis." *Journal of Cleaner Production* 355 (June 25): 131796.

Black, S., A. Liu, I. Parry, and N. Vernon. 2023. "IMF Fossil Fuel Subsidies Data: 2023 Update." Working paper 2023/169, International Monetary Fund, Washington, DC.

Boehm, S., K. Lebling, K. Levin, H. Fekete, J. Jaeger, R. Waite, A. Nilsson, J. Thwaites, R. Wilson, A. Geiges, C. Schumer, M. Dennis, K. Ross, S. Castellanos, R. Shrestha, N. Singh, M. Weisse, L. Lazer, L. Jeffery, L. Freehafer, E. Gray, L. Zhou, M. Gidden, and M. Gavin. 2021. *State of Climate Action 2021: Systems Transformations Required to Limit Global Warming to 1.5°C.* Washington, DC: World Resources Institute.

CemNet.com. 2022. *The Global Cement Report*, 14th ed. Dorking, UK: Tradeship Publications. https:// www.cemnet.com/Publications/Item/187049/the-global-cement-report-14th-edition.html.

Cho, R. 2019. "How Climate Change Impacts the Economy." *State of the Planet* (blog), June 20, 2019. https://news.climate.columbia.edu/2019/06/20/climate-change-economy-impacts/.

Climate Watch. 2023. "World Greenhouse Gas Emissions in 2019 by Sector, End Use and Gases (static)." *Climate Watch,* June 2023. https://www.climatewatchdata.org/key-visualizations?visual ization=3.

CPI (Climate Policy Initiative). 2021. "Global Landscape of Climate Finance 2021." CPI, San Francisco. https://www.climatepolicyinitiative.org/wp-content/uploads/2021/10/Full-report-Global -Landscape-of-Climate-Finance-2021.pdf.

CPI (Climate Policy Initiative). 2022. "Global Landscape of Climate Finance. A Decade of Data: 2011–2020." CPI, San Francisco. https://www.climatepolicyinitiative.org/wp-content/uploads /2022/10/Global-Landscape-of-Climate-Finance-A-Decade-of-Data.pdf.

Czigler, T., S. Reiter, P. Schulze, and K. Somers. 2020. "Laying the Foundation for Zero-Carbon Cement." McKinsey & Company, Chemicals Practice, New York, May 2020.

Dall'Olio, A. M., T. K. Goodwin, M. Martinez Licetti, A. C. Alonso Soria, M. A. Drozd, J. A. K. Orlowski, F. A. Patiño Peña, and D. Sanchez Navarro. 2022. "Are All State-Owned Enterprises Equal? A Taxonomy of Economic Activities to Assess SOE Presence in the Economy." Policy Research Working Paper 10262, World Bank, Washington, DC.

Damania, R., E. Balseca, C. de Fontaubert, J. Gill, K. Kim, J. Rentschler, J. Russ, and E. Zaveri. 2023. *Detox Development: Repurposing Environmentally Harmful Subsidies.* Washington, DC : World Bank.

Dunz, N., and S. Power. 2021. "Climate-Related Risks for Ministries of Finance: An Overview." Coalition of Finance Ministers for Climate Action, Washington, DC.

Eberhard, A., and T. Kåberger. 2016. "Renewable Energy Auctions in South Africa Outshine Feed-In Tariffs." *Energy Science & Engineering* 4 (3): 190–93.

Ellis, L. D., A. F. Badel, M. L. Chiang, R. J.-Y. Park, and Y.-M. Chiang. 2020. "Toward Electrochemical Synthesis of Cement: An Electrolyzer-Based Process for Decarbonating $CaCO_3$ while Producing Useful Gas Streams." *Proceedings of the National Academy of Sciences* 117 (23): 12584–91. https://pubmed.ncbi.nlm.nih.gov/31527245/.

EPA (Environmental Protection Agency). n.d. "Climate Impacts." EPA, Washington, DC. https://www.epa.gov/climateimpacts.

European Commission. 2011. "Antitrust: Commission Fines Producers of Washing Powder €315.2 Million in Cartel Settlement Case." Press release IP/11/473, European Commission, Brussels, April 13, 2011.

FitchRatings. 2021a. "Chinese Coal, Steel, and Cement Firms to See Further Consolidation." FitchRatings, September 16, 2021. https://www.fitchratings.com/research/corporate-finance/chinese-coal-steel-cement-firms-to-see-further-consolidation-16-09-2021.

FitchRatings. 2021b. "Fitch Affirms Indonesia's PLN at 'BBB'; Outlook Stable." FitchRatings, August 12, 2021. https://www.fitchratings.com/research/corporate-finance/fitch-affirms-indonesia-pln-at-bbb-outlook-stable-12-08-2021#:~:text=Issuer%20Profile,portion%20amounts%20to%2045.9GW.

Foster, V., and A. Rana. 2019. *Rethinking Power Sector Reforms in the Developing World.* Washington, DC: World Bank.

Gamper, C., B. Signer, L. Alton, and M. Petrie. 2017. "Managing Disaster-Related Contingent Liabilities in Public Finance Frameworks." OECD Working Paper on Public Governance 27, OECD Publishing, Paris.

Ge, M., J. Friedrich, and L. Vigna. 2020. "4 Charts Explain Greenhouse Gas Emissions by Countries and Sectors." World Resources Institute, February 6, 2020. https://www.wri.org/insights/4-charts-explain-greenhouse-gas-emissions-countries-and-sectors#:~:text=The%20Energy%20Sector%20Produces%20the%20Most%20Greenhouse%20Gas%20Emissions&text=The%20energy%20sector%20includes%20transportation,emissions%20and%20other%20fuel%20combustion.

Global Commission on Adaptation. 2019. *Adapt Now: A Global Call for Leadership on Climate Resilience.* Washington, DC: Global Center on Adaptation / World Resource Institute.

Global Commission on Adaptation. 2022. *State and Trends in Adaptation Report 2022.* Washington, DC: Global Center on Adaptation / World Resource Institute.

Günster, A., M. Carree, and M. A. van Dijk. 2012. "Do Cartels Undermine Economic Efficiency?" Paper prepared for the American Economic Association 2012 Annual Meeting, Acapulco, January 8, 2012.

IEA (International Energy Agency). 2018. "Cement Technology Roadmap Plots Path to Cutting CO_2 Emissions 24% by 2050." *IEA News*, April 6, 2018. https://www.iea.org/news/cement-technology-roadmap-plots-path-to-cutting-co2-emissions-24-by-2050.

IEGCF (Independent Expert Group on Climate Finance). 2020. *Delivering on the $100 Billion Climate Finance Commitment and Transforming Climate Finance.* Report for the UN Secretary-General. New York: IEGCF.

IRENA (International Renewable Energy Agency). 2017. *Renewable Energy Auctions: Analysing 2016.* Abu Dhabi: IRENA.

Isungset, E. 2022. "State Ownership and Climate Change: Can State Ownership of the Economy Reduce Greenhouse Gas Emissions? A Quantitative Study." Norwegian University of Science and Technology, Faculty of Social and Educational Sciences, Department of Sociology and Political Science, Trondheim.

Kirchberger, M., and K. Beirne. 2021. "Concrete Thinking about Development." Trinity Economics Paper 0621, Trinity College Dublin, Department of Economics, Dublin.

Kling, G., U. Volz, V. Murinde, and S. Ayas. 2021. "The Impact of Climate Vulnerability on Firms' Cost of Capital and Access to Finance." *World Development* 137 (January): 105–31.

Lehne, J., and F. Preston. 2018. *Making Concrete Change Innovation in Low-Carbon Cement and Concrete.* Chatham House Report. London: Royal Institute of International Affairs.

Li, Xia. 2022. "Physical Climate Risk and Firms' Adaptation Strategy." Questrom School of Business, Boston University, Boston, MA.

Ligthart, A. 2003. "The Cement Industry in China: Present Structure Restructuring Program Opportunities." Cement Distribution Consultants, Presentation for the Intercem Workshop "Today's Challenges: Tomorrow's Opportunities," London, June 25, 2003. https://cementdistribution.com/wp-content/uploads/2016/10/cement_industry_in_china.pdf.

Montrone, L., N. Ohlendorf, and R. Chandra. 2022. "The Political Economy of Coal in India." In *The Political Economy of Coal: Obstacles to Clean Energy Transitions*, edited by M. Jakob and J. C. Steckel, 137–39. London: Routledge.

Naran, B., J. Connolly, P. Rosane, D. Wignarajah, E. Wakaba, and B. Buchner. 2022. "Global Landscape of Climate Finance: A Decade of Data 2011–2020." Climate Policy Initiative, San Francisco.

OECD (Organisation for Economic Co-operation and Development). 2020. "Executive Summary of the Hearing on Sustainability and Competition." Annex to the Summary Record of the 134th Meeting of Competition Committee held on December 1–3, 2020. M(2020)2/ANN2/FINAL. Directorate for Financial and Enterprise Affairs Competition Committee. OECD, Paris. https://one.oecd.org/document/DAF/COMP/M(2020)2/ANN2/FINAL/en/pdf.

OECD (Organisation for Economic Co-operation and Development). 2022. *Climate Finance Provided and Mobilised by Developed Countries in 2016–2020: Insights from Disaggregated Analysis.* Paris: OECD Publishing.

Parry, I., S. Black, and N. Vernon. 2021. *Still Not Getting Energy Prices Right: A Global and Country Update of Fossil Fuel Subsidies.* IMF Working Paper WP/21/236, International Monetary Fund, Washington, DC.

Prag, A., D. Röttgers, and I. Scherrer. 2018. "State-Owned Enterprises and the Low-Carbon Transition." OECD Environment Working Paper 129, OECD Publishing, Paris. http://dx.doi.org/10.1787/06ff826b-en.

Richmond, M., J. Choi, R. Padmanabhi, and A. Lonsdale. 2021. "Financial Innovation for Climate Adaptation in Africa." Global Center on Adaptation and Climate Policy Initiative, Rotterdam.

Ritchie, H. 2020. "Sector by Sector: Where Do Global Greenhouse Gas Emissions Come from?" *Our World in Data* (blog), September 18. https://ourworldindata.org/ghg-emissions-by-sector.

Ritchie, H., M. Roser, and P. Rosado. 2020. "CO₂ and Greenhouse Gas Emissions." *Our World in Data* (blog), August 2020. https://ourworldindata.org/co2-and-greenhouse-gas-emissions.

Röller, L.-H., and F. Steen. 2006. "On the Workings of a Cartel: Evidence from the Norwegian Cement Industry." *American Economic Review* 96 (1): 321–38.

Ruppert Bulmer, E. R., K. Pela, A. Eberhard-Ruiz, and J. Montoya. 2021. *Global Perspectives on Coal Jobs and Managing Transition Out of Coal.* Washington, DC: World Bank.

Śniegocki, A., M. Wasilewski, I. Zygmunt, and W. Look. 2022. "Just Transition in Poland: A Review of Public Policies to Assist Polish Coal Communities in Transition." Resources for the Future, Washington, DC. https://media.rff.org/documents/Report_22-06_June_1_2022.pdf.

Springer, C., D. Shi, and A. Kudrimoti. 2022. "The Political Economy of Coal: The Case of China." In *The Political Economy of Coal: Obstacles to Clean Energy Transitions*, edited by M. Jakob and J. C. Steckel, 117–35. London: Routledge.

Tall, A., S. Lynagh, C. Blanco Vecchi, P. Bardouille, F. Montoya Pino, E. Shabahat, V. Stenek, F. Stewart, S. Power, C. Paladines, P. Neves, and L. Kerr. 2021. "Enabling Private Investment in Climate Adaptation and Resilience: Current Status, Barriers to Investment and Blueprint for Action." World Bank, Washington, DC.

Talukdar, D., and C. Meisner. 2001. "Does the Private Sector Help or Hurt the Environment? Evidence from Carbon Dioxide Pollution in Developing Countries." *World Development* 29 (5): 827–40.

Thomas, E. 2021. "Fine China." *World Cement,* October 21. https://www.worldcement.com/asia -pacific-rim/05102021/fine-china/.

UNEP (United Nations Environment Programme). 2022a. *Adaptation Gap Report 2022: Too Little, Too Slow—Climate Adaptation Failure Puts World at Risk.* Nairobi: UNEP. https://www.unep.org /adaptation-gap-report-2022.

UNEP (United Nations Environment Programme). 2022b. *The Six-Sector Solution to the Climate Crisis. Based on Emissions Gap Report 2020.* Nairobi: UNEP, November 2022. https://www.unep .org/interactive/six-sector-solution-climate-change/.

Vagliasindi, M. 2023. "The Role of SOEs in Climate Change." Background paper for this report, World Bank, Washington, DC.

World Bank. 2016. *Breaking Down Barriers: Unlocking Africa's Potential through Vigorous Competition Policy.* Washington, DC: World Bank.

World Bank. 2021. *State and Trends of Carbon Pricing 2021.* Washington, DC: World Bank.

World Bank. 2022a. "Achieving Climate and Development Goals: The Financing Question." Development Committee, World Bank and International Monetary Fund, Washington, DC.

World Bank. 2022b. "China Country Climate and Development Report." World Bank, Washington, DC.

6. A Practitioner's Guide for When (Not) to Use BOSs

Introduction

New evidence generated for this report and findings from previous studies provide guidance to practitioners on whether and how (not) to rely on businesses of the state (BOSs) as tools for development policy. The objective here is to support policy makers in getting the most from BOSs and at the same time highlight potential risks and propose reform options to improve expected outcomes. This chapter offers principles and practical checks on how to proceed.[1]

State ownership of enterprises is part of the toolkit that governments use to correct market imperfections and institutional failures. But, as this report argues, the best policy response rarely requires mobilizing state ownership. Fiscal and regulatory policies can provide incentives to private firms so that they provide universal access to services or protect the environment. And, when confronted with macroeconomic fluctuations or crises, governments often find that fiscal policy and monetary policy are better suited for stabilizing an economy.

In reality, reliance on BOSs can create good, bad, or ugly outcomes, as illustrated with the following examples:

- *Good outcomes.* Some BOSs perform well. They effectively meet valid policy objectives, create markets, and innovate. BOSs with majority private ownership can provide market discipline that contributes to higher productivity.
- *Bad outcomes.* A bad outcome could be that some BOSs' good performance is driven by preferential treatment. This can enable them to meet their objectives but can be inefficient and costly and prevent crowding in private investment.
- *Ugly outcomes.* An ugly outcome—a worst-case scenario—can occur when some BOSs underperform and do not have a social mandate justifying state ownership. These entities may fail to fulfill their intended social objective, become a fiscal drain, engage in anticompetitive practices, or are heavily protected from competition. Such BOSs can inhibit innovation by private investors or suffer from political patronage and corruption.

Evidence in this report confirms that outcomes across markets can indeed be good, bad, and ugly, providing motivation to revisit policy approaches. The features that distinguish BOSs from private firms—the soft-budget constraint, the nonprofit objectives, and the favorable regulatory environment—affect those outcomes. And the way BOSs affect outcomes depends on how they interact with market imperfections and institutional failures in the rest of the economy. Because BOSs are unlikely to go away, it helps to clarify when relying on them can be viable.

Five Guiding Principles for Engagement with BOSs

The impact state participation in markets has on an economy is shaped by three factors: the type of public-private ownership characterizing BOSs, the structure of the markets they operate in, and the broader policies and institutions that regulate state ownership. Hence, when policy makers decide whether to rely on BOSs to attain specific development objectives, they should be guided by principles that bring to the surface the least visible parts and risks of the state's involvement in business at the country, sector, and enterprise levels.

This report proposes five principles for government engagement with BOSs:

1. Develop a nationwide mapping of BOSs under various line ministries and agencies and in different sectors, and monitor their performance and fiscal cost.
2. Apply the subsidiarity principle economywide, which calls for a limited role of the state if private firms are interested and capable of supplying goods and services that fulfill demand adequately.
3. Put in place strong institutions to regulate sectors and address the risk of capture by insiders.
4. Ensure competitive neutrality of regulations and policies and their enforcement, including labor regulations, the separation between commercial and noncommercial roles of BOSs, and implicit and explicit support to BOSs and privately owned firms.
5. Prepare phase-out strategies for BOSs that are no longer needed.

Principle 1: Ensure Transparency and Monitoring of the Entire State Footprint in the Economy

The first step is to gauge the true extent of the state's footprint. For example, uncovering indirect ownership stakes in other firms, across markets, and in value chains can unveil upstream and downstream relationships and vertical integration issues that can inhibit competition and create fiscal risks.

The transparency of BOSs fosters accountability and fiscal sustainability at the aggregate level, creates a level playing field at the sector level, and provides confidence to private investors. It is especially important in countries with a large state presence, with conglomerate groups whose operations are not easy to grasp, and with sovereign wealth funds.

The transparency of BOSs' operations requires timely and full disclosure of their financial reports. It is good practice to define and subsequently monitor the fulfillment of a BOS firm's immediate-term objectives and targets in relation to its main economic and, where relevant, public policy objectives. These mandates should be translated into financial, operational, and nonfinancial indicators that are specific, measurable, and timebound (table 6.1) and are subsequently reported in an annual aggregate report (OECD 2022).

Having a clear picture of the advantages the state grants to each BOS firm in direct transfers, consumption or production subsidies, tax exemptions, and other preferential treatments is crucial. Transparency also involves the explicit costing of the public service obligations for each company with state ownership, as well as an assessment of its contingent liabilities.

Principle 2: Apply the Subsidiarity Principle Economywide

The economic rationale for BOSs needs to be carefully assessed and can be guided by the subsidiarity principle (box 6.1 and box 6.3). The subsidiarity principle calls for the state to play a subsidiary role in economic activities. It must assign scarce public resources to the most critical needs that cannot be supplied by markets. If private firms are interested and capable of supplying goods and services that fulfill demand adequately, the state should be limited to a supervisory role. The state should provide goods and services only when the private sector cannot do an adequate job (OECD 2009; Ruiz, Martinez, and Quintana 2006).

TABLE 6.1 Financial and Nonfinancial Targets and Outcomes for a Reporting Year

FINANCIAL TARGETS AND OUTCOMES FOR REPORTING YEAR

Enterprise name	*Profitability* (Return on equity, or other relevant metrics)	*Capital Structure* (Equity/assets ratio, or other relevant metrics)	*Dividends* (Based on earnings, or other relevant metrics)
	Targets vs outcomes	*Target vs outcomes*	*Target vs outcomes*
Aggregated by portfolio	*Share of SOEs that achieved profit targets (achieved, partly achieved, not achieved, no targets)*	*Share of SOEs that achieved capital structure targets (achieved, partly achieved, not achieved, no targets)*	*Share of SOEs that achieved dividend targets (achieved, partly achieved, not achieved, no targets)*

PUBLIC POLICY TARGETS AND OUTCOMES

Enterprise name	*Public policy target adopted*	*Target level*	*Outcome*
	Enterprise-specific public policy targets	*Expressed as percent, share, other relevant metrics*	*Expressed as percent of target achieved per reporting year*
Aggregated by portfolio	*Share of SOEs that achieved public policy objectives (achieved, partly achieved, not achieved, no targets)*		

Source: OECD 2022.

Note: SOE = state-owned enterprise.

Subsidiarity Principle

According to the subsidiarity principle, the state plays a subsidiary role in the provision of economic activities. This principle is grounded in both economic and social considerations. The state's resources are limited and must be assigned to the most valuable objectives. The principle of subsidiarity represents a limit to state action in the market, as it establishes that the state can only intervene in the market with a state-owned enterprise if the private supply is insufficient or nonexistent. If private agents are interested and capable of supplying goods and services to attend demand, then the best means for the state to intervene in those markets is by supervising and controlling the behavior of those private agents. Meanwhile, the direct intervention of the state focuses on (1) supplying essential goods and services that will not be provided by private agents, that is, the social role of the state driven by distributive and welfare objectives; or (2) on those activities that, according to the country's highest ranking laws, cannot be performed by the private sector. In parallel, complementary regulatory reforms are implemented for goods and services to be provided in a competitive manner. Deregulation should be implemented to incentivize entry and foster a competitive private sector.

This means that the best policies rarely require state ownership. However, state interventions in markets could be necessary in rare cases. One is supplying essential goods and services not being provided by private firms, such as public goods that embody the social role of the state and are driven by distributive and welfare objectives. Another is economic activities that for other strategic reasons cannot be performed by the private sector, such as national security or strategic natural resource activities.

Although state ownership of commercial businesses is rarely the best policy response, governments still choose to rely on BOSs to achieve certain objectives, even if those objectives could be attained through better policies. For example, BOSs are often used to deliver on socially valuable tasks not privately profitable, such as providing service coverage for lower-income households and those in remote areas or advancing the decarbonization of the economy. Alternatively, however, the financial resources to accomplish these goals could be channeled through the demand side rather than the supply side.[2] BOSs are also used as an industrial policy tool, with the goal of solving market failures in emerging sectors and jump-starting economic activity in lagging areas. But other policy instruments are likely to achieve the same goals with lower risks of resource waste or political capture.

A key question is whether the public resources devoted to these social or development goals would be used more effectively if channeled through private firms rather than BOSs. For service delivery, there are risks that public utilities will be overstaffed relative to their private counterparts, and that they will have lower responsiveness to customers. Universal service coverage may be mandatory for privately run utilities;

however, when that coverage is unprofitable, governments could use budget transfers to fill the gap rather than operating BOSs. For climate-related goals, taxes, subsidies, and standards can incentivize the adoption of green technologies by the private sector. Similarly, instead of relying on using BOSs as instruments for industrial policy, governments can use subsidies to make private firms internalize the positive network spillovers they generate in emerging sectors, or their positive externalities in lagging areas. Direct support to universities can compensate for the difficulties of appropriating the benefits from basic research. Private innovation efforts toward social goals can become profitable with advance purchase commitments.

Any protocol related to using BOSs should identify the least distortive policy alternative to attain specific social goals. Doing so requires understanding the trade-off between state ownership and potential unintended consequences and recognizing that state participation in the production of goods and services is not always necessary to solve market imperfections or address institutional failures.

Principle 3: Put in Place Strong Institutions to Regulate Sectors

The overall quality of governance in a country is likely to determine whether BOSs deliver good, bad, or ugly outcomes. Preventing an excessively loose budget constraint requires good fiscal institutions and being able to transfer resources to BOSs only when justified. But support should be based on performance, which should be assessed to ensure that targets are indeed being met. Avoiding bailouts of BOSs requires solid debt management capabilities, so that BOSs' liabilities and risks can be evaluated in real time. And providing incentives for BOSs' management to perform as expected requires strong accountability mechanisms, including the ability to reward or dismiss those in charge of delivering, from chief executive officers down to technical cadres and workers.

At the heart of the institutional quality in which BOSs operate is the strength of the competition regulatory framework. That framework needs to include BOSs under the provisions and oversight of the competition agency authority and sector regulators. Beyond the regulatory framework, effective enforcement—free of political influence—is key to exercising market discipline and deterring anticompetitive practices.

Around the world, BOSs operate in a range of sectors that differ both in their market structure and in the way competition among market players is regulated. The World Bank's *Businesses of the State and Private Sector Development: Policy Toolkit for Practitioners* identifies sector-specific policy considerations depending on whether BOSs operate in competitive, partially contestable, or natural monopoly markets (World Bank, forthcoming; also see annex 6A). For example, unless market regulation ensures a level playing field, a strong presence of BOSs in competitive or partially contestable markets runs the risks of undermining private sector entry, fostering market consolidation, and slowing innovation.

Principle 4: Ensure the Competitive Neutrality of Regulations and Policies, and Their Enforcement

In parallel to the subsidiarity principle, complementary regulatory reforms should be implemented for competitive provision of goods and services. Competitive neutrality principles should be incorporated across BOS-related laws, regulations, and policies to avoid explicit or implicit preferential treatment for BOSs.

The regulatory advantages of BOSs are often associated with unfair competition with private firms. Such advantages typically reflect a conflict of interest. As a policy maker the government has a broader responsibility toward the public. Its regulation of the market and its enforcement of competition law should increase economic efficiency and ensure a fair distribution of its benefits. But as an owner of BOSs the government has an interest in maximizing their revenues and distributing them in politically advantageous ways. These conflicting roles raise the possibility that the state will make decisions that advantage BOSs over their competitors.

The blurred lines between public interest and financial gain call for a careful examination of the regulatory environment in which BOSs operate. This is especially needed in competitive markets, where there is no strong economic rationale for state participation. Because the state may not adequately protect against anticompetitive behavior or prevent undue exercise of market power by the businesses it owns, the assessment needs to go beyond the letter of the law.

Measures to limit conflicts of interest and guarantee independence of the regulators are essential. Responsibilities for market regulation and oversight of BOSs should not lie with the BOSs or any other entities or actors involved in the day-to-day management of these firms' commercial activities. Anticompetitive regulations are less likely when a specialized agency that operates at arm's length from BOSs designs and enforces the regulations. This kind of separation is less frequent in middle-income countries than in high-income countries.

Given the limited fiscal space and the goals of minimizing market distortions and maximizing the effectiveness of public interventions, competitive neutrality should be embedded in BOS firm governance and operations and be an overall requirement for targeting state support. Because evidence presented in this report shows BOSs with higher state ownership and direct state ownership perform worse than minority state-owned firms, a greater detachment of the owning state authority from day-to-day BOS firm management could increase BOSs' efficiency.

It matters which state agency or government body is in charge of BOSs. The exposure of BOSs to state influence is greatest when ownership rights are exercised by a line ministry and lowest when they are exercised by a specialized agency that operates at arm's length from the government. Less-developed countries have a higher proportion of BOSs with a greater state influence through ownership exercised by the line ministries in charge. High-income countries are more likely to have safeguards to ensure that BOSs' chief executive officers are appointed by board members rather than public authorities, which reduces the propensity for government to influence day-to-day decision-making.

For BOSs' operations, there should be a separation of commercial functions from public service obligations (unbundling) to ensure that the allocation of public funds does not cross-subsidize commercial activities and potentially distort pricing mechanisms in markets. Cost-allocation mechanisms should guide unbundling.

Principle 5: Prepare Phase-Out Strategies for BOSs

Governments can make a solid case for using BOSs as policy instruments when outcomes are good—BOSs perform well following the first four principles—and when the best options are out of reach or take time to implement. But what about when outcomes are bad, as when BOSs fulfill their objective but operate inefficiently and generate fiscal costs, or if BOSs perform well because of preferential treatment? Then the government could pursue reforms to improve on the first four principles, ranging from strengthening BOSs' corporate governance to enforcing competitive neutrality in the markets where they operate.

What about when outcomes are ugly? That can happen when BOSs underperform, have no social objective, or do not fulfill it and are a fiscal drain. It can also happen when BOSs behave anticompetitively and crowd out private investment, and when they suffer from political patronage and corruption. In such cases, the prospect for successful reforms in the short to medium term may be slim. Charting a sunset path for these weak BOSs should then be a central tenet of development policy. Options range from greater private sector involvement to divestiture and to outright closure (box 6.2).

BOX 6.2

Framework for BOS Reforms for Practitioners

The World Bank's *Businesses of the State and Private Sector Development: Policy Toolkit for Practitioners* proposes a new framework for reforms related to businesses of the state, or BOSs (World Bank, forthcoming)—see figure B6.2.1. The private sector has opportunities to engage in and benefit from such reforms. The framework goes beyond privatization and broadens the type of instruments for reform that governments can use to foster private sector–led growth. Reforms to restore market-based incentives and foster contestable and efficient markets focus on promoting the private sector

- *As a market player (competing alongside BOSs),* by abolishing and reforming policies and regulations that otherwise inhibit private entry and investment in relevant market

(Box continues on the following page.)

Framework for BOS Reforms for Practitioners *(continued)*

FIGURE B6.2.1   BOS Reform Options

Nature of ownership change	None	None	Partial	Partial/Full
Role of private sector	As **market player** (competing alongside BOSs/SOEs)		As **manager** and/ or **temporary owner** of BOSs/SOEs	As **long-term** manager and owner of BOSs/SOEs
Policy instrument	Corporate governance, ownership policy, restructuring, and performance management	Pro-competition regulatory frameworks and strengthened market institutions	Management contract and public-private partnerships	Ownership transfer by divestiture and privatization
Reform objectives	• To ensure transparent government structures and accountability • To establish legal basis for the presence of BOSs/SOEs across sectors through a state ownership policy • To improve performance of BOSs/SOEs • To improve debt, expenditure, and revenue management	• To level the playing field between BOSs/SOEs and private investors • To promote competition and market reforms to enable private entry and investment • To enable reform through national and sectoral laws and regulations	• To bridge investment gaps without transferring ownership of strategic assets • To enable private operation and/or ownership in sectors that traditionally have been served by BOSs/SOEs and realize efficiency gains	• To partially or fully transfer ownership to private sector that provides fiscal revenues to the government from sales of assets • To restructure BOSs/SOEs to increase asset value or liquidation in case of potential insurmountable issues
Potential issues or problems	• Lack of oversight and poor corporate governance • Lack of framework to justify presence of BOSs/SOEs or the creation of new ones • Poorly performing BOSs with low credit ratings • Poorly managed debt and fiscal implications (including contingent liabilities)	• Entry and/or operation is restricted • Anticompetitive laws and regulations • BOSs/SOEs benefiting from undue advantages • BOSs are also the sectoral regulator • High prevalence of BOSs in competitive sectors	• Underperforming BOSs/SOEs with regard to efficiency, service delivery, affordability, reach, and maintenance • Lack of performance incentives • Underinvestment due to lack of fiscal space or poor credit ratings	• High prevalence of BOSs/SOEs in competitive or partially contestable sectors with unclear rationale for state ownership • Underperforming BOSs/SOEs in competitive markets • Lack of market incentives, legacy issues, and political patronage

Source: World Bank, forthcoming.

Note: BOSs = businesses of the state; SOEs = state-owned enterprises.

(Box continues on the following page.)

BOX 6.2

Framework for BOS Reforms for Practitioners *(continued)*

> segments, or regulatory provisions that grant specific protections and privileges that upset the playing field, which is particularly relevant in competitive and partially contestable sectors;
>
> - *As a manager of a BOS firm*, as a temporary owner-manager of state-owned assets through concessions or public-private partnerships, which can fill important investment gaps and bring in private sector investment in sectors with high perception of risks or uncertainty including the development of new technologies (for example, green energy production); and
> - *As a long-term owner-manager* through divestiture measures.

Private actors can be mobilized through various mechanisms. Management contracts retain state ownership but delegate operational decisions to private investors for a specific period. They are particularly useful when service delivery involves public goods for which delivery is relatively straightforward to monitor, as for waste management. Public-private partnership (PPP)[3] arrangements and concessions transfer assets or stakes to the private sector. They are especially well suited for BOSs in sectors such as transportation, power generation, or telecommunications.

Ownership changes are, however, neither a necessary nor a sufficient condition for reforming sectors with a BOS firm presence. Just as state participation in markets does not necessarily solve market failures, private sector ownership is not a panacea either. Reforms that privatize BOSs or open state-dominated markets to private participation can create new opportunities for collusion if effective anticartel enforcement does not accompany liberalization. Reforms should start by setting the preconditions for proper market functioning. Doing so includes removing rules that limit or deter entry of the private sector, such as legal monopolies or bans on foreign direct investment, even before discussing divestiture options.

The institutional capacity and the implementation of competitive neutrality across markets also matter when transitioning BOSs to private sector players (box 6.3). Governments have several measures at hand to implement this transition effectively for the benefit of consumers and businesses. Effective pro-competition regulation of incumbents that were former BOS monopolies is essential to ensure sector transformation and further benefits from transition to the private sector.

The Subsidiarity Principle for BOS and Market Reforms: The Case of the Peruvian Telecommunications Market

In Peru, during 2001–02, Indecopi's Free Competition Commission analyzed state-owned enterprises in a variety of sectors, including the postal service, commercial aviation, ship building, and the commercialization of coca leaves. This helped reform these sectors and bring in private investment. For example, the commission applied the subsidiarity principle when it opened up the telecommunications sector. In line with this principle, the commission established a strong regulatory and institutional framework to guarantee a proper transition from the state-owned dominant player. The state granted a concession contract for provision of telecommunications services to a private player, initially for a five-year period, including a national monopoly in fixed telephony and domestic and international long distance.

During this period, the concessionaire was to expand and improve fixed telephony service, public service telephony, and universal service obligations in rural areas. Competition was permitted in other services, including mobile telephony, pay phones, beepers, and cable television. Additionally, the contract set specific investment goals to build the infrastructure (new lines) and thus decrease the price and increase the quality of the service for consumers. The concession contract included an explicit competition clause stipulating that the concessionaire was obliged not to abuse its dominance position, not to engage in tying practices, not to discriminate in allowing other service providers access to the network, and to eliminate cross-subsidies between long distance and local telephony services. The telecommunications regulator played a fundamental role in the transaction. It participated in all the final stages of the privatization and renewal of contracts to make sure that the contract adhered to competition principles.

This strategy resulted in successful bidding for the concession, over US$2 billion (almost four times more than the minimum asked price), an additional 1.19 million lines in the first five years, reduction of cross-price distortions between services (that is, rebalancing of rates) with a recompositing of the structure of operating earnings, completion of calls from 35 percent to over 95 percent, digitization of the network from 30 percent to over 90 percent, significant reduction in the cost and time of installing a line (from more than US$1,500 and several years to get a fixed line installed), more efficiency in the number of employees, and reduction in the allocation of its costs to wages and salaries, which was estimated at about 40 percent. The impact on consumer welfare was also significant. An important regulatory improvement after privatization was the guidelines established by the ministry and regulator for the full opening of the market, setting up rules for new market concessions to competing firms, tariff policies such as the application of the total factor productivity factor to reduce rates, cost-based models to set interconnection rates, interconnection policy, access to infrastructure and essential facilities, new obligations for expanding the network's connectivity and penetration, spectrum access, network digitization and quality of service, and revision of compliance with competitive regulations.

Sources: Congreso de la Republica del Perú 2002; Government of Peru Decreto Supremo 020-1998-MTC; OECD 2004; Torero 2002; Torero et al. 2003; UNCTAD 2004.

Scorecard to Identify Strengths and Weaknesses of BOSs

Although state ownership of commercial businesses is rarely the first-best policy response to any development challenge, there may be circumstances in which governments still choose to rely on their BOSs to attain certain goals. Whether they can expect good outcomes from this choice, and contain the ensuing risks, depends on the characteristics of the BOSs and how they interact with the rest of the economy. Therefore, it is worth assessing the strengths and weaknesses of individual BOSs before deciding to rely on them for economic policy.

A key prerequisite for relying on BOSs is to have transparent and reliable information on their finances and performance, which is not always available. But characteristics of the broader economic environment, the sectors they operate in, and the BOSs themselves can also make a significant difference for the expected outcomes.

The findings in this report suggest that outcomes of individual BOSs are determined by four major dimensions: (1) the transparency of the information available about them, (2) the broader institutional environment ensuring their accountability, (3) the structure of the markets they operate in, and (4) their own characteristics as firms.

So, when deciding whether to rely on BOSs to attain specific development objectives, policy makers could use country, sector, and enterprise indicators for BOSs to prepare a scorecard, in addition to assessing the footprint of BOSs in their economies (table 6.2).

TABLE 6.2 A Suggested Scorecard with Indicators to Assess BOSs

Dimension	Indicator	Rating
Data transparency and performance monitoring	1. Financial reports are timely, reliable, and publicly available. Direct and indirect government support is quantified and systematically monitored. Debt and its service are adequately documented. BOSs' efficiency and performance with specific key performance indicators (KPIs), execution of performance contracts, and achievement of other goals (for example, sustainability and resilience) are monitored. KPIs include the return on equity and equity/assets ratio, dividend policy, share of employment, portfolio value, labor productivity, and utilization of production capacity.[a]	0–10
Company characteristics	2. State ownership rights are exercised by a specialized agency rather than by a line ministry. The BOS firm has a competitively selected private partner with a stake in its performance. Board members representing the state are appointed based on professional rather than political criteria.	0–10
	3. The management of the BOS firm is appointed based on professional rather than political criteria. Sound corporate governance principles are followed. The personnel of the BOS firm are subject to the same labor regulations that apply to private firms. Dismissal for underperformance is feasible.	0–10
	4. The commercial and noncommercial activities of BOSs are clearly separated, and the costs of each activity can be properly identified and allocated. The commercial activity of BOSs yields rates of return like comparable private businesses over a reasonable period to prevent private sector competitors from being undercut.	0–10

(Table continues on the following page)

TABLE 6.2   A Suggested Scorecard with Indicators to Assess BOSs *(continued)*

Dimension	Indicator	Rating
Sector characteristics	5. The sector is a natural monopoly or is characterized by positive or negative externalities. Some potential for contestability by private entrants exists.	0–10
	6. The agency in charge of regulating the sector operates at arm's length from the company. Efficiency, equity, and security are its most important goals.	0–10
	7. Effective competition policies apply to the sector. Mergers leading to anticompetitive effects are prevented, and abuse of significant market power is penalized. Regulatory neutrality applies (for example, equal treatment for corporate and commercial law).	0–10
Institutional context	8. Transfers of resources from the government are linked to well-specified mandates. The BOS firm is not automatically supported if it underperforms. The compensation paid by the public authorities to the BOS firm for the delivery of public service obligations is transparent and limited to the minimum necessary to avoid cross-subsidization. Mechanisms of adjustments and compensation should balance out the BOSs' preferential access to finance through state-owned banks or government guarantees. The transfers to BOSs are assessed, monitored, and captured in published subsidies data.	0–10
	9. The buildup of contingent liabilities by the BOS firm and its potential to create systemic risk are adequately assessed, regularly monitored, and captured in overall contingent liabilities disclosures.	0–10
	10. There is reasonable control of corruption in the country, including disclosure of beneficial ownership for procurement contracts. The chances that the BOS firm will be used for private gain are limited. The access of the BOS firm to public contracts and their overall treatment during public procurement is open, transparent, and nondiscriminatory.	0–10
Overall	Aggregate score	0–100

Source: Original table for this report.

Note: BOSs = businesses of the state.

a. A good practice is to evaluate the fulfillment of individual BOSs against financial and nonfinancial targets set by the state-owner and disclosure of noncommercial assistance (OECD 2022).

The table illustrates how a simple scorecard can be adapted to each country context and BOS firm. It can be complemented with specific key performance indicators (KPIs). KPIs go beyond financial performance indicators and should include efficiency measures. Efficiency KPIs measure the degree of efficiency in using resources (labor, management, and capital) to generate output and revenue (for example, labor productivity and utilization of production capacity). In the table, the larger the aggregate score, the higher the probability that good outcomes will be attained, and the lower the risk of bad—or even ugly—consequences for the rest of the economy. This aggregate score is not a statistically rigorous predictor but more of a heuristic tool.

This approach can make the BOSs in a country more visible and help build a consensus on their various strengths and weaknesses. The rating exercise would also provide guidance on whether a specific BOS firm could or should be used for policy purposes. And it would help identify the areas where further policy reforms are needed to maximize the chances of obtaining good outcomes.

Key Lessons from Previous BOS Reforms

This report builds on lessons learned from BOS reform strategies during the 1970s through the 2000s, when such reforms focused primarily on privatization and governance improvements. Seven country case studies prepared for this report illustrate past reform priorities and reflect the BOS reform histories across countries, income groups, and regions.

For every BOS reform, the case studies illustrate how country context matters. They describe reform episodes and the main lessons learned from Costa Rica, Ethiopia, Kazakhstan, the Republic of Korea, Pakistan, Serbia, and Uzbekistan. Some describe key reform episodes when countries underwent major medium-term structural changes and switched from a state-led economy to a market-based economy. Others describe BOS reforms that were part of larger fiscal or economic reform packages in answer to acute crises. They also reflect the importance of the political economy of the BOS reform episodes described.

The goals of past BOS reform approaches (of privatization and strengthening corporate governance) were to boost economywide productivity and growth either by handing back to the private sector some of the economic functions of BOSs or by improving BOSs' performance. Although privatization efforts focused on reducing the state footprint in the economy by providing more space to the private sector, which operates under market incentives, the assumed impact of BOS governance reforms was as follows.

To improve public service delivery and resource allocation, BOSs should be managed more like private firms in the same economy. By following similar professional corporate governance practices as in the commercial sector, BOSs would become more efficient, with positive spillover effects to the rest of the economy.

As BOSs perform better, fiscal risks in relation to BOSs could be better managed and the fiscal burden to support BOSs reduced. Evidence across countries suggests that better governance and more competitive and transparent management can make investments in those entities more attractive. This reform strategy could also help steer BOSs away from competitive markets where the private sector is better positioned to provide goods and services. This shift could lead to economywide benefits of higher productivity growth and economic expansion.

Important benefits of privatization were in the medium term reduced fiscal risks. Consumers also benefited from better service delivery. Privatization reduced losses of BOSs and improved financial performance, yet success varied across different sectors and gains were unevenly distributed (ADB 2022). The benefits accrued to new owners, whereas losses were suffered by workers, consumers, and sometimes other stakeholders. Legitimate concerns also arose about opacity and corruption in privatization processes (ADB 2020).

Efforts to improve BOSs' corporate governance continued, but improvements to BOS firm oversight and governance did not consistently improve BOSs' performance (World Bank 2014). BOSs face distinct governance challenges. At one end of the spectrum, directly owned and majority-owned BOSs can experience overly hands-on and politically motivated ownership interference, leading to unclear lines of responsibility, a lack of accountability, and efficiency losses in operations. At the other end of the spectrum, the lack of oversight by the state can weaken the incentives of BOSs and their staff to perform in the best interests of the enterprise and the general public and raise the likelihood of self-serving behavior by corporate insiders (OECD 2015). So far, corporate governance requirements for when the state is an owner have been applied primarily to majority-owned and directly owned BOSs. In line with the new strategies of partial divestiture of state ownership, they should also be applied to minority-owned and indirectly owned BOSs. Annex 6B illustrates these continuous governance challenges by examining six state-owned airlines that received technical advice from the World Bank.

For crowding in a productive private sector, reforms from corporate governance to privatization programs need to be accompanied by broader reforms to institutions and competition. Over time, recognition has grown that traditional BOS reforms cannot replace facilitating market discipline and creating other sustainable business models. An Independent Evaluation Group evaluation highlights both institutions and competition as essential conditions for successful engagement to support BOS reforms (IEG 2020).

That evaluation notes that, first, better institutions and control of corruption are key for improving the effectiveness of BOS reforms. Second, BOS reforms have more impact, and BOSs perform better, when competitive market conditions prevail that reinforce market discipline and competitive neutrality at the market and enterprise levels. However, only seven countries and one subregion had comprehensive competition analysis for more than 1,000 projects analyzed across 142 countries when supporting BOS reforms (IEG 2020). Given the changes in the BOS landscape over the past two decades, key BOS reform strategies are being redrafted.

Emphasis on stronger regulation to ensure competitive neutrality and competition is expanding the traditional firm-level BOS reform agenda and links it firmly to broader private sector development strategies. This shift is consistent with moving from a more firm-driven policy agenda of BOS privatization and governance reforms toward market-level approaches, like creating an enabling environment for private sector development that focuses on a level playing field between all actors in the economy, whether state owned or privately owned. A particularly important aspect regarding a strengthened regulatory framework for competition and enforcement is capacity building for competition agencies or commissions. However, the focus on stronger regulation does not mean more regulation, and the importance of strong regulation differs for markets with a BOS presence (and that importance is greater for competitive sectors).

In sum, what it is critical for maximizing the potential gains of BOS reforms for growth and private sector development is having in place policies and regulations that ensure a level playing field among market players, including incumbents and new entrants. Even with full privatization, if market discipline and market incentives to perform are not in place, BOS reforms might have limited results. The incentives for BOSs or private firms to reach their full potential are shaped by the rules in the market including corporate governance, performance contracts, pro-competition regulation, and proper enforcement and monitoring (World Bank, forthcoming).

Annex 6A Reform Priorities for Competitive, Partially Contestable, and Natural Monopoly Markets

Competitive Markets

Ensuring that effective legal and policy reforms create a level playing field is a priority for competitive markets.

A large presence of BOSs in competitive sectors points to the potential risk for crowding out private investments when the regulation, governance, and market conditions to ensure a level playing field are not in place. As a starting point, governments could, therefore, reform rules in competitive sectors (those typically with low barriers to entry and a weak economic rationale for state ownership) that shield BOSs from private entry (for example, import monopolies, legal monopolies, price regulations, and specific subsidies) or that increase the costs for private firms to operate. Competition authorities can use competition advocacy tools such as market assessments to identify the most restrictive regulations and promote more pro-competition reforms.

If BOSs operate in competitive sectors with poor performance, the most pragmatic reform option is likely to analyze whether some business lines of the loss-making BOSs can be made profitable. The options are to unbundle these business lines and turn their performance around through governance and management reforms. For those business lines deemed unprofitable in the long run and impossible to turn around, divestiture is likely the most sensible option.

Divestiture in competitive sectors should follow the subsidiarity principle. Divestiture (either full or partial) may be desirable to transfer loss-making BOSs in competitive sectors to private owners, where neither externalities nor the public good nature of services calls for involvement of BOSs. Under "free market conditions" private ownership ultimately could lead to performance improvements and income to the government in the form of tax revenues.

The subsidiarity principle may be a useful tool in assessing both ex ante and ex post the adequacy of state presence in a given sector. At the same time, it is important to keep in mind that regulatory reforms should be carried out to prevent the private sector from enjoying protections or preferential treatment and to embed competitive neutrality principles (that is, in primary laws and relevant sector-specific provisions). Doing so requires strong coordination not only with the competition authority but also with relevant regulators mandated to determine rules in the market.

Partially Contestable Markets

For contestable sectors the reform priority is to explore potential management contracts or PPP arrangements for BOSs.

BOSs operating in contestable sectors such as transportation, power generation, or information and communication technology infrastructure could also benefit from management arrangements or PPPs, including concessions[4] to attract private investment and associated skills and expertise. Management contracts allow the government to retain control over assets but transfer the day-to-day management and business operations to the private sector, allowing for increased efficiency in service delivery. As noted earlier, management contracts are particularly useful when service delivery involves public goods for which the delivery is relatively straightforward to define and measure, for example, waste management.

PPP arrangements typically transfer more risk and responsibilities to the private investor, including rehabilitation and maintenance as well as design, build, and (time-bound) ownership of the asset, for example, under build-own-operate-transfer contracts. PPPs find their application in transportation infrastructure (for example, toll roads) and services (for example, rail cargo), or power generation (for example, through independent power producer arrangements). A review and reform of the PPP framework may be necessary to attract private investment, along with reforms to rules that restrict or inhibit entry of the private sector (for example, sectors reserved for BOSs). Further meaningful oversight and open tenders are required to ensure a competitive and transparent process, including appropriate frameworks for unsolicited proposals (World Bank 2017).

PPPs, like BOSs, are not immune to political patronage and corruption. As with BOSs, PPPs can increase fiscal risks (see chapter 4), especially since PPPs are off budget. For that reason, PPPs need to operate in an environment of adequate regulation of such contracts to minimize fiscal risks.

Natural Monopoly Markets

In natural monopoly markets, BOSs' operations should complement and crowd in private sector activity.

BOSs that operate in natural monopolies (for example, water distribution and transmission lines) can be supported through enhancements in the regulatory and policy environment; in BOSs' internal governance, operational, and financial performance (such as raising commercial capital); and in investments to improve service delivery. Alternatively, the service that these BOSs deliver can be transferred to private operators through PPPs (or other hybrid models) to improve performance, which requires careful regulation and proper enforcement mechanisms.[5]

Support to BOS reform should leverage the full range of instruments in carefully sequenced interventions, ranging from (1) regulatory and policy change (including the review of tariff models, least-cost development plans, regulatory and supervisory bodies, and so on), to (2) improving BOSs' internal governance and performance (strengthening governance, professionalizing boards of directors, automating business processes, achieving higher revenue collection, and enhancing better credit ratings), to (3) investments and credit lines to support investment programs or enable performance improvements in service delivery.

Private investments in the sector allow private firms to operate these natural monopolies and allocate those rights based on open and competitive tenders (for example, PPPs, including concessions, or a simple management arrangement assigned through bids). Competition for the market can attract multiple interested stakeholders and grant the rights to the provider with the best offer (for example, in terms of capacity, investment plans, or service delivery).

Regulations to avoid abuse of the dominant position of private monopolies (for example, price controls or quality controls) and stronger enforcement mechanisms (for example, strengthening the sectoral regulator and competition authority capacity) should be considered an essential part of such reforms. Rules and design of concessions should minimize negative effects in other markets (for example, access regulation or account separation in the case of vertical integration and even more when receiving compensation for public service obligations). Regulatory requirements that integrate the public service obligations of state-owned enterprises (SOEs) will also be needed to safeguard the public interest as ownership and service delivery are transferred to private owners or operators.

Annex 6B Corporate Governance in the Airline Industry: A Case Study

The airline industry is a capital-intensive industry with high barriers to entry. In many countries, it started as a state-owned sector characterized by a national carrier that operated using bilateral agreements with limited or no competition among market

---

This case study is based on findings from six World Bank engagements that assisted state-owned airlines, with most engagements consisting of assessing the financial viability of the enterprise with the objectives of de-risking and limiting their fiscal burden.

players. The deregulation of the US market in 1978, the privatization wave of the 1990s, the financial crisis of 2008, and the recent COVID-19 (coronavirus) crisis have shaped the industry and transformed it into a highly competitive sector with a focus on cost control and profit maximization.

The corporate governance practices of successful airlines have evolved alongside their business models. Today, the ownership structure is dominated by publicly listed companies and privately held groups, but in many developing countries state ownership remains the prevalent form of ownership.

State ownership of airline companies has benefits and drawbacks, with differences observed across regions. However, adequate corporate governance practices have been shown to reduce the overpoliticization, bureaucracy, and overstaffing in state-owned airlines.

Airlines with the best governance practices have a more balanced approach toward hedging, de-risk decisions, behave in a more agile manner, and are more likely to reduce fleet size and staffing to control costs. Research by Chen, Chen, and Wei (2017) finds that non-state-owned airlines dominated and outperformed the state-owned companies, whereas Duppati, Scrimgeour, and Stevenson (2016) observe that a government holding in the Asia-Pacific region had a positive effect on airlines. Regardless of airline ownership structure, these studies conclude that good corporate governance makes it more likely that airlines will adopt performance management methods that improve financial performance.

In many countries, the national-level legal and regulatory framework lacks a unified corporate governance policy and accountability mechanisms for state-owned airlines. Often the government has weak capacity to act as a competent owner and to support the management board in identifying and implementing necessary measures for restructuring. It also lacks mechanisms to hold management accountable for reforms with the goal of reducing airlines' losses. Governments face difficulties in implementing severe cost-cutting measures, so the measures are often watered down.

State-owned airlines often lack professional nonexecutive boards of directors. Board members are frequently nominated from the overseeing ministries rather than selected independently on the basis of relevant professional expertise. Independent experts, when invited to the board of directors, often cannot adequately support the company because they lack the professional, technical, or industry profile required by good practice standards to be effective in such a position. This practice is partly due to weak bylaws and governance policies that could empower management to execute decisions without political interference. Most publicly held airlines with external support have improved their performance.

Many state-owned airlines have limited or no fiscal and financial transparency, have weak audits that are mostly performed by state audit organizations or finance ministries with weak capacity, and do not have transparent public procurement procedures. Although in many countries SOE regulatory frameworks stipulate that the ministry of finance is responsible for exercising the government shareholder responsibilities and fiscal oversight of SOEs, the discharge of such responsibilities is often uneven and undermined by lack of data that track SOEs' financial performance. Oversight responsibility is often fragmented or delegated to the relevant ministries the SOEs belong to, creating conflicts of interest because the oversight body is often represented in the management team of the SOE. Most countries have no centralized or publicly available SOE database with recent financial results and debt profiles, including contingent liabilities and expenditure arrears. External audits mostly focus on compliance with local regulations and laws, and do not provide adequate information about the reliability of financial results and compliance with internationally recognized financial reporting standards. Moreover, audit reports are not publicly disclosed.

Most airlines lack a complete enterprise resource planning solution and have weak financial and accounting tools. Financial management information systems are often inadequate to support management reporting and strategic planning with identifiable objectives and measurable metrics. The periodic reports issued by the airlines for the management and board are not prepared using a comprehensive enterprise management solution or uniform project management software to track basic project actions: duration, costs, human resources, and expected completion. This has contributed to a lack of synchronized action plans and comprehensive reporting.

In addition to being often overstaffed when compared with well-performing industry peers, state-owned airlines in many countries lack performance management plans for employees and lack incentivized remuneration. Regardless of the digitization of airlines in the past 10 years, the airline industry remains people-centric, and performance management is an important catalyst of success if accompanied by good communication and continuous training of staff. Performance management helps transform the corporate strategy and business priorities into executable and measurable activities by ensuring that employees understand what is expected of them and when, that they have access to adequate tools, and that their level of completion of deliverables is measured periodically. For example, Southwest Airlines, the airline with the best human resource performance in the industry, has evolved performance monitoring from once a year to a continuous process, and has transformed managers into leaders and coaches for staff (HCI 2020).

These governance and management weaknesses perpetuate the cycle of poor performance of several state-owned airlines that results in debt accumulation and contributes to significant fiscal risks and costs for the government. Along with a dearth of periodic management reporting on key performance indicators, the absence of periodic controls monitoring means management does not receive adequate and timely feedback on the drivers of poor financial performance and compliance gaps, and thus cannot sufficiently address the causes of poor performance that resulted in the build-up of losses. In addition, airlines—as capital-intensive entities purchasing high-value equipment and services—require transparent and competitive public procurement procedures and digital platforms.

Key reform recommendations for improving governance build on best practice from successful international public and private airlines' strategies and align with the *Guidelines on Corporate Governance of State-Owned Enterprises* (OECD 2015):

- Incorporate at least one expert with international airline experience in the board of directors, familiar with airline turnarounds and restructuring of financial debt.
- Establish a chief financial officer and financial controller role as part of the executive board and upgrade the organizational structure for full compliance with international best practice, to reflect the direct connection between the accountable manager and all nominated persons, as well as the level of accountability among the different management roles.
- Upgrade the management and develop and implement company processes establishing detailed corporate governance guidelines focusing on transparency, leadership culture, management information, and performance management.
- Upgrade management information systems, focusing on integrated enterprise management solutions and accounting and manpower management solutions. Implement project management software, training staff to use Microsoft Project, Smartsheet, or other simple tools, to improve task monitoring and offer a complete perspective on project duration, costs, human resources, and expected completion.
- Capacitate the workforce to perform effectively and minimize staff turnover of the airline, streamlining personnel needs to avoid excessive personnel costs.
- Acquire external support for the implementation of a performance management strategy, with tailored solutions for the aviation industry.
- Develop a publicly available procurement manual in line with airline purchasing requirements and facilitate a digital platform, owned or through the government's electronic platform, to create a transparent process and attract a higher number of international bidders.
- Use International Financial Reporting Standards to ensure financial reporting accuracy and ease in international transactions, or potential attraction of foreign investors and international financing.
- Conduct annual financial statement audits and publicly disclose the audit report.
- Adhere to transparent and competitive procurement practices to maximize value for money and minimize rent-seeking behavior. Publicize invitations to tenders and awards.

Notes

1. The chapter draws on *Business of the State and Private Sector Development: A Policy Toolkit for Practitioners* (World Bank, forthcoming).
2. This is not possible in cases when the provision of the good or service is not available in the first place.
3. A PPP is "a long-term contract between a private party and a government entity, for providing a public asset or service, in which the private party bears significant risk and management responsibility, and remuneration is linked to performance" (World Bank 2017, 5). PPPs differ from management contracts, which typically involve no or very limited risk transfer.
4. Concession is mostly used to describe a user-pays PPP.
5. Independence of the sectoral regulator and strong competition agencies are among the success factors for this alternative.

References

ADB (Asian Development Bank). 2020. *Reforms, Opportunities and Challenges for State-Owned Enterprises*. Mandaluyong City, Philippines: ADB.

ADB (Asian Development Bank). 2022. "Privatization of State-Owned Enterprises. A Summary of Experience." The Governance Brief, Issue 47. ADB, Mandaluyong City, Philippines.

Chen, S.-J., M.-H. Chen, and H.-L. Wei. 2017. "Financial Performance of Chinese Airlines: Does State Ownership Matter?" *Journal of Hospitality and Tourism Management* 33: 1–10.

Congreso de la Republica del Perú. 2002. "Informe Especial de Investigación – El Proceso de Privatización de las Empresas." Lima.

Duppati, G., F. Scrimgeour, and R. Stevenson. 2016. "Corporate Governance in the Airline Industry: Evidence from the Asia-Pacific Region." University of Waikato, New Zealand.

HCI (Human Capital Institute). 2020. "Southwest Airlines New Performance Management, July 2020." Podcast. https://www.hci.org/podcast/continuous-performance-management -southwest-airlines.

IEG (Independent Evaluation Group). 2020. *State Your Business! An Evaluation of World Bank Group Support for the Reform of State-Owned Enterprises FY08–18*. Washington, DC: World Bank.

OECD (Organisation for Economic Co-operation and Development). 2004. "Peru: Peer Review of Competition Law and Policy." OECD Country Studies, OECD, Paris.

OECD (Organisation for Economic Co-operation and Development). 2009. "State-Owned Enterprises and the Principle of Competitive Neutrality." *Policy Roundtables*. OECD, Paris. https://www .oecd.org/daf/competition/46734249.pdf.

OECD (Organisation for Economic Co-operation and Development). 2015. *Guidelines on Corporate Governance of State-Owned Enterprises*. Paris: OECD Publishing.

OECD (Organisation for Economic Co-operation and Development). 2022. "Monitoring the Performance of State-Owned Enterprises: Good Practice Guide for Annual Aggregate Reporting." OECD, Paris. https://www.oecd.org/corporate/ca/Monitoring-performance-state-owned -enterprises-good-practice-guide-annual-aggregate-reporting-2022.pdf.

Ruiz, G., M. Martinez, and E. Quintana. 2006. "El Carácter Subsidiario de la Actividad Empresarial del Estado desde una Perspectiva de Políticas de Competencia." *Boletín Latinoamericano de Competencia* 22: 107–25.

Torero, M. 2002. "Peruvian Privatization: Impacts on Firm Performance." IDB Working Paper No. 186, Inter-American Development Bank, Washington, DC.

Torero, M., E. Schroth, A. Pasco-Font, M. Urquiola, and R. J. Lüders. 2003. "The Impact of Telecommunications Privatization in Peru on the Welfare of Urban Consumers." *Economia* 4 (1): 99–128.

UNCTAD (United Nations Conference on Trade and Development). 2004. "Perú: Informe sobre las necesidades y prioridades en el área de Políticas de la Competencia." United Nations, New York.

World Bank. 2014. *Corporate Governance of State-Owned Enterprises: A Toolkit*. Washington, DC: World Bank.

World Bank. 2017. *PPP Reference Guide*. Version 3. Washington, DC: World Bank.

World Bank. Forthcoming. *Business of the State and Private Sector Development: A Policy Toolkit for Practitioners*. Washington, DC: World Bank.